RISE ABOVE IT

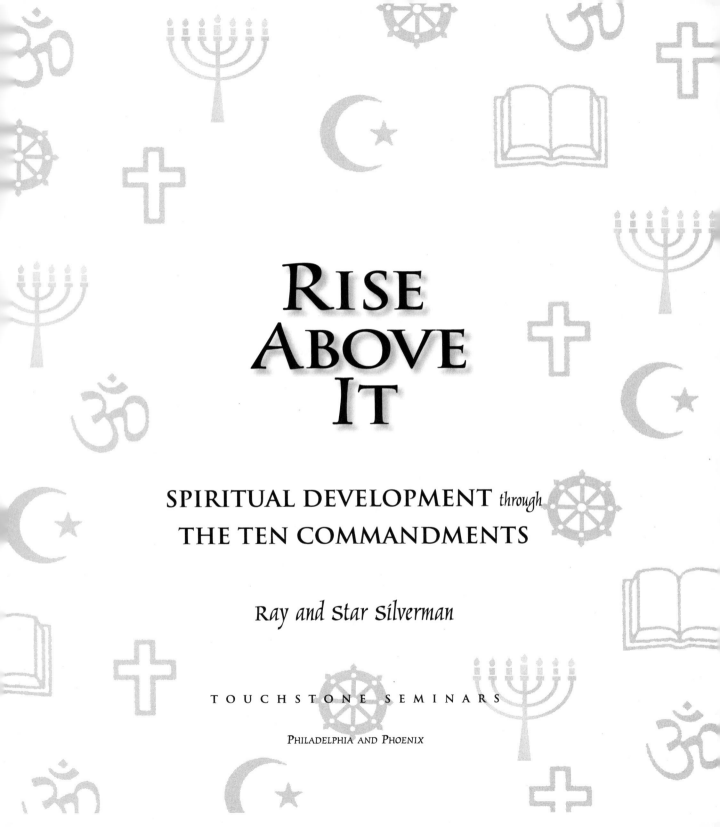

RISE
ABOVE
IT

SPIRITUAL DEVELOPMENT *through*
THE TEN COMMANDMENTS

Ray *and* Star Silverman

TOUCHSTONE SEMINARS

PHILADELPHIA AND PHOENIX

RISE ABOVE IT

Spiritual Development through the Ten Commandments

Ray and Star Silverman

T O U C H S T O N E   S E M I N A R S

"A right idea of God . . . is a kind of touchstone."
— EMANUEL SWEDENBORG

Editor: Mark Pendleton
Cover and book design: Yvonne Reyes
Cover photograph: Gregg Krantz

The authors are grateful for permission to reprint excerpts from the following material:

Meditation: A Simple Eight-Point Program for Translating Spiritual Ideals into Daily Life, by Eknath Easwaran, © 1991 by Nilgiri Press, Petaluma, California. Reprinted by permission of Nilgiri Press.

Tears and Laughter, by Kahlil Gibran. Translated from the Arabic by Anthony Rizcallah Ferris, © 1949 by Philosophical Library, Inc., New York. Reprinted by permission of Philosophical Library.

The Holy Bible: Containing the Old and New Testaments. All scripture quotations, unless otherwise indicated, are taken from the New King James Version. © 1982 by Thomas Nelson, Inc., Nashville, Tennessee. Used by permission. All rights reserved.

Publisher's Cataloging-in-Publication Data
Silverman, Ray
    Rise above it : spiritual development through
the ten commandments / Ray and Star Silverman. –
1st ed.
      p. cm.
      Includes bibliographical references and index.
      Library of Congress Catalog Number: 99-71073
      International Standard Book Number: 0-9670768-0-3

     1. Religious ethics — Comparative studies.
  2. Ten commandments. 3. Spiritual life.
  I. Silverman, Star. II. Title

BJ1188.S55 2000   291.5
                               QB199-1760

In honor of our parents,
Mack and Allegra; Harry and Gertrude.

We dedicate this book to our children,
Serena, Sasha, Skyler, Aria, Spring, Celestyn, and Shiloh.

Each of you is a precious gift in our lives.

If you want to enter into life,
keep the commandments.
—MATTHEW 19:17

Acknowledgements

WHEN WE MET and fell in love in 1976, we experienced an extraordinary change in our lives. Our love for each other opened us to the presence of God and led us into a search for truth. It was the beginning of an incredible journey. We explored many religions until we came across a little known revelation by an eighteenth century theologian named Emanuel Swedenborg. It was through this revelation that we discovered a religion that was deeply spiritual and immediately practical. We learned about the nature of God, the symbolism of Sacred Scripture, and the spiritual dimension in marriage. This revelation brought us to a path that was neither mysterious nor unfamiliar. It was the Ten Commandments, tried and true, containing the wisdom of the ages in a Divinely ordered sequence. In striving to apply the Ten Commandments in our daily lives, we experienced the joy of unexpected breakthroughs in our marriage and in our relationships with others. Eager to share our discovery, we decided to put together a seminar on the Ten Commandments.

Our first seminar was presented in Pittsburgh, Pennsylvania, in the spring of 1989. Since then we have had the opportunity to present this seminar to numerous people across America and in several foreign countries. Along the way, people from a wide variety of religious backgrounds have participated in the seminar and given us generous feedback about how we might continue to refine this course. We are especially grateful to those participants who were willing to share their journal entries with us so that we might make their insights and experiences available to others. It is a rare privilege to be a part of each person's unique—yet universal—journey. We wish to express our sincerest gratitude to those who opened up their lives so that we might learn from their experiences.

We are deeply indebted to Mark "the Pen" Pendleton who poured heart, soul, and mind into the editing and revising of this manuscript. We are grateful for his valuable insights, inspiration and encouragement. We are also grateful to David Deaton, Tom

Rose, Hugo Henderson and our daughters, Serena and Sasha, for excellent editorial assistance. We appreciate the valuable support of Michael David who helped us sort through computer challenges, and who created an on-line classroom for this seminar. "*Gracia*" to William Piccirillo, Gabriel D'Amato, and the staff at *Centro Studi sulle Nuove Religioni* (Torino, Italy) for helping us translate Italian idioms. We would especially like to thank our graphic designer, Yvonne Reyes, for her magic touch in translating our vision into artistic reality. Yvonne's gentle spirit and inner confidence brought great peace during times of stormy seas and computer crashes!

Several people have provided valuable doctrinal assistance in the development of this manuscript. These include Chris Bown, Stephen Cole, Andrew Heilman, Willard Heinrichs, Kent Junge´, Dick Keyworth, John Odhner, J. Durban Odhner, Peter Rhodes, Bruce Rogers, Prescott Rogers, Don Rose, Frank Rose, Jonathan Rose and Erik Sandstrom. Thank you to Sam McBride for introducing us to the wisdom of the Islamic Scriptures. We are also grateful to Kate Hammond and Rosie and Terry O'Sullivan for their insights into Buddhist and Hindu teachings.

We wish to acknowledge Kay Alden, Erik Buss, Peter Buss, Jr., Vera Dyck, Clark Echols, Karin Elder, Nathan Gladish, Cedric King, Stephen Morley, Mary Jane Odhner, Mark Pendleton, Terry Schnarr and Ned Uber, all of whom have led Ten Commandments seminars in America. We also acknowledge Alain Nicolier who has introduced this seminar in France and in French speaking West Africa, and Mutsuo Oga who has translated and introduced this course in Japan. We are especially pleased to acknowledge five college students: Athena Childs, Francis Darkwah, Jeremy Henry, Sasha Silverman, and Anna Woofenden who participated in this seminar in America and then brought it to the people of Ghana on Africa's "Gold Coast."

We want to express our gratitude to Karl Boericke, Eleanor Jean Dillard, Michael Grubb, Jinny Latta, Phyllis Pitcairn, Marge Rose, Tamar King, Lori Nelson, Ruth Zuber, Marilyn Payne, Joe Deters, Frank DiMaria, and Terry Roach for their ongoing support. Many thanks to Matthew O'Donnell for his literary gifts and brotherly inspiration. Special thanks to "the Sunrise Crew"—Peggy and Bob Merrell, Jane and Hugo Henderson, Julie and David Conaron, and Beryl and Paul Simonetti—for their work in helping us to present this seminar at the Sunrise Summer Camps in New Hope, Pennsylvania. At a time when we were uncertain about the publication of this book, John Gladish and Nick Morley were there to encourage us and to provide solid direction. There are many others, too numerous to mention, who have supported us in bringing this work to fruition. Each of you is a part of this book and a part of our lives. We are grateful.

It is our prayer that this book may in some small way articulate the profound insights of the great theologians and mystics in language that is simple, clear and comprehensible to the millions of people who struggle to apply the teachings of Sacred Scripture in their everyday lives. May the ancient wisdom stored up within the Ten Commandments provide profound, fresh and applicable insights for a new millennium.

Finally, we want to thank our children, Serena, Sasha, Skyler, Aria, Spring, Celestyn, and Shiloh. We appreciate how perceptively and how gently you have reminded us to *Rise Above It*. We are grateful for your acceptance, support, and love through all these years.

This book is in many ways one of our "offspring." Just as children come through us but do not belong to us, so, too, do our best ideas and most creative insights. We realize, therefore, that whatever is of value in this work, and whatever blessing it may contain, is from God alone and not from us. It is with this in mind that we now send forth this book—our "spiritual offspring"—praying that it may be a blessing to many, and that many may come to know the truth: that there is One God, infinitely loving and wise, who has given us the Divine commandments, along with the power to live according to them, so that our lives may be filled with joy.

Ray and Star Silverman

Great peace have they who love Thy law,
and nothing shall offend them.

— PSALM 119:165

Table of Contents

And the Lord spoke to you out of the midst of the fire . . . .
He declared to you His covenant which He commanded you to perform,
that is, the Ten Commandments; and He wrote them on two tablets of stone.

THE OLD TESTAMENT—DEUTERONOMY 4:12-13

 And Jesus said to him, "If you want to enter into life,
keep the commandments . . . .
You shall not murder, You shall not commit adultery, You shall not steal,
You shall not bear false witness, Honor your father and your mother,
and You shall love your neighbor as yourself."

THE NEW TESTAMENT—MATTHEW 19:17

 In the Tablets of the Law [The Ten Commandments]
all matters are commanded and explained . . . .

THE QUR'ĀN 7:145; 2:38

 Right speech is to abstain from lies . . . .
Right acts are to abstain from taking life, from stealing, and from lechery.

THE BUDDHA—THE NOBLE EIGHTFOLD PATH

 The Ten Commandments contain, in brief summary, all things of religion.
Through them the conjunction of God with man, and man with God,
takes place. There is nothing more holy.

EMANUEL SWEDENBORG—TRUE CHRISTIAN RELIGION 283

The Way of the Divine Commandments

O nobly born, the time has now come for thee to seek the Path.
—THE TIBETAN BOOK OF THE DEAD

One way or many?

P EOPLE TEND TO believe that their chosen path is the "one right way" or "the only true religion." It would probably be more accurate for people to say that the particular religion or spiritual path they have chosen is the right one *for them*. When people feel strongly about their chosen way, even to the point where they are eager to recruit others, it is usually because their religion works for them in their lives. Like the various forms of music, it may suit their taste; like the many approaches to education, it may match their learning style. This is perhaps why there are many religions—each with its unique external forms, traditions, and Sacred Scriptures, but all leading to the same destination.

Religion, then, like music, is adapted to different cultural backgrounds and various states of consciousness. Just as there is not "one right song" or "one right flower" or "one right tree," there is not "one right religion." Any religion that leads to God is "right" because, ultimately, this is the aim of religious life—to find a way that leads us away from selfishness and into the presence of the Divine.

Whether we speak about the way to the presence of the Divine, or the way to the Promised Land of Judaeo-Christianity, or the way to the Pure Land of Buddhism, we are speaking about the same thing. The roads may vary, but the destination remains the same—because the real destination is not in the world of time and space. It is the "Kingdom of God." As Jesus said, "The Kingdom of God does not come with observation; nor will they say, 'Here it is,' or 'There it is,' for indeed, the Kingdom of God is within you" (Luke 17:21, 22).

Still, even though the Kingdom of God is within us, we sometimes have difficulty discovering it on our own. So we may search for a particular religion, and try to find a reliable guide. This might be compared to going to a travel bureau for assistance and directions as we prepare for a journey. A well detailed, annotated "map" that describes the journey accurately is essential. In addition, a personal guide—minister, rabbi, guru, shaman, imam, etc.—can be most helpful. Because they have "been there," they can help us make it over perilous terrain, and warn us of hidden dangers along the way. They also know where we can find nourishment and springs of fresh water so that we can continue our journey. And they can recommend places where we can find rest. A personal guide offers encouragement, helps us interpret the map, and offers gentle reminders when we misread it, forget to use it, or wander off the path.

The many religions of the world provide a wide variety of colorful maps for their followers. In this book we will try to show how the Sacred Scriptures of the various religions are really one map, and that all the great religions, when understood more deeply, are really one religion. This is because they all teach the same fundamental message: *There is One God, infinitely loving and wise, Who is leading each of us, at every moment, into all the love and wisdom we are willing to receive.* As the Dalai Lama has said, "Every major religion of the world has similar ideals of love, the same goal of benefiting humanity through spiritual practice, and the same effect of making their followers into better human beings."[1] In brief, every major religion seeks to aid its adherents in finding their way to the Kingdom of God.

Our map to the mountaintop

Entering the Kingdom of God is sometimes compared to climbing a mountain. Even though we know that the Kingdom of God is within us, the metaphor of God

1. Jeffrey Moses, *Oneness: Great Principles Shared by All Religions* (New York: Fawcett Columbine, 1989), front cover.

waiting for us at the top of the mountain is useful. We can visualize God as a loving Parent compassionately looking down on each of us as we make our way up the mountain from every side. Waiting there at the top of the mountain, watching those who are traveling upwards by various routes, with various guides, with various maps, and speaking various languages, God understands that all ways leading upward—however various—are really one. For God is always there with open arms, ready to receive us, no matter what map we use and no matter how long it takes.

As the authors of this book, we have chosen the time honored ethical code of the Ten Commandments as our "map" to the mountaintop. We have found it to be simple, practical, and universal. The Ten Commandments are not mysterious. They can be easily understood by anyone, in any culture, male or female, young or old, rich or poor. In fact, the Ten Commandments might be considered humanity's most trustworthy map, because in essence these commandments are the foundation of every true religion. In the Old Testament they appear in Exodus 20:1-17 and in Deuteronomy 5:6-21. Though there are slight differences in the wording of the two versions, the sequential order and essential message remain the same, as does the wording of the Divine Prologue:

> I AM THE LORD YOUR GOD, WHO BROUGHT YOU OUT OF
> THE LAND OF EGYPT, OUT OF THE HOUSE OF BONDAGE.

Following this prologue, the Ten Commandments are given as follows:

> YOU SHALL HAVE NO OTHER GODS BEFORE ME.

> YOU SHALL NOT MAKE FOR YOURSELF ANY CARVED IMAGE,
> OR ANY LIKENESS OF ANYTHING THAT IS IN HEAVEN ABOVE, OR
> THAT IS IN THE EARTH BENEATH, OR THAT IS IN THE WATER
> UNDER THE EARTH; YOU SHALL NOT BOW DOWN TO THEM NOR
> SERVE THEM. . . .

> YOU SHALL NOT TAKE THE NAME OF THE LORD YOUR GOD IN
> VAIN, FOR THE LORD WILL NOT HOLD HIM GUILTLESS WHO
> TAKES HIS NAME IN VAIN.

REMEMBER THE SABBATH DAY, TO KEEP IT HOLY.
SIX DAYS YOU SHALL LABOR AND DO ALL YOUR WORK, BUT THE
SEVENTH DAY IS THE SABBATH OF THE LORD YOUR GOD. IN IT
YOU SHALL DO NO WORK. . . .

HONOR YOUR FATHER AND YOUR MOTHER THAT YOUR DAYS MAY
BE LONG UPON THE LAND WHICH THE LORD YOUR GOD
IS GIVING YOU.

YOU SHALL NOT MURDER.

YOU SHALL NOT COMMIT ADULTERY.

YOU SHALL NOT STEAL.

YOU SHALL NOT BEAR FALSE WITNESS AGAINST YOUR NEIGHBOR.

YOU SHALL NOT COVET YOUR NEIGHBOR'S HOUSE.

YOU SHALL NOT COVET YOUR NEIGHBOR'S WIFE,
NOR HIS MANSERVANT, NOR HIS MAIDSERVANT,
NOR HIS OX, NOR HIS DONKEY, NOR ANYTHING
THAT IS YOUR NEIGHBOR'S.

The heavenly curriculum

The Ten Commandments appear in one form or another in all the great religions of the world. Sometimes the first commandment is divided into two commandments (the first forbidding the worship of other gods; the second forbidding the worship of graven images). Sometimes the ninth and tenth commandments are combined as one (forbidding coveting). Although this book follows the numbering of the commandments that is practiced in some Judaic, Catholic and Protestant (Lutheran) traditions, we acknowledge that *keeping the commandments* is vastly more important than reaching a consensus about their precise numbering. It is also noteworthy that in the Old and

New Testaments, the commandments are never referred to by number. While the language of Sacred Scripture often refers to the "third day" or the "fourth angel" or the "seventh year," we never hear about the "third," "fourth" or "seventh" commandment. Therefore, instead of speaking about "the third commandment" or "the seventh commandment," we will be speaking about "the Sabbath commandment," or "the commandment against stealing," etc.

We believe that the Ten Commandments, for all their brevity, are a Divinely given framework that contains the totality of spiritual truth. Furthermore, we believe that because they are given in a Divinely ordered series, they are more than a mere collection of ethical laws. We regard them, in fact, as a heavenly curriculum "written by the finger of God," and intended for the spiritual development of humanity. We do not insist that the way of the Ten Commandments is the only way, but we do believe that from beginning to end—from the first word to the last—the Ten Commandments are a continuous stream of Divine Truth, and that this curriculum has been prepared by the Master Teacher—the One True God of heaven and earth.

From Egypt to the Promised Land

According to the Old Testament story, the Ten Commandments were given at a significant time in the history of the Hebrew people. The Hebrew nation had been sojourners in the land of Egypt for four hundred and thirty years (Exodus 13:40). For most of that time they had been forced to serve as slaves, working for harsh, unreasonable, and often merciless taskmasters. Finally, God raised up Moses through whom the Hebrew nation would be delivered from their hard bondage. Moses would lead them out of Egypt and take them to the Promised Land. Along the way they would come to Mt. Sinai, the place where Moses would receive the Ten Commandments.

The occasion was a dramatic one. We are told that the whole mountain shook. There was lightning, thunder, and the long blast of a trumpet which became louder and louder as the God of the universe descended upon the mountain in a flame of fire. The Divine Prologue to the Ten Commandments identifies this God as the God of deliverance—the God who had delivered the children of Israel from Egyptian captivity and bondage. As it is written, "I am the Lord your God who brought you out of the land of Egypt, out of the house of bondage."

But what kind of bondage is being referred to here, and what is meant by captivity in "the land of Egypt"? In order to answer these questions it is important to know that in Old Testament times the land of Egypt was seen as a great center where ancient knowledge was stored up and preserved. The land of Egypt, therefore, was called "the storehouse of knowledge"—the intellectual and academic capital of the world. People would come from far and wide to study, to learn, and to satisfy their thirst for knowledge. For this reason the phrase "land of Egypt" came to symbolize "stored-up knowledge"—that knowledge which is learned and stored up in the human mind. The time comes in each of our lives, however, when we must leave the "land of Egypt" and journey onward to the Promised Land—the Pure Land of useful service. As it is written in the Sacred Scriptures, "Out of Egypt, I called my son" (Hosea 11:1; Matthew 2:15).

This same symbolism applies today. If we merely remain in the state of acquiring knowledge—*without using it to serve God and others*—we become "slaves" in Egypt. This can take place in several ways. For example, as we acquire and store up more and more knowledge, we may begin to take pride in our own intelligence and feel superior to others. Infatuated with learning for its own sake, we forget that the purpose of knowledge is for a life of useful service. As our self-love and conceit grow into full blown egocentricity, we are tempted to use whatever knowledge we have accumulated to serve our own ends and our own selfish purposes—to win an argument, to manipulate others, to justify wrong doing, or to realize our private ambitions. On the other hand, we may feel so insecure and so intimidated by the vast stores of knowledge with which we are confronted that we never venture forth to use it in our lives. Overwhelmed by all there is to learn, we may choose to remain perpetual students, always accumulating knowledge and discussing it, but never really using it to improve ourselves or to serve others. These are some of the ways that we can become "slaves" in "the land of Egypt," and never leave "the house of bondage."

The "Promised Land," on the other hand, represents our higher possibilities, the elevated consciousness in which we feel the profound love of God for all humanity, and for all creation. It is a state of mind in which our learning is seen, not only as a way of "improving ourselves," but more importantly as a way of spiritual development which allows us to be as useful as possible in our efforts to benefit mankind. We are all born for others; we are born to be of service and to play our part in the great drama of mankind's spiritual rebirth and development. All the mystics of the world and all the great religions declare that the Kingdom of Heaven is a kingdom of useful service—a beautiful kingdom that we are not only preparing for, but are also participating in at this very moment. As Helen Keller says, "The old thought tells us we are given earth to prepare for heaven, but there is truth in seeing it the other way around. We are given a knowledge of heaven to fit us better for earth. The Vision of Beauty must come into the workshop of Nazareth."[2] And as Mother Theresa writes, "The fruit of love is service."[3]

Although everyone is invited to take the journey from Egypt to the Promised Land, and although everyone is offered a wondrous map that may be called "The Ten Commandments," not everyone accepts the invitation or uses the map. In some cases people do accept the invitation, and begin to use the map, but are overcome by fear. Take, for example, the story of the children of Israel. According to the Biblical account, after receiving the Ten Commandments they remained at the foot of Mt. Sinai for another fourteen months (Numbers 10:11). It was in the second month of the second year after they had come to Mt. Sinai that the Lord gave them a sign indicating that it was time for them to begin their journey to the Promised Land. After only eleven days they arrived at Kadesh-Barnea, the border of the Promised Land. It was at this point that God told Moses to select twelve men (one from each tribe) to cross the border and "spy out the land." After remaining in the land for forty days and forty nights, the spies returned. Of the twelve spies, only two—Caleb and Joshua—came back with a positive report and with evidence that it was a good land, flowing with milk and honey. The other ten spies focused on "the giants in the land" and frightened the children of Israel. Caleb and Joshua tried to assure the people that there was nothing to fear, and told them that with God they could certainly overcome the giants. But the people, frightened by the stories about the giants, refused to listen. Instead, they chose to believe the reports of the ten other spies, and would not enter the land.

Because they gave in to their fears—refusing to believe the report of Caleb and Joshua—the children of Israel did not enter the Promised Land. Instead they had to wander in the wilderness for thirty-eight more years. This is a dramatic illustration of what happens to each of us spiritually whenever we listen to, and are led by, our fears. An eleven day journey can take thirty-eight years! But God, through the Ten Commandments, comes to deliver us from our fears, to free us from bondage, and to encourage us to cross over—today—into a land flowing with milk and honey.

---

2. Helen Keller, *Light In My Darkness,* edited and revised by Ray Silverman (West Chester, PA: Chrysalis Books, 2000), 91.
3. Mother Theresa, *A Simple Path* (New York: Ballantine Books, 1996), 1.

The journey from Egypt to the Promised Land, then, is the journey of each of our lives. It is the journey from selfishness to selflessness, from natural life to spiritual life, from worldly knowledge to the wisdom of service, from earth to heaven. To return to our original metaphor, it is a journey to the top of the mountain, to the Kingdom of God, where we can receive our full spiritual inheritance and become all that we are intended to be. As we ascend the mountain of God, we find ourselves rising above the clouds and obscurity—the fears, feelings and thoughts that have kept us in bondage. We find ourselves rising into the clear light of higher consciousness where the sun is always shining, and where there are limitless opportunities for joyful service.

The Seminar

In the final analysis, no amount of thunder on the mountaintop is going to convince us that the Ten Commandments are Divinely given laws. We must experience this for ourselves. We can't just study the commandments, as one would study a map; we must live them, and follow where they lead. A map to the Promised Land, even if it is the best and most accurate map, is not the Promised Land. Just as there is a difference between pointing to the moon and actually landing on it, there is a difference between reading the map and taking the journey.

So it is with religion. The Divine test of who we really are is not a mere matter of theology; nor is it a matter of what cultural background or religious organization we belong to; rather, it is a matter of how we apply our beliefs to life. God does not ask what our religion, race, or nationality is. God only asks what we have loved with all of our hearts, and how we have expressed that love in our lives. In the Sacred Scriptures of India we read, "No *Brahmin* is a *Brahmin* by birth; a *Brahmin* is a *Brahmin* by his deeds" (*Dhammapada* 26:11). And Emanuel Swedenborg writes, "In the spiritual world, into which everyone comes after death, no one is ever asked, 'What is your religion?' but rather, 'What is your life?' for everyone's life is his religion" (*Divine Providence* 101).[4]

This book, then, is more than a discourse on theology; it is a book about life—a book that encourages us to bring our understanding of the Ten Commandments into every detail of our lives. The information contained in these pages is the basis for a seminar that we call "*Rise Above It: Spiritual Development through the Ten Commandments.*" As we have already pointed out, *rising above* refers to rising above

4. *Angelic Wisdom about Divine Providence* (New York: Swedenborg Foundation, 1975), 101. Note: the numbers which follow Swedenborg's works refer to *paragraph* numbers, not to *page* numbers.

merely natural existence and entering higher states of consciousness—states that are closer to God—so that we may see clearly the circumstances and situations in which we find ourselves. We get a new view from a higher vantage point.

As we proceed through each of the commandments, ascending the mountain of God, our understanding is elevated above the promptings of our lower nature, and we are able to make choices that are consistent with the truth that we know. Through the effort of continually choosing to live according to the truth as we understand it, a new nature is born within us. This new nature grows steadily, even as a child grows, from infancy to childhood, and finally comes into full maturity. Although this is sometimes referred to as being "born again," it is important to point out that for most people this is a gradual process. Although deaf, blind, and mute from an early age, Helen Keller was able to understand this process clearly, and to articulate it eloquently. In her spiritual autobiography, she writes, "We are not born again suddenly, as some people seem to think. It is a change that comes over us as we hope and aspire and persevere in the way of the Divine Commandments."[5]

This seminar has been presented in a variety of contexts: in maximum security prisons to men and women from a wide variety of religious backgrounds; in college and university settings as courses in "Christian Ethics" and "Moral Life"; in several church groups around the United States and Canada; in African villages; via e-mail with participants from around the world; before a fireplace with couples striving to enrich their marriages; around kitchen tables with mothers who are trying to apply the Ten Commandments to their child-rearing; in summer camps; and in our own home with our children and their friends. The idea behind the seminar, no matter what the environment, age group or culture, remains the same: to give people the opportunity to develop spiritually through *keeping* the commandments.

In each class of the seminar a commandment is introduced, its various levels of meaning are explained, and an assignment is given. It is recommended that participants keep journals in which they can record their experiences of examining themselves in the light of the particular commandment that is being studied. After a period of time spent focusing on one of the commandments, the participants return to class ready to share their experience of putting that commandment into practice. Sometimes they read from their journals or just talk about their experiences. Although time is allowed for important theological discussions, we keep our focus on the *actual experience* of bringing a

---

5. *Light In My Darkness*, 78.

particular commandment into the details of our lives, and on sharing what opened up for us as a result of doing this. We also talk about the thoughts and feelings that came up for us along the way. In a word, our focus is on *keeping* the commandments, not just learning about them and discussing them. As we pointed out when we discussed what it means to be a slave in the land of Egypt, our emphasis is not just on learning and stockpiling truth; rather, it is on applying that truth to every aspect of our lives, and, in so doing, entering the Promised Land.

In this book you will be reading journal entries written by seminar participants, and used with permission. Some of the details have been altered or omitted to protect privacy; grammar and spelling has been corrected to prevent misunderstanding and to increase clarity. Nevertheless, the journal entries are actual accounts of how people have striven to put the Ten Commandments into practice in their lives.

Getting the most out of this book

In order to get the most out of this book, we recommend that you study the commandments in sequential order. The study of each commandment begins with a series of quotations taken from the Sacred Scriptures of the major world religions (Judaism, Christianity, Islam, Buddhism, and Hinduism). The quotations show how every religion of the world has specific and central teachings about each of the Ten Commandments. In addition, each set of introductory quotations is summed up and synthesized in a quotation from Emanuel Swedenborg, an eighteenth century Christian theologian, whose writings demonstrate how the various world religions, when understood more deeply, are really one religion. As the French novelist Honoré de Balzac has written, "Swedenborg undoubtedly epitomizes all the religions—or rather the one religion of humanity."[6]

Begin by reading through each chapter and noting the various levels at which the particular commandment may be kept. Pay special attention to the journal entries within the chapter. This will give you an idea of how others have been striving to apply these commandments to their lives. Next, use the commandment as an opportunity to "rise above" your normal level of consciousness. Examine yourself carefully and honestly in the light of the particular commandment you are studying. As the Chinese philosopher Lao-tzu has said, "He who knows others is discerning; he who knows himself is wise" (*Tao Te Ching* 1:33). Finally, and most importantly, practice putting that commandment

---

6. *Oeuvres completes de H. de Balzac*, tome XVII (Paris: Michel Levy Freres, 1870), 7.

to work in your life each day. Record your experience of keeping the commandment in your journal.

There is great benefit in getting together with others to work on these commandments. Beyond merely discussing the commandments, the group atmosphere can provide support and encouragement. It also provides an incentive to keep working because you will have the opportunity to report your results to other members of your group each time you meet. Participants often find that reporting their experience of keeping a commandment helps them to be honest with themselves and with others. Participants also discover that they are not so different from other people as they might have thought, that we all struggle with similar issues, and that honest reporting of these struggles in a confidential setting can be of great benefit to one's self and to others.

Not all people have the time, opportunity or inclination to take part in a group process. As we have already said, just as there is a wide variety of religious paths, there is also a wide variety of learning styles. Some people like to make their way up the mountain in a group; others prefer to travel alone. There are many ways to the Promised Land. Therefore, the "Suggestions for Further Reflection and Application" at the end of each chapter are designed for individual or group use, and are suitable for either venue. Whether you choose to work alone or with a group, we encourage you to use the suggestions at the end of each chapter as vehicles for seeing broader applications of the commandments in your daily life.

We would especially encourage you to practice the meditation on the Lord's Prayer which is given at the end of each chapter. Meditating on Sacred Scripture is a time-honored spiritual discipline that helps us develop what the Hindus call "one-pointedness" (*Samadhi*)—the art of steadying and staying our mind on God and on the Sacred Scriptures. In the Jainist teachings it is written, "Righteous concentration is contemplation on the subject matter of Scriptural teaching . . . ." (*Tattvartha Sutra* 9:36). In the Sacred Scriptures of Islam we read, "And to thy Lord turn all thy attention" (*Qur'ān* 94:8). And in the Old Testament it is written, "Thou wilt keep him in perfect peace, whose mind is stayed on Thee" (Isaiah 26:3; King James Version).[7]

---

7. The pronouns "thou," "thy," and "thine" appear occasionally throughout this book, especially in well-known Scriptures (e.g. "*Thou* wilt keep him in perfect peace," "*Thy* will be done," and "For *Thine* is the kingdom"). Until the 17th century these pronouns were used to express informality—as when we address an intimate friend or close relative. Although modern English has almost entirely abandoned the use of these pronouns, they are often retained in certain poetic and religious expressions. It is also interesting to note that the word "thou" was used as a *singular* pronoun. In other words, the phrase, "Thou shalt not," suggests that God is speaking to each of us *individually*.

The narrow path

In this introduction we have been stressing the idea that there are many ways to the Kingdom of God, and that the Ten Commandments summarize those ways. We should also note that the way of religion, and especially the way of the Ten Commandments, is sometimes seen as a "narrow path." People often associate such narrowness with narrow-mindedness and rigid life-styles. They may refer to it as "the straight and narrow path" and see it as a solemn and difficult way to go through life. Such thinking may arise from a misunderstanding of Jesus' words, "Enter by the narrow gate; for wide is the gate and broad is the way that leads to destruction, and there are many who go in by it. Because narrow is the gate and difficult is the way which leads to life, and there are few who find it" (Matthew 7:13, 14). At first reading this certainly sounds as though the way of religion is straight, narrow, and difficult.

In another passage, when Jesus was journeying through the villages, He was asked, "Lord are there few who are saved?" His answer begins with the word "strive": "Strive to enter through the narrow gate, for many I say to you will seek to enter and will not be able" (Luke 13:22-24). In the original Greek the word that is here translated as "strive" is actually "agonize." This gives a clearer picture of the kind of effort that is required as we strive to live truly and fully according to our best understanding of God's will.

Ultimately, the important questions are not "How many are saved?" or "Is the path easy or difficult?" Instead, the important questions are, "Do you believe in God?" and "Have you courageously striven to live according to your faith with all your heart, soul, mind and strength?" A good life is a matter of belief combined with concentrated effort. This is the "narrow path." It calls each of us to keep our focus on God and on keeping the commandments. It prevents us from wandering too far "to the left" or "to the right" and thereby "broadening" the path. As it is written in the Old Testament, "Be strong and very courageous, that you may observe to do according to all the law that Moses My servant commanded you; do not turn from it to the right hand or to the left, that you may prosper wherever you go" (Joshua 1:7).

The central premise of this book is that we cannot "love the Lord" by merely saying or thinking that we do. The thoughts of our hearts and the words of our lips must be grounded in the actions of our lives. That is why Jesus told the disciples, "Not everyone who says to me 'Lord, Lord,' shall enter the Kingdom of Heaven, but he who does the will of My Father in heaven" (Matthew 7:21); and "If you love Me, keep My commandments" (John 14:15). When a rich young ruler asked Jesus what he must do in order to inherit eternal life, Jesus said, "*If you want to enter into life, keep the commandments*" (Matthew 19:17). In brief, to keep the commandments is to love God. As Emanuel Swedenborg writes in *Apocalypse Explained* 981:

> *To love the Lord is to love to keep the commandments of the Decalogue; in proportion as a person, from love or affection, keeps and does them, in the same proportion the person loves the Lord. The reason is that the Ten Commandments are the Lord with man.*

In summary, we believe that the Ten Commandments are a heavenly curriculum, ordered and designed by the Greatest Teacher of all. We believe that they are intended to lead all who keep them into the experience of heavenly life—even while on earth— for the Ten Commandments are God's presence with each of us. Though at first they may seem to be a "narrow path," they open the way to the greatest possible freedom. But you must see for yourself. We invite you, therefore, to try this curriculum and to experience your own transformation along the way.

You shall have no other gods before Me.

OLD TESTAMENT—EXODUS 20:3

 You shall worship the Lord your God,
and Him only you shall serve.

NEW TESTAMENT—MATTHEW 4:10

 The Lord hath decreed that ye worship
none save Him.

QUR'ĀN 3:1

 In Me alone fix thy mind,
let thy understanding dwell in Me:
in Me alone shalt thou live hereafter.

BHAGAVAD—GITA 12:8

 The commandment, "Thou shalt not make to thee other gods,"
includes not loving self and the things of the world above all things;
for that which one loves above all things is his god.

APOCALYPSE EXPLAINED 950:3

One True God

You shall love the Lord your God with all your heart,
with all your soul, and with all your strength.
—EXODUS 20:3

The nature of the One True God

AFRIEND OF ours was once asked, "Do you believe in God?" He answered, "No, I don't *believe* in God. I *know* God!" His response reminds us that there is probably no single concept or idea in the whole world that is more important to us than our concept of God. It is not sufficient to merely believe in God. We must *know* God—that is, we must know God's true nature.

If, for example, we have the idea that God is angry and vengeful, we, in turn, may feel justified when we respond to life's circumstances in angry and vengeful ways. If we believe that God punishes us, or turns away from us when we do not obey the commandments, we will be inclined to be punitive in our child rearing and withdraw our love when our children do not obey us. If we believe that God's love is conditional and depends on our performance, we may be inclined to be over-achievers, striving to earn the love of God and the approval of others.

On the other hand, if we have the idea that God is an infinitely loving Parent Who provides for all our needs, Who watches over us tenderly, Who guides us gently,

Who loves us abundantly without expecting anything in return, and Who forgives us unceasingly, we will be inspired to act similarly as we respond to others and to life's circumstances.

In the book of Genesis we read, "So God created man in His own image; in the image of God He created him" (Genesis 1:27). We are made in God's image—a rather pleasing thought. But trouble arises whenever we begin to attribute our fallible, human inclinations to God. When we do not "know" God, we tend to see the Divine nature as a reflection of our own human nature. Our impatience, anger, self-pity, greed, fear or resentment become the various lenses through which we see God, and we project our own shifting moods on the One who does not change. As a result, we do not really see ourselves as being created in the image of God; instead we create God in the image of ourselves. For example, an angry parent might say to her child, "God is very disappointed in your behavior," or "God is going to punish you for this." In reality, what we say about God may reveal more about our own nature than about God's true nature. Whenever we clothe God in our own infirmities, attributing to a perfect God what rightfully belongs to our imperfect human nature, we are worshipping a false god.[1]

It is important, therefore, that we have a right idea of God. The True God is the One God of all nations and of all people. The True God is all powerful, all wise, and ever present. The essential nature of the One True God is pure love, pure wisdom, and pure energy for useful service. The One True God has created us all, loves us all, and is continually and forever urging us to open ourselves so that we might receive the blessings of the Heavenly Kingdom. Whether we realize it or not, it is the One True God whom we seek, and whatever prevents us from experiencing the immediate presence of the One True God in our lives may be called a "false god." This could be a false idea of God, an attitude we have chosen, an object that we long for, a person whom we idolize or fear, or anything that we allow to stand between us and our God.

It is a touchstone of all the great religions that we should love God above all things and our neighbor as ourselves. In this first commandment, then, we are given an opportunity to examine what it is that we love above all things—our God and our

---

1. In this seminar, the term "false god" will be used to refer to any thing, any person, or any concept that stands between an individual and the immediate experience of God. According to the Islamic scholar 'Abdullah Yusuf 'Ali, false gods include idols, deified men, false ideas and superstitions. *The Holy Qur'ān: Text, Translation, and Commentary* (Maryland: Amana Corporation, 1989), 400, note 1167. In the index to the *Qur'ān*, the term "false gods" is used as a general category for all references to the worship of any other god, or any other thing, except Allah (p. 1732). In the Old Testament, "false gods" are generally referred to as "other gods," and "strange gods." And in the New Testament we find the terms "false prophets," "false christs" and "false witnesses."

neighbor, or our selves and the material possessions of the world. As it is written by Emanuel Swedenborg, "That which one loves above all things is his god" (*Apocalypse Explained* 950:3).

Total devotion to God

This commandment begins with the simple words, "I am the Lord your God." In these opening words, the One True God is speaking directly to us, using the same name that was used when God said to Moses at the burning bush, "I AM WHO I AM. . . . Thus you shall say to the children of Israel, 'I AM has sent me to you'" (Exodus 3:13-14). This is the great God of the universe, speaking to all people at all times, saying, "I am the Lord your God, who brought you out of the land of Egypt, out of the house of bondage. You shall have no other gods before Me."

As we mentioned in the introduction, all religions teach that God is continually bringing us out of what is represented by "the land of Egypt" and "the house of bondage." That is, God is continually delivering us from our imprisoning pre-occupation with our selves and our enslaving attachments to the things of the world. As it is written in the Hindu Scriptures, "Those who surrender to God all selfish attachments are like the leaf of a lotus floating clean and dry in the water. Sin cannot touch them" (*Bhagavad Gita* 5:10-12). Such a person is called a *Brahmin*: "Him I call a *Brahmin* who, casting off attachment to human things, rises above . . . all attachments" (*Dhammapada* 26:35). In focusing completely on God, in losing one's self entirely in God, one rises above all selfish attachments—even the attachment to life itself. This is what Jesus meant when He said, "Whoever desires to save his life will lose it, and whoever loses his life for My sake will find it" (Matthew 16:25). And in another place, emphasizing the importance of total devotion to God, above every materialistic craving and every earthly relationship, Jesus says, "Everyone who has left houses, or brothers or sisters or father or mother or wife or children or lands, for My name's sake, shall receive a hundredfold, and inherit everlasting life" (Matthew 19:29).

"Losing our lives" and "leaving houses, brothers or sisters or father or mother or wife or children or lands" does not mean that we must lose our physical lives, or physically leave our families, homes or native lands. It does mean, however, that we must be willing to focus on what is higher than all these things. It means that we must be willing to sacrifice everything of selfish pride and ambition so that we may truly worship God alone. We must be willing to focus on that which is higher than our need to be right, our longing for approval, or our inordinate desire for worldly wealth. We must be willing to focus on that which is higher than any self-serving allegiance to family, career or country. In brief, we must "seek first the kingdom of God" (Matthew 6:33). This idea is beautifully expressed in the following poem written by a prisoner. Notice how clearly he identifies those things that stand between him and his direct relationship with the One True God:

We search for a God we can touch.
In our longing for such a God we often create false gods
Who seem not so demanding.

It is hard for us to admit the truth
That what we worship and serve really is lord of our lives.

The God I was trying to love
Was too demanding — so I looked
For other gods who would ask less of me,
And in uncovered corners of my heart,
I found them.
Possessions, recognition, power!
I bowed before them, but my hunger only deepened.

The God I was trying to escape
Was too loving.
The gospel He preached was too hard.
"Love your enemy," He taught . . .
And so I turned to other gods.
This God that I had tried to love and tried to escape,
This God who was too demanding and too loving,
Gathered up my false gods:
My reputation; my pride; my honor and prestige; my possessions;
My success; my own glory; my time; my friends; even my daughter —
He gathered up all these lords of mine
He gathered up all my lies and held them close to me —

So close I lost all sight
Of my true God for a while.

But my true God never lost sight of me —
(and therein lies my salvation).
For in one desperate moment,
Smothered by gods who couldn't save me,
I prayed for a God who would.[2]

Out of Egypt

In the great opening to the Ten Commandments, we read about the God whose leading quality is that of Savior. "I am the Lord your God who brought you out of the land of Egypt, out of the house of bondage." The Hebrew verb is here translated in the English past tense as "*brought you out.*" This suggests that we have already been delivered from spiritual captivity. But if this is true—if we have indeed been delivered from spiritual captivity—why does it sometimes feel as though we are still in bondage? Why does it feel as though the battle is still raging, and that we are in the very midst of it? Why does this "new life" at times feel so much like the old one we left behind in "the land of Egypt" when we were in the "house of bondage"?

This is because *we still must do our part.* Although we are "out of Egypt" we are not yet in the Promised Land. God has indeed (just as this commandment states) brought us out of spiritual bondage. But note carefully where God has led us: to the foot of Mt. Sinai. We no longer need to be enslaved by ideas and emotions that formerly held us captive. We have been brought out of captivity and set free—free to learn the truth, free to live according to that truth, and free to become all that we are intended to be. The truth will set us free. That truth, given at Sinai, is the Ten Commandments. These Divinely given laws are a perfect progression, a wonderfully connected sequence that, if followed, will take us step by step into the Promised Land. Every time we make a decision to live according to the Divine truth—*and actually do it*—we claim the victory which has already been won for us. As a result, we are gradually "brought out" of bondage to selfish and worldly attachments, and led into states of deeper love and greater wisdom.

---

2. Unpublished poem written by Matt O'Donnell. Used with permission.

In the original Hebrew, the verb that is translated "brought you out" actually refers to completed activity in the past, present or future.[3] Therefore it might be better translated, "I am the Lord your God who *brought* you out of the land of Egypt, *is bringing* you out of the land of Egypt, and *will bring* you out of the land of Egypt." This is why we speak of spiritual development as a continuous journey, filled with battles that are fought and won yesterday, today and tomorrow. And yet the higher truth, transcending all sense of the past, present or future, is that "The battle is the Lord's, and He will give it into our hands" (1 Samuel 17:47). In this way the Lord our God is, was, and always will be our Savior—the God who continually leads us out of bondage, out of slavery, and into true freedom.

The first step

The first step on the journey, as basic as learning the number "1" in mathematics, or the letter "A" of the alphabet, is to know that God exists. "I am" says our God. It is the simplest possible way to express the Divine Identity. "I am the Lord your God," the One who brought you out of spiritual captivity. This is why we are told, "You shall have no other gods before Me."

At the time when this commandment was given, it was common to worship a plurality of gods such as the god of rain, the god of fertility, the god of war or the god of harvest. Therefore, in the historical context, this commandment was given to remind the people of Israel that the God who brought them out of the land of Egypt was the greatest God of all—to be worshiped before all other gods. This was an accommodation to their state of mind. They weren't quite ready for the idea of *one* God; but the idea of the Savior God as the greatest one of all was an important and crucial step for them to take. The people were solemnly warned, "You shall make no graven images," and "You shall not bow down to them." Again, they were to keep their focus on the Savior God, the God who had redeemed them from their enemies.

In today's society not many of us actually bow down to graven images, worship rain gods, or pray to the god of fertility. But we can still violate the spirit of this commandment whenever we find ourselves dwelling obsessively on the material things

---

3. The Hebrew verb used in this passage is "*Yatsa*" which means "to go out," "to cause to go out," or "to lead out." Although the form of the verb suggests completed activity, this may be a completed activity in the past, present or future. In other words, God has already won the battles which we have faced in the past, are facing in the moment, or will face in the future.

of the world (cars, televisions, computers, etc.), as well as upon other people and our relationships with them (bearing grudges, wondering what kind of an impression we are making, worrying about our popularity, etc.). In essence, we violate this commandment whenever we allow ourselves to be governed by thoughts or ruled by feelings that do not come from God. We call such thoughts and feelings "other gods" or "false gods" because these incessant demands prevent us from feeling and experiencing the immediate presence of the One True God in our lives.

This first commandment, then, invites us to examine ourselves, to notice what occupies our minds, and to discover what cuts us off from feeling the joy of God's presence. This commandment invites us to identify and name the "occupants" of our minds—the thoughts and feelings that demand our attention, the things that we dwell on, the attitudes and opinions that have taken up more or less permanent residence within us. This is a call to fearless, honest self-examination. It is perhaps what the Irish poet William Butler Yeats meant when he wrote, "Why should we honor those who die on the field of battle? A man may show as reckless a courage in entering into the abyss of himself."[4]

Identifying our false gods

Whatever we spend the most time thinking about can become a false god. Our mind keeps drifting back to that subject—whether it is an idea that fascinates us, a person who has hurt our feelings, or an event that we consider unjust. Our conversations seem to keep coming around to that topic; we may find that people say things that remind us of our favorite subject, our "pet peeve," or our persistent complaint. If you love sports or politics or music, notice how easy it is for you to find a way to bring up that topic in a conversation. If someone has hurt you, notice how much time and energy you give toward mentally nursing your wound, or "discussing it" with others. An emotion or a thought may be so overpowering that it "rules over" you and "controls" you. You can't shake it off; you can't stop thinking about it. Though you may be temporarily distracted, your mind finds a way of returning to those same thoughts and dredging up those same emotions. Those thoughts and emotions become your master, and you become their slave. Whenever we find ourselves "obsessing" about something, we can be sure that we have returned to the "house of bondage."

---

4. Quoted by Maynard Mack in "The World of Hamlet," *The Yale Review* 41 (1952): 523.

When any activity, person or thing becomes an obsession, it may be called a "false god" because it dominates our lives. On the altar of our minds it commands the central place; in our hearts it reigns supreme. Nothing is more important than our obsession—not even God. In the following journal entry, a thirty-year-old prisoner describes his fifteen-year addiction to alcohol, calling it "the center of his life." He writes:

> *While on the streets my god was alcohol. I did everything for that god and loved it with all my heart, soul, and mind. I went to work to make money to give to my god, and I did give generously. When I'd have problems in my life, or felt angry about someone or something, I'd go directly to my god for comfort. When something good happened in my life, you got it, time to celebrate with my god. It was the center of my life. It was my life! I'd worship my god and do whatever it wanted me to do, because it was in total control of me.*

A forty-four-year-old female prisoner writes:

> *Having "no other gods before Me" means that we shouldn't serve images and idols, and that we are only supposed to serve our Father in Heaven. In the days past I have served drugs, man, and money. Those were the things I worshiped. When I got up in the morning, instead of saying thanks to God, I put a needle in my arm, or just went and broke the law for money.*

Another female prisoner, age twenty-nine, writes:

> *Every day for the past fifteen years of my life I have worshiped my god. This god even killed my father, and I still fall down on my knees twenty or thirty times a day and worship my guts out. My god is cigarettes.*

Addictions and obsessions are "false gods." They drive us with incredible, relentless power until we eventually submit to their demands. They rule over us like harsh taskmasters, and we bow down to them and serve them. People who have become addicted must eventually admit that their addictions have totally consumed them, that they have been unable to break free, and that most of their mental energy is devoted to finding ways to "appease" the insatiable appetites of these false gods. This is especially true in cases of addiction to cocaine, heroin, and other highly addictive substances. Sometimes, however, the addiction can be more subtle. Consider, for example, the following journal entry of a class participant who recognized marijuana as his false god:

I always believed that if marijuana were used properly, it could be regarded as a sacred substance. In fact, I prided myself on the fact that I used it very seldom—only once or twice a year, and only to gain a closer communication with God. Over the years I learned that it was best not to make any major decisions until I had smoked up and opened my mind entirely to God. My encounters with marijuana had always been positive and joyful. I had learned things about myself and about other people that I felt I could have never learned in any other way. For example, I once was so mad at my wife that I almost became physically violent with her. Instead, I decided to smoke some marijuana. As soon as I smoked up I came into an entirely different state of consciousness. I understood my wife, and I realized that I didn't have to be angry. Over the years I used marijuana in this way to help me better understand other people, and to make important career decisions. It was my special "link" to God.

What I didn't realize, however, was that all through those years, when it came to making major decisions in my life, I had never risen above my need for marijuana. I would tell myself, "Well, before I make a decision about that, I will have to get loaded and see what God has to say." How could I have been so blind and deaf? I had convinced myself that my sacred "pow-wows" were holy times—times when I could experience God directly and get immediate direction from Him. I didn't realize that in trusting that marijuana would connect me with God, I had, in fact, made this substance my "false god."

To sum up: I had trusted in marijuana rather than in God. I had limited my experience of God's presence to once or twice a year, rather than trusting that I live and breathe and move in God's presence every moment.[5]

In this person's case, the appearance was that he had been able to "control" his marijuana usage—using it only once or twice a year, and only for "sacred purposes." In

---

5. Terence Gorski and Merlene Miller have identified eight basic categories of addictive behavior (besides alcohol and drug addiction). These include the compulsive need to diet or overeat (anorexia/bulimia); the compulsive need to take risks (gambling); the compulsive need to keep busy, accomplish things and excel (overachieving); the compulsive need to stimulate the body through physical exertion (over-exercising); the compulsive need to have sexual experiences (sexaholism); the compulsive need to experience intense stress or thrills (thrill seeking); and the compulsive need to buy or acquire possessions (overspending). See *Staying Sober: A Guide for Relapse Prevention* (Independence, Missouri: Herald House / Independence Press), 120-121.

reality it had become a false god. Because he trusted in marijuana as his "link" to the Divine presence, he had lost faith in the myriad ways that God was actually present and leading him in every moment of his life.

Another false god that can keep us "in bondage" is the addiction to watching TV. A pastor, the leader of a large congregation, writes:

> *The other day I put on the TV to see what was on. It was a movie I had already seen about ten times. I had other things that I really wanted to do, and needed to do, but I couldn't break away from watching the TV. There was a certain scene in the movie that I wanted to see again. It was about an hour into the movie and I told myself that I would just watch that scene and then shut off the TV. When the scene came I watched it and just couldn't stop. I kept on watching till the movie was over. The TV was in total control of me. I was totally captivated. I sat there for three hours, in bondage—a slave in Egypt.*

Though addictions are a fairly typical example of how "false gods" can show up in our lives, there are other ways too. In the following example, a thirty-four-year-old housewife describes a kind of idolatry she fell into by putting others on a pedestal:

> *Recently some friends of mine said that they were going to get a divorce. I was shocked, dismayed and saddened. I had idealized their lives, their relationship, and their position in society. But maybe this attitude didn't allow them enough space to air their feelings. After all, they couldn't let any crack show because of the husband's very public position. If we had allowed them to have flaws, without being shocked, would it have made a difference? I don't know. But in the future I will try to admire people's good qualities without putting them on a pedestal or altar. Only the Lord walks on water.*

Expecting perfection is a widespread yet well-hidden form of idolatry. The worship of this false god, when undetected, can be most harmful. A thirty-eight-year-old mother of four children writes:

> *One of my numerous false gods is that of perfection. I want/expect my life to be perfect. The perfect home, the perfect car, the perfect wife, mother, teacher, perfect husband, children, even dog! Needless to say, I never feel that I can reach my goal, and I find myself becoming angry, dissatisfied, sad, impatient,*

etc., with those in my life who are not striving for my idea of perfection. How dare they not play their role in my "reality"? I have been bowing down to the false god of perfection.

Beginning at a young age

Identifying our false gods can be difficult. Often, and especially when we are young, we first see false gods in *others* before we begin to see them in *ourselves*. This is not necessarily a bad thing, and it may not mean that our children are being overly critical when they observe improper behavior in others. In fact, it can be a useful first step in beginning to recognize false gods in themselves. In the following example, a ten-year-old boy talks about a false god he sees in others during a school athletic activity.

Today in recess we played a game called "knockout." One person is picked to be the bumper. That was me. The kids picked on me and got mad at me because I am not very good at being a bumper. The bumper's job is to bump the ball out of the net. I'm not good at it, but the kids who are good at it get mad at me. Just me, not at the other kids. They are bowing down to the "mean god."

A twelve-year-old girl notices that she may have a tendency to serve the false god of "being right." She is well on her way to learning what it means to be more tolerant of other people's viewpoints:

In school I found myself saying, "No, that couldn't be right." I realized afterwards that they might be right. My false god is not considering what others think. I think I am always right.

A nine-year-old boy, examining himself in the light of this commandment, observes what he does when he gets mad at someone:

My false god is the "evil eye." Whenever I am mad at someone I squint my eyes and go "ooooooooooooohhhhhhhh." Once a boy named Andrew tripped me on purpose and I gave him the evil eye. My false god makes me give the "bad-eye," "evil-eye" look.

Earlier, we read of a person who compared his TV watching to being "in bondage—

a slave in Egypt." Here a ten-year-old boy also realizes that his desire to watch television may be a form of slavery to a false god:

> *Whenever I ask my Mom if I can watch TV she says, "No." But I don't take "No" for an answer. Sometimes when the false god begins to rule over me a whole lot I sneak and watch TV when my parents are not in the room. It feels like a false god because I have to watch it or else my day is not a good day.*

A seventeen-year-old high school student observes that she has been too much of a "people pleaser." She writes:

> *My false god is wanting to please other people. I am always worried about what people think about me and what they will say about me. Sometimes I just can't put these worries out of my mind. They stay with me for a long time. I keep wondering, "What did they think about me?" and, "Did I say the right thing?" I go over it again and again in my mind. This concern about what other people think is really a false god.*

A nineteen-year-old African identifies a false god that is familiar to us all. He calls it, quite simply, "Me-ism":

> *"Me-ism" is my false god. Everything that I have done, I thought that it comes from me. I had thought that I don't need God to help me because I can do everything by myself. You know this god is a thief because he really steals the truth and the good of God. I learned that I must be aware of this false god because he pulls you slowly away from the true God. This god was ruling me. He was part and parcel of my life. But now I am saying thanks to God who saved me from this false god. Now I am saying, "No more, no, no, no, no, no other gods."*

Bowing down to other people's false gods

We have said that having "no other gods" before the One True God means that we should be led by God alone, rather than by our own selfish desires. However, this also means that we should be careful about being led by, or dominated by, the selfish desires of other people. For example, a small child should be able to say "No" when a friend suggests that they steal some candy from the neighborhood store. A worker should be able to refuse to join in when her co-workers engage in destructive gossip about another employee. A man should be able to say "No" when his legal advisors suggest that he shade the truth in order to make his case look better. Each of these people should be able to refuse to bow down to someone else's false god. As it is written in the Old Testament, "You shall not follow a crowd to do evil" (Exodus 23:2).

In the following example a prisoner refuses to "bow down" to the false god of an old neighborhood friend. Referring to his friend as his "homeboy," he writes:

> *Tonight at the Wednesday Night Bible Study, one of my homeboys came into the study, sat down, and we talked for a minute. He asked me to write a statement about the prison dentist, stating that the dentist is a racist and not giving the inmates fair treatment. He explained that the dentist had done some dental work on him, but had refused to give him a plate. He said that the dentist said some things that were not professional. As I listened to him the spirit said, "Remember your assignment, You shall not bow down to false gods."*
>
> *Now this brother is my personal homeboy. I went to school with him, and it wasn't easy to say, "I can't." He looked at me funny, but I said, "I can't write a statement against this man. He hasn't done anything to me, and I just can't say he did it because you said he did this to you."*
>
> *I was hoping that he would understand my point, but I could see in his eyes that he was very disappointed with me, but I can't worry about how he feels. He will get over it. As it says in the Bible, "We ought to obey God rather than man." As this came to mind, I said to myself, "I ought to obey God rather than my homeboy."*

At another level we might sometimes find ourselves being deeply influenced by philosophical or psychological systems, or the teachings of a particularly enlightened individual. These systems and teachers can be quite helpful in our spiritual development. In fact, one of the ways that God's teachings come to us is through the minds of great thinkers and writers everywhere and at all times. But a word of caution is necessary. Although the words of these wise people may be intended to lead us to God, they must not take the place of God. They may show us the way to a deeper understanding of God's love for us, but they are not the *Way* itself. They may provide useful and illuminating insights about how we might apply the truths of revelation to our lives, but they are not the *Truth* itself. They may lead us more deeply into spiritual life, but they are not *Life* itself. Our many teachers along the way, in every branch of knowledge, serve us well and are a vital part of our spiritual journey. They are provided by God to help us in our journey to the Promised Land. Nevertheless, while the thoughts of friends, philosophers, psychologists, and other great thinkers may be helpful in our spiritual development, we must always return to the Source: we must return to God and to the Sacred Scriptures for direction and inspiration.

In the New Testament a story is told about the apostle, John, who was banished to the Isle of Patmos. While he was there an angel came to him and showed him wonderful things. John says, "When I heard and saw, I fell down to worship before the feet of the angel who showed me these things." But the angel corrected John, saying, "See that you do not do that. For I am your fellow servant, and of your brethren the prophets, and of those who keep the words of this book. Worship God" (Revelation 22:8-9). The words of the angel remind us that we must not worship or bow down to anyone or anything except the One True God.

The Rumpelstiltskin Effect

From time to time we may experience overpowering desires to think unkindly of others, to spread malicious rumors, to disparage our parents, to criticize our children, to brag about our accomplishments or to grovel in our misery. All these desires can become "false gods," especially when they rule over us and make us serve them. Therefore, it is of utmost importance that we learn to accurately "name" these false gods. It is not sufficient to say, "I feel upset." We must try to be as specific as possible. For example, some of the false gods that we might identify are anger, impatience, self-righteousness, the need for approval, the need to be right, and the need to control. In the following journal entry we are given a graphic and *specific* example of how a modern mother "sacrifices" her children at the altar of self-righteousness, as she bows down to the god of anger. She writes:

> *The way I seem to serve this god of anger might be called my "morning worship." This god of anger seems to like sacrifices, especially children and their self-esteem. There are many mornings when this false god is well pleased with*

me. Yelling at my children is the way I praise and glorify his name. Harsh tones are his hymns, and I sing them too well. Anger is really something I have to work on. I don't like it when I serve this god. My insides feel awful. But I keep giving daily tribute to it when I think thoughts such as, "I'm right," "I'm always right," "I'm never wrong."

Often, parent-child relationships provide ample opportunities to identify our false gods. In the following journal entry, a woman comes to the realization that she has allowed her mother to come between her and her relationship with the One True God. This realization came during a "Rise Above It" class when we invited the participants to stand up on their chairs to gain a sense of what it might feel like to rise above a false god. She writes:

I have been working on my relationship with my mother for the past twenty years of my adult life. Even though she has passed away, I have not been able to allow myself to be free of her control, and so you might say that I have been in bondage—a slave in Egypt. I have always felt terribly controlled and terribly intruded upon by her. I was raised with the idea that my parents are in the place of God and that I must honor them. I have always felt ashamed that I could not fully honor her. What I see now is that this depends on my parents' view of the Lord. A gentle God is O.K., but not a punishing and controlling one.

I have been able to appreciate the good things my mother gave me, but they have been overshadowed by her domination and my shame, anger, and guilt. I knew that my mother had come between my God and me. I had tried to move her off to the side, but it didn't work. Her influence was still there. When I physically stood up on a chair, and got a different perspective on the situation (when I "rose above it"), I could actually feel that my mother was no longer an influence "over" me. And what I found was that the Lord was above me. She had continued to be an influence over me until I stood up on that chair. Identifying her as a false god helped me to "name it" without shaming her or me. I no longer felt ashamed or angry. When I got up on that chair, I felt finally free.

After writing this journal entry the participant shared the following insight with the seminar participants: "I realized that I had been trying to *move my mother*. The difference was that I didn't need to move my mother in order to stand up on the chair. Instead of trying to move my mother, *I moved!*"

There is real power in being able to accurately name the false god that is ruling over us. We are reminded of the fairy tale in which a young woman is held captive, kept under the spell of a wicked little man. The only thing that can free the young woman from the spell is the remote possibility that she can discover the man's true name. This, however, is not likely since his name is an unfamiliar and unusual one. The situation becomes desperate when the wicked man tells her that if she does not discover his name within three days, he will take her first-born child. Through a series of coincidences she discovers the little man's name, and at the last minute she says to him, "Your name is Rumpelstiltskin!" The little man is shocked and enraged. The spell is broken, and he flees away—never to return. The young lady keeps her child and is freed from the oppression of the petty tyrant who had so dominated her life.

This fairy tale contains a valuable lesson about the importance of naming our false gods. *As soon as the young lady was able to name the man, he lost his power over her!* It is similar in the realm of spirit. It is not sufficient for us to be vaguely aware of our spiritual states, or to make a general confession that we are "sinners." We must be specific; we must be able to identify the false god that is ruling over us; we must be able to *name it*. Naming it is the first step to overcoming it. We call this "the Rumpelstiltskin Effect."

A participant taking the seminar via e-mail writes:

> *This idea of giving a name to the obsession which blocks spiritual growth is very helpful. I like the idea of knowing its name so that, like Rumpelstiltskin, it might be deprived of its power. The false god that controls me might be called ESR—Energizer of the Self-Righteous. It manifests itself as anger towards others and vindictiveness, especially when others flout the behavioral standards that I feel compelled to fulfill to the letter. Why is this false god so addictive? Because it doles out quick jolts of energy. It provides the reward of smug self-satisfaction, the feeling of being superior to others. ESR masquerades as true righteousness, but really it is a cluster of contempt, conceit and arrogant self-righteousness.*

A young mother, also taking the seminar via e-mail, writes:

> *Hopelessness is the name of my false god. I have had a string of nights with children who wake up one after the other, and with one child who has such a chronic sleep problem that he stays up most of the night before we can get him*

to sleep at all. When I finally get to sleep myself I wake up feeling tired, overwhelmed, and convinced that nothing will work, that I can't possibly do the housework, that I can't play with the children, that my paperwork is too deep to be waded through, and that NOTHING WILL EVER CHANGE. This feeling of hopelessness overwhelms me so much that I just sit around playing computer games or watching TV.

Last night I realized what was happening to me, and in one hour I got more done than in the last three days put together! This morning the children and I cleaned all the bedrooms, did all the laundry, and then went to the mall for a wonderful afternoon together.

What was the difference? I just chose not to believe that it was hopeless. I was still exhausted, but that didn't prevent me from having a productive day. Now it is only 10:30 p.m. and two of my three little ones are asleep. The last (the one with real struggles in this area) is resting quietly in front of a movie, cuddling with his dad.

This young mother felt overwhelmed by a feeling which she named "hopelessness." Fortunately, she was able to recognize the extent to which she was in bondage to this state of mind, and she saw how it had been enslaving her. When she began to realize what was actually happening to her, she named her state of mind. In that moment the spell was broken, Rumpelstiltskin (her hopelessness) departed, and she was free to enjoy her family. She had successfully identified the false god.

The assignment: Identify false gods / Self-examination

This commandment invites us to take time for reflection. Notice what consumes your mental energy. Notice what feelings or thoughts about people or things rule over you and occupy your mind. Is there a person, a substance, or an activity in your life that controls you or about which you are obsessive or compulsive? Do you find yourself dwelling on troublesome people, political problems, or financial concerns, while leaving little room for God? Do you find yourself being ruled by the god of fear, anger, hatred, greed, lust, self-pity, hopelessness, or resentment? Pay careful attention to whatever it is that separates you from the experience of God's immediate presence. *Identify it* as a false god and *name it.*

Assignment

Identify false gods / Self-examination

When you notice a false god ruling over you, name it.

In your journal, record your experience of keeping this commandment.

SUGGESTIONS FOR FURTHER REFLECTION AND APPLICATION

MEDITATION: "OUR FATHER WHO ART IN HEAVEN"
The opening phrase of the Lord's Prayer, "Our Father who art in heaven," reminds us that there is One True God. Try using this phrase as a meditation, repeating it silently, over and over again, as you practice the spiritual discipline of keeping this commandment. Set aside a period of time each day to find a quiet place where you can stay your mind on the simple words, "Our Father who art in heaven." As you do so, keep in mind that there is One True God who loves you with an everlasting love, who will never leave you comfortless, and who will keep you in perfect peace.

ACTIVITY: TRAINING THE MIND
While there are many forms of meditation, we have found that the ancient practice of meditating on Sacred Scripture is simple, powerful and safe. We have also found that the best time for us is early in the morning—just as we awaken—before embarking on our worldly responsibilities. At that time our minds are most receptive and relatively uncluttered with worldly concerns. It is a good time to allow a specific passage from Sacred Scripture to sink into the depths of our consciousness and to remain with us throughout the day. Another good time to meditate (or simply to read and reflect on Sacred Scripture) is in the evening, just before going to sleep.

Meditation should be an enjoyable process, not a chore. Think about it as gently disciplining your mind, and training it to stay focused. When seeing-eye dogs are being trained, they must learn to walk beside the trainer without a leash, and not stray from the path. Recently, two seminar participants acquired a cute Golden Retriever puppy named "Izzie." This was because Izzie had flunked out of a special training school for seeing-eye dogs. As the story goes, Izzie's downfall came when he saw a squirrel and chased it! Izzie needed to learn to be focused, to stay by the trainer's side, to control impulses, and not allow distractions to enter. Think of your mind as an impulsive puppy that needs to be trained, and the Sacred Scriptures as the Master's voice. Train your mind to stay by the Master's side, and to keep to the path. When it wanders, gently bring it back. You can even tell it to "stay."

JOURNAL REFLECTIONS: AN EXPLANATION
At the end of each chapter we write, "In your journal, record your experience of keeping this commandment." Journal keeping is a time-honored spiritual discipline that can assist us in the work of honest self-examination. In our journals we write to remember. We put our experiences and our responses to these experiences into written form so that we can reflect on them and learn from them. These journal entries are for you alone—much like a personal diary. Still, there is value in sharing your insights with others as we all travel together on the road of self-discovery. Enjoy the process!

JOURNAL REFLECTION
As a *young person*, what was your idea of God? Did you see God as kind? loving? angry? vengeful? forgiving? punishing? Did you have a picture of God in your mind? an awareness of the sound of God's voice? a feeling of God's presence? Was your experience of God an intimate one or a distant one? In your journal, or with a friend, describe your understanding of God—or your relationship with God—when you were young.

JOURNAL REFLECTION
Describe your current relationship with God.

JOURNAL REFLECTION
Describe one area of your life in which you need help right now. For example, in a particular relationship, facing an addiction, addressing some particular fear, etc.

ACTIVITY: SHARING "4 BY 4" STYLE

The *Rise Above It* seminar is usually presented as a series of ten classes that meet once a week for two hours. During this time we provide an opportunity for sharing in small groups that we refer to as "4 by 4's." We break into groups of four people who are randomly selected. Each person in the group has four minutes to share his or her recent experience of keeping the commandment. (For a complete explanation of the "4 by 4" process, see *Appendix: Conscious Reporting: the "4 by 4."*)

ACTIVITY: MAKE A LIST

Make a general list of "other gods" or "false gods." Identify as many as you can think of, whether they apply to you or not. Then go back and identify those that apply to you in particular, or to situations in your life. Do you see any patterns? Try spending time on this assignment on your own. When finished, you may compare your list to the one on the next page.

ACTIVITY: NAME THE FEAR

You may take the previous activity to an even deeper level by looking at each of your "false gods" and determining or naming the underlying fear. Does your false god stem from a fear of abandonment or rejection? Is it rooted in a fear of disappointing others or a fear of failure? Could it perhaps be linked to a fear of being vulnerable or a fear of facing the truth? What about a fear of the unknown, or a fear of all of the things that could possibly go wrong? For example, if you identify "anger" as your false god (especially when dealing with one of your children), you might be able to see that the anger comes from a fear of failure—the fear that your child will make the same mistakes in life that you made. Another example: one of your false gods might be "anxiety" manifesting as the need to eat whenever you feel anxious. If you look more closely at this false god, you may discover that this is actually related to a fear of rejection. Identifying false gods in terms of the underlying fears can be a helpful self-examination tool. In your journal, describe what comes up for you as you do this activity.

FALSE GODS

A SAMPLING

anger	perfectionism	nicotine
self-pity	cynicism	alcohol
control	misery	drugs
accomplishment	doubt	sugar
fear	lust	food
judgment	pride	discouragement
impatience	greed	contempt
jealousy	resentment	criticism
approval	rage	workaholism
gossip	power	sex
anxiety	recognition	money
laziness	possessions	reputation
dwelling on the past	dwelling on the future	worry

You shall not take the name of the Lord your God in vain.

OLD TESTAMENT—EXODUS 20:3

 Whoever calls upon the name of the Lord shall be saved.

NEW TESTAMENT—ROMANS 10:13

 He is Allah and there is no other God, the Sovereign Lord, the Holy One, the Source of Peace, the Guardian of Faith, the Preserver of Safety, the Exalted in Might, the Irresistible, the Supreme. . . . To Him belong the Names most beautiful.

QUR'ĀN 59:23-24

 They call Him Indra, Mitra, Varuna, and Agni . . . To what is One the sages give many names.

RIG VEDA I:164, 46

 The name of anyone means not only his name but his whole characteristic quality.

TRUE CHRISTIAN RELIGION 300:1

CHAPTER TWO

The Name of God

Now, O prince, I shall recite the Names of the Lord. Listen carefully, and they will remove fear and evil from your life.

—WORDS OF BHISHMA TO PRINCE YUDHISHTHIRA,
FROM THE MAHABHARATA—SABHA PARVA 36:28

A name represents a person's inner quality

IN OUR STUDY of the first commandment we focused on the Lord our God who "brought us out of the land of Egypt, out of the house of bondage." Our assignment was to identify the false gods we serve, to name them, and to observe how much of our mental and emotional energy is devoted to "bowing down" before them. These were the false gods that kept us in bondage and prevented us from experiencing the presence of the One True God. You may have noticed that, like "Rumpelstiltskin"— the petty tyrant who tried to take the young woman's child, the false god that kept you in bondage suddenly disappeared when you named it. In the fairy tale about Rumpelstiltskin, the little man became so upset when his name was discovered that he ran away and never returned. By correctly *naming* the wicked man, the spell was broken, and the young lady was able to keep her child.

Sometimes, however, merely naming a false god is not enough. Certainly it is an excellent *beginning*, but when a false god refuses to go away, and continues to enslave us—even after it has been named—we may need more help. That's why we are given the next commandment. In this commandment our focus shifts from identifying and naming our false gods to calling upon the name of the One True God. As we enter into this commandment, it is useful to keep in mind Emanuel Swedenborg's teaching: "The name of anyone means not only his name but his whole characteristic quality."[1]

In many cultures, the name that is given to a person represents a unique quality or personality characteristic. In the Native American tradition, for example, children are given names that are symbolic of inner qualities—names like Brave Eagle, Laughing Waters, Swift Arrow, and Peaceful Dove.[2] When we offered this seminar in Africa, we met people who were named Peacemaker, Goodwill, Wisdom, Welcome, Gladness, and Purity. While we were there, we were given honorary Zulu names: *Thandazani* (Pray Together) and *Thandanani* (Love Each Other). And the four American college students who presented the seminar in Ghana were given honorary Twi names: *Anigye Nkoaa* (Joyful), *Asumdoe* (Peaceful), *Akomapa* (Good-Hearted) and *Abutare* (Patient).

People from various religious traditions go through a similar naming process. In the Jewish tradition, newborn sons are named on the eighth day, at the time of circumcision. During the ceremony the *Moyle* (literally, "one who circumcises") invokes the Hebrew names of the child's ancestors and then asks the parents to name their child. At a ceremony that we were invited to attend, the Hebrew names of the parents and grandparents were invoked, and their significance explained, before the child was named. When the time came to name the child, the parents said that his name was to be "Gabriel," which means "one who is devoted to God." In the Hindu tradition, a *Jyoti* (literally, "one who brings the light") gives the child a Sanskrit name that accords with the child's inner spirit or "God quality." Later, if the child chooses to enter a monastic order, a new name, *representing a new quality*, is given to the child. Similarly, during the Christian sacrament of infant baptism, the priest or minister often asks, "Will you now name this child?" The name given to the child at the time of baptism often represents a particular quality that the parents hope their child will have. And later, at the time of Christian confirmation, the child may once again receive a new name—often the name of a Christian saint. Many of these naming practices are beautifully summarized in the

---

1. *True Christian Religion* (London: The Swedenborg Society, 1950), 300:1.
2. In some of the more primitive Native American religions a person's name was considered a vital part of a person's soul. It was believed, therefore, that the malicious handling of a person's name could produce actual physical injury—even death! Similarly, the ancient Israelites (as well as primitive Hindus and Australian aborigines) believed that blessings and curses could be given merely by the way a person's name was spoken. This is why primitive people were so careful to avoid the abuse of a person's name, and were especially concerned about not taking the name of God in vain. See James Frazer, *The Golden Bough: A Study in Comparative Religion*, Vol. 3 (New York: Macmillan, 1935), 318.

Book of Revelation, where we read of a "new name"—a new inner quality—which is given to everyone who overcomes: "To him who overcomes I will give some of the hidden manna to eat. And I will give him a white stone, and on the stone a new name written which no one knows except him who receives it" (Revelation 2:17).

In the following journal entry, a thirty-seven-year-old clergyman describes how his name has taken on a deeper significance for him over the years. It further illustrates the idea that a name can represent an inner quality:

I haven't realized it until now, but as soon as I've begun to reflect on my name and what it means to me, I realize that my name is sacred to me. My name embodies all that I am, and is not to be tampered with.

It hasn't always been this way. When I was young I didn't particularly like my name. I felt embarrassed about it, and at times when I would say my name to myself, or when I heard it used in a television program or movie, I felt a bit uncomfortable and even "yucky" inside.

But that has changed as I've grown up, and as I've learned more and more about myself and about my name. My name means "warrior," and it's interesting to me that when I was in fifth grade my first and favorite hymn from my church's liturgy was titled, "As Warriors True." I loved that song for the strength and courage that were depicted in it:

> *As warriors true, before the Lord we stand*
> *In battle front, awaiting His command. . . .*

I loved that song (I still do), enough so that as a fifth grader I taught myself to plunk out the melody of the first few lines on our piano at home. I played them often to myself.

Later in my life I read the best seller by Betty Eadie, Embraced by the Light *—a long description of her near death experience and the effects that it had on her life. In the middle of that book Betty describes a particular type of angel that she got to see and learn about as part of her near death experience. She says that these angels are called "warrior angels." Everyone, she says, has associate angels present with them and helping them at all times, but in especially difficult times we need these "warrior angels" to be present with us; and they are* *available to us through prayer. She says that the warrior angels are magnificent to behold. They are bigger and more muscular in appearance than other angels, and they actually wear headdress and armor. She says that they are swifter than other angels, and that one of the striking things about them is their utter sense of confidence—nothing evil can daunt them, and they know it! Betty was also struck by the looks of compassion that she saw in these angels' faces. At one point in her experience, she saw them speed off in a certain direction on some undisclosed mission; and as she watched them depart, she knew—and they knew—that they would not return until their mission was completed.*

I love the description that Betty Eadie has written about these "warrior-angels." Each time I tell it to a friend I get a little choked up inside. Part of the reason I get choked up is because this is the kind of person I think I have always been— a warrior from the grass roots up—and this is the kind of angel I would love to be. I love the exhilaration of a good fight for a good cause. I love justice and standing by what is right. And through all my years of growing up, I have felt compassionate and protective toward people whom I've seen picked on and bullied by others.

Through these experiences I have come to believe that I am aptly named, and I have come to love my name. It embodies all that I have ever been, all that I am, and all that I hope to be. My name is sacred to me, and it is not to be tampered with—not by anyone.

Holy Names

In the great spiritual traditions, and in the Sacred Scriptures associated with each tradition, the name of God is always most holy because it refers to God's sacred qualities. In the Old Testament, for example, God is called "Wonderful," "Counselor," "Mighty God," "Eternal Father" and "Prince of Peace" (to name just a few). Muhammad, the founder of the Islamic faith, begins every chapter of the *Qur'ān* with the words, "In the Name of Allah, the Merciful, the Compassionate." And followers of this religion (Muslims) hallow "the Ninety-Nine Beautiful Names of Allah."

The names of Allah, like the names of Jehovah, stand for the innermost qualities of

God. In the *Bhagavad Gita* we read: "The different qualities have their source in Me: Discrimination, Wisdom, Understanding, Patience, Truth, Self-control, and Calmness" (10:4). It is these *qualities* that are to be regarded as holy, not the mere names apart from the qualities. Even the name *Bhagavad Gita* has a sacred significance. It comes from two words: "*Bhagavat*," meaning "Lord," and "*Gita*," meaning "song." Therefore, the phrase "*Bhagavad Gita*" means, "Song of the Lord."

Whenever we talk about "holy names" in our seminars, we pay special attention to the name "Jesus Christ," and we try to explain why this sacred name has such tremendous power and significance. We explain that the first half of the name—"Jesus"—comes from a Hebrew word meaning "Jehovah saves" and refers to the compassionate, forgiving, ever-merciful aspect of God who "saves us from our sins." This is why the Christmas story opens with the words of the angel to Joseph: "You shall call His name 'Jesus,' for He will save His people from their sins" (Matthew 1:21). Therefore, when we think of the name "Jesus," the proper association is with Love, Goodness, Compassion, Mercy, and especially the *Salvation of Souls*. All of these qualities constitute the Divine Goodness.

Now let's consider the second half of this holy name—"Christ." In ancient times when a person became a king, oil was poured on his head as part of the ceremony. This "anointing" was the official sign that the individual was to become the ruler of the kingdom. He was therefore called "the anointed one." In Greek, the word for "anointed" is "Christ"; in Hebrew it is "Messiah." So when Jesus was recognized as the promised king of Israel, people called Him "the Messiah" or "the Christ." They referred to Him as Jesus the Anointed One, Jesus the Promised King, Jesus the Christ, or simply, Jesus Christ.

Although many people expected Jesus—the Anointed One—to be the new King of Israel and to lead the people to victory over the Romans, Jesus said, "My kingdom is not of this world" (John 18:36). In other words, Jesus came to teach the laws of the spiritual world, not the laws of economics, politics or civil government. He came to be a teacher of spiritual truth, and to show the way to live in the Kingdom of Heaven. Just as a worldly king governs his kingdom by means of natural laws, God governs His spiritual kingdom by means of spiritual laws. Therefore, when we think of the name "Christ," the proper association is with the "Anointed One"—the Divine Law by which each of us is governed. This is why the name "Christ" refers to the kingly aspect of God—the teaching, administration and government of the Divine Truth.

When these two names, "Jesus" and "Christ," combine as one holy name, we take it to represent the whole universe of Divine Goodness (Jesus) and the whole universe of Divine Truth (Christ). These are the *qualities* that we associate with the One True God of the entire universe—the omnipresent God of all people, and for all time. Helen Keller writes:

> *I had been told by narrow people that all who were not Christians would be punished, and naturally my soul revolted, since I knew of wonderful men who had lived and died for truth as they saw it in the pagan lands. But when I read Swedenborg's* Heaven and Hell, *I found that "Jesus" stands for Divine Goodness wrought into deeds, and "Christ" symbolizes Divine Truth, sending forth new thought, new life, and joy into the minds of all people; therefore no one who believes in God and lives right is ever condemned. . . .*

> *The idea that vast multitudes are excluded from the blessings of salvation through Jesus Christ is giving way to a more generous understanding that God has "other sheep who hear His voice and obey Him" (John 10:16). He has provided religion of some kind everywhere, and it does not matter to what race or creed people belong if they are faithful to their ideals of right living. The one principle to be remembered by all is that religion is to live a doctrine, not merely to believe one.[3]*

To "call upon the name of God" is more than simply reciting a holy name—it is to pray that God's qualities might come into us; it is to pray that God might give us those qualities that are represented by, and contained within, the holy names *Jesus* (Divine Goodness), and *Christ* (Divine Truth). It is to pray for qualities such as Love, Mercy, Compassion, Patience, Forgiveness, Understanding, Courage, Strength, and Peace. It is not enough merely to believe that these qualities exist; we must pray that these qualities might become manifest in our lives. The Word must become flesh and dwell among us.

Call upon the name of God

In this commandment we are invited to reflect on the various qualities of the One True God. These will include everything associated with the Divine Goodness (Love, Mercy, Compassion, Forgiveness, etc.) and everything associated with the Divine Truth

3. *Light in My Darkness*, 74.

(Wisdom, Understanding, Discernment, Perception, etc.). Whether your faith teaches that "Allah's are the fairest names; invoke Him by them," or "Call upon the name of Jesus and you will be saved," we are all invited to call upon the name of God—that is, we are all invited to ask that God's qualities come into our lives. For example, when we notice the false god of fear trying to control us, we are invited to ask for the qualities of Courage or Trust to come into our lives—qualities of the One True God. In place of the false god of anger, we might ask for the qualities of Love, Compassion, or Understanding to come into our lives. In place of the false god of anxiety, we might ask for the Prince of Peace to govern our inner world. In place of the false god of *self-*righteousness, we might ask for the kingdom of God and *God's* righteousness to rule in our lives. Whenever we call upon the name of God and ask for God's qualities to come into our lives, these qualities will be given to us—as much as we are willing to receive. As Jesus said, "Whatever you ask the Father in My name, He will give you. Until now you have asked nothing in My name. Ask and you shall receive, that your joy may be full" (John 16:23-24).

In the following example, a thirty-year-old secretary on vacation feels upset by the rudeness of a motel owner. Normally she would have just avoided the motel owner or have been curt to her. Instead, she remembers to "call upon the name of God"—to ask God for the qualities of Love and Kindness:

> *This past weekend I went to the shore for four days and three nights. I stayed at a motel. The room was a bit shabby. The screens were torn, the lamps were missing light bulbs, and there was sand in the bureau drawers. On my way out for dinner I stopped by the front desk to ask for light bulbs. I was also planning to ask to have one of the screens fixed, and if I could have some extra towels. The owner came out and angrily said that I was interrupting her dinner. I apologized and told her what I needed. She gave me the light bulbs.*

> *On the way to dinner I told my friend about the incident, and she was shocked at how rude the owner was towards me. Now, normally I would just avoid a person like that motel owner, or else I would be curt to her the next time I saw her. But I remembered the Lord's qualities of love and kindness. I decided to not serve the false god of avoidance, or the false god of feeling rejected. So, after eating, on our way back to the motel, I ran into a flower shop and bought her a festive flower which was gaily wrapped. My friend said I was crazy and that I had wasted my money.*

When we got back to the motel, I went over to the owner's office and handed her the flower, saying, "You seemed a little stressed earlier. I hope this brightens your day." She actually smiled and thanked me, saying that she is always stressed. Well, from that point on she always smiled when I saw her, and when I was checking out she said that I could take as long as I wanted. She didn't even charge me for the three local calls I made. What a miracle, huh?

The true miracle here is not the free phone calls, but the miraculous change of attitude that took place within the young woman on vacation as well as the effect it had on others. When the young woman recognized a desire arising within her that made her want to avoid the motel owner, she named it the false god of "rejection" and "avoidance." Naming these false gods was the first step in refusing to serve them. She then "called upon the name of God." She prayed for Love and Kindness, and her prayer was answered. As a result of her prayer, she experienced a change of heart and the joy of seeing a smile on the face of the motel owner.

In the following example, a prisoner had spent a year praying that his cell-mate, with whom he did not get along, would be transferred. After hearing about this commandment, he realized that he should not be praying for a change of cell-mates, but rather for a change of heart. He writes:

For the past year my cell-mate has been making my life miserable. In class we talked about calling upon God and not taking God's name (God's qualities) in vain. We were supposed to pray, to ask God to give us the qualities of Love, Compassion and Patience. When the teacher told me that I could pray for a heart of love, I was really surprised. For the past year I've been praying that my cell-mate would be transferred. I hadn't realized that God had perhaps given me a beautiful opportunity.

So I accepted the assignment, "You shall not take God's name in vain." My prayer this week was to pray for a heart to love my cell-mate. I really began to pray for this guy. And what do you think happened? He got transferred!

The answer to this inmate's prayer was not really the change of his cell-mate's location in the prison. Rather, it was the change that took place at the core of his being as he prayed for a heart to love his cell-mate.

In the following journal entry a forty-two-year-old mother recognizes her need to pray for God's qualities and not take them in vain. She is in her car waiting for her daughter, who is late. Describing herself as "angry, frustrated, and upset," the mother talks about her struggle to clear her mind and pray for the qualities that she is lacking. She writes:

I went to pick up my teenage daughter after her softball practice. I got to the high school at about the time I usually arrive for pick-ups; but she wasn't there. I waited 15 minutes . . . still no Bethany. I had other children to pick up soon at a different location and not a lot of time or emotional energy to keep on waiting. I could feel my anxiety level rising and my anger growing. "Why couldn't she be more responsible?" I was sure I had the correct time and place.

Checking with another parent, I discovered that the team had an away game but should be back "any minute." So I sat in my car feeling angry at my daughter, and frustrated and upset because I had no ability to control this situation. Then I remembered my assignment from class: "Do not take the name of the Lord your God in vain. Remember to pray." It was like a shock went through my body. It hardly seemed possible to change my state of mind now, but heaven knew I really needed it!

*So I prayed, and prayed, and prayed. I realized how assuming I was, how blaming, how controlling, and how I was justifying it all. I prayed for patience, for understanding, for acceptance, and for love for my daughter. The thought came that I too had made others wait at different times in my life; I too had forgotten to leave a message; and my daughter **really** is a wonderful person. I have often said how lucky I am to be her parent. So why crucify her now?*

I turned on the radio and tried to be patient, still feeling very emotional about all these insights that were coming to me. Forty-five minutes later my daughter's bus pulled up. When she got into the car I could see that she was worried. I met her worried eyes with a smile. She asked, "Mom, are you mad?"

"No," I answered. (I had calmed down, and by now was actually feeling genuine love for her.)

She replied, "Why not?"

I answered simply, "I knew if you weren't here there must be a good reason."

She melted. "I'm really, really sorry," she said. "Have you been waiting long?"

"Forty-five minutes," I said. (There was no blame in my voice.)

She apologized again, and we lovingly hugged. I realized that prayer kept me from blasting her with my "justified" anger, and it gave her the space to say that she was sorry rather than be defensive. What an important lesson in my life.

This mother was upset while "waiting for her daughter." But everything changed when she remembered to call upon the name of God. Her willingness to recognize her anger and frustration opened the way for her to ask for, and to receive, the Kingdom of Heaven—Patience, Understanding, and Acceptance. She writes, "*The thought came that I too had made others wait . . .[that] my daughter really is a wonderful person . . . how lucky I am to be her parent.*"

We know that God's qualities are Patience, not impatience; Understanding, not resentment. If we ask for God's Patience and Understanding, we shall receive. Similarly, we can choose to be Courageous rather than fearful; Bold rather than timid; filled with Love and Kindness rather than complaints and criticism. This is not new knowledge; it is ancient wisdom. As it is written in the Old Testament: "I have set before you life and death; blessing and cursing; therefore choose life" (Deuteronomy 30:19).

In the New Testament we receive a similar message, "Ask, and it will be given to you; seek, and you will find; knock, and it will be opened to you" (Matthew 7:7). What is it that we will be given? What will we find? What will be opened to us? Nothing less than the Kingdom of Heaven! And that Kingdom is made up of God's many qualities. These gifts are made available to each of us at every moment as a continuous Divine endowment. This is what is meant by the words, "Come, you blessed of My Father, inherit the kingdom prepared for you from the foundation of the world" (Matthew 25:34). It is all there—the fullness of life—just waiting to be claimed. It is all there, just a prayer away. As one seminar participant put it, "Claim your prize!"

Finally, it should be noted that prayer must be specific. In the last chapter we were asked to be specific about the name of the false god that we might be serving. Similarly, in this next commandment we are asked to be specific about the quality that we are lacking whenever we find ourselves bowing down to a false god. A college professor writes:

It's the start of a new semester. I haven't wanted to leave summer; I didn't get enough time to really recharge. Two new textbooks to deal with, a messy, inconvenient schedule, large additional chores on top of my teaching schedule, scary political machinations that I don't really understand, my computer at home gone belly-up, and what appeared to be a need for a root canal. It seemed like everything and everyone was taking a piece out of me. Normally, under such circumstances my prayers would be more like inarticulate howls. I figured that God would understand. But now my prayers are quite specific, as in, "OK, Lord, I need some enthusiasm," or "Lord, I need to approach X without foaming at the mouth. Could you get me into a little better order than I'm in at the moment?"

The beginning of the week was orderly and quiet. One morning, as I drove past the corn fields on the way to school, I prayed for peace and certainty. That day a talk I was scheduled to give went well. I was able to comfort a friend who was also confronting massive work-overload with the recollection of an old hymn: "Blessed are they whose spirits long, whose trust is in the Lord, and on whose lips is praise unending." Life is good.

Indeed, life *is* good—whenever we remember to "call upon the name of God."

Taking the Lord's name in vain

Unfortunately, even though God's qualities are there "for the taking," we often "take them in vain." Notice what is said in this commandment: "You shall not take the name of the Lord your God *in vain*, for the Lord will not hold him guiltless who takes His name *in vain*." In this brief commandment the phrase "in vain" appears twice. This emphasizes the fact that God wants to give us wonderful qualities, as much as we ask for—but these qualities must be *put to use*! Otherwise our prayers are empty; they are no more than "vain repetitions." We may call ourselves "Christians," "Muslims," "Hindus," "Buddhists" or "Jews," but if we do not make use of the Divine qualities that are continually available to us from God, whatever name we ascribe to that Divinity is taken in vain. We are like a child who asks for a new bicycle only to let it rust in the rain, or for a new dress only to leave it crumpled up on the floor of the closet. God's qualities are there for us, not merely to ask for, but to use.

This idea, that we can take God's name in vain by not making use of God's qualities, has many applications. In the following examples, people from a wide variety of cultures and religious traditions speak about the different ways they have taken God's name in vain. A prisoner observes how he "takes God's name in vain" at meal times:

> *This negative thing is really rooted deep within my personality. My false god loves to complain. I even ask the Lord's blessing on my food and then turn and complain about the meal!*

A familiar way that people take God's name in vain is to attend a service of worship, or to receive religious instruction, but not use what they have received. An inmate reflects on the difference between his behavior during a morning church service at the prison, and his behavior after returning from that service:

> *Taking God's name in vain is like going up that hill to the chain gang church service here, and then coming back down that hill to chase down one of my buddies to get a skin book [pornography] from him. When I'm holding that book with the same hands that I lifted in the air to praise God with, I know that I am "taking God's name in vain."*

In the next example, a young African observes how his religious instruction was "taken in vain":

> *When I started school, my teacher used to teach us what was called "ezenkolo," which means "religious education." I would not pay attention when she taught us without showing any pictures. When she was finished what she was saying, I wouldn't remember even one thing. I was taking the name of God in vain.*

In the Sufi tradition we find the following story:

> *When Mustafa came home from his religious studies, his parents asked him to speak about what he had learned from the Holy Qur'ān that day. Mustafa told his parents all about one of his classmates who did not listen to the instruction that was being given. Mustafa's parents listened patiently to their son's complaints. When he was finished, they told him that if this was all that he had learned from that Holy Book, it would have been better for him not to have heard the Qur'ān at all.*

These examples remind us that real prayer is more than simply asking for God's qualities to come into our lives; rather, it is to make use of those qualities in every aspect of our lives. Otherwise we take God's name "in vain."

Remembering to pray

While all religions acknowledge that prayer is an essential aspect of spiritual life, many of us need help remembering to pray. Therefore, when we explain this commandment in the *Rise Above It* seminar, participants each receive a pack of small "Post-it" notes to be used as prayer reminders. They are asked to write the word "Pray" on each note. When they get home they post the "Pray" notes at various strategic places as reminders that we can pray anytime, anywhere. A young mother writes:

> *I placed my "Remember to Pray" notes in obvious places like on my bathroom mirror and over my kitchen sink. The one that caught my attention the most times during the week, however, was the one I put on the door of our bedroom at eye level so that I would see it every time I left our room. It said to me, "You are leaving your personal space to go out to be with others: REMEMBER TO PRAY." It was interesting to me that this note was one that I just stuck there, seemingly on a whim. And yet it became the most important one for me. The Lord works in wonderful ways.*

An e-mail participant, reporting a similar experience, writes:

> *On Saturday my husband and I both wanted to be on the computer. I was already on it and not feeling very charitable or giving. My husband kept coming back and asking me if I was finished yet. I could feel the tension building. Negative thoughts were coming into my mind, so much so that when he came back in for the fourth time, I spoke to him in anger and said things that I wanted to swallow and take back, even while I was saying them. He reacted, and we were off to a petty argument.*
>
> *As we were arguing I kept seeing my Post-it notes that said "Pray," "Call upon the name of God," "STOP and PRAY." I found myself getting more frustrated and I walked out of the room because I didn't want to be reminded of what I*

should be doing instead of arguing. However, I did such a good job of putting Post-it notes all around the house that I couldn't escape them! Everywhere I looked there was a reminder to call upon the the name of God. So I finally shut up and started to listen. By being quiet I could see how stupid our argument had become, and by listening patiently the argument ended.

I am thankful for this exercise. If the Post-it notes had not been there as a gentle reminder, who knows how long my false gods would have hung in there with their arguments and destruction.

The remember-to-pray notes can often be just what we need—gentle reminders to call upon the name of God. Yet there may be times when no matter how many reminders are in front of us, praying is the last thing we want to do. A seminar participant writes:

It was a tough week—one in which I knew prayer to the Lord would be valuable to me. The curious thing about the mental state I was in was that at times I was so low that when I rationally thought to pray, I would say to myself "BUT I DON'T FEEL LIKE PRAYING!" So I had to pray about being led into a state of mind in which I could pray to God with an open heart.

It felt like I was "in the basement," needing to claw my way to the first floor so that I could get some fresh air and clear my head.

Well, praying to be in a good mental state worked. It enabled me to see those little Post-it notes and "pray on the fly," as well as in a more meditative state. I really believe that connecting with God and the angels through prayer is what brought me to a healthier state of mind by the end of the week.

This journal entry reminds us of one of the more sobering facts along our spiritual journey: *At those times when we need to pray the most, we may be the least willing to do so!* It is a good time to remember that the false gods of stubbornness, self-will, and hard-heartedness may be ruling over us. These harsh task-masters must be identified and replaced by humbler, gentler qualities. Sometimes, when we do not feel like praying, all we can ask for is the willingness to pray. It may not seem like much, but it is an important step along the path of spiritual development.

Finally, it must be emphasized that "calling on the name of God" is not a magic formula. There is no magic in the mere recitation of a holy name apart from a genuine understanding of what that name represents. *The "name of God" represents the qualities of the Living God*—the God who is always with us, pressing to be received, urging us to invite the Divine qualities into our lives. Our task is to open ourselves to these qualities, to pray that we might receive them, and to make use of them in our lives. They are always there "for the taking"—but we must ask!

The assignment: Do not take God's name in vain / Pray

In the commandment against worshipping other gods, we took time for self-examination. We noticed the many "false gods" we served, and we saw to what extent we were in bondage to them. This kind of self-examination prepares the way for the next commandment. When we find ourselves being ruled by a false god, and when merely naming it is not enough, we need more. This is the time to "call upon the name of God." This is the time to pray. Pray to receive the quality that you are lacking at the moment. That quality will become God's presence with you. And when you do pray, be specific. Ask for God's Courage, or God's Patience, or God's Perseverance, or God's Compassion, or God's Righteousness, etc. In other words, *Call upon the name of God. Do not take God's name in vain.*

Assignment

Do not take God's name in vain / Pray

**When you notice a false god ruling over you, name it.
Then pray for the specific quality that is lacking.**

In your journal, record your experience of keeping this commandment.

SUGGESTIONS FOR FURTHER REFLECTION AND APPLICATION

MEDITATION: "HALLOWED BE THY NAME"

While the opening words of the Lord's Prayer remind us that there is One True God, the next section tells how we are to address God: "Hallowed be Thy name." Try using the words, "Hallowed be Thy name" as a meditation as you practice the spiritual discipline of keeping this commandment. Set aside a few minutes each day to stay your mind on the simple words, "Hallowed be Thy name," remembering as you do so, that "the name of God" represents the many qualities of the One True God.

JOURNAL REFLECTION

In your journal, write about what your name means to you. What stories do you remember about why you were given your name? Over the years, has your name taken on a different meaning, significance, or quality in your life?

ACTIVITY: IDENTIFY GOD'S QUALITIES

Make a list of the various names of God. Identify a particular quality associated with each of these names. For example, "Father" may represent the qualities of Trust or Respect; "Holy One" may represent the qualities of Compassion or Wisdom.

JOURNAL REFLECTION

Describe your early experiences of prayer as well as your current experience of prayer. Has prayer been a part of your life? In what way? Is prayer a part of your life now? How do you pray? When and where do you pray? Are you comfortable with prayer?

ACTIVITY: PUT UP "POST-IT" NOTES

Purchase a pack of small "Post-it" notes (1.5" x 2" works well). Write the word "PRAY," "PRAYER," or "PRAY for_____ (Peace, Patience, Courage, etc.)" on the first note. Put this Post-it note in a place where it will remind you to pray. When/where do you need it most? In your car? On your computer? By the kitchen sink? On the door frame of your bedroom? etc. Fill your surroundings with as many reminders as necessary to actually have prayer become an integral part of your life—like breathing. (If you are not able to purchase Post-it notes, you can use paper and tape.)

ACTIVITY: CHOOSE LIFE!

Go back and examine your list of "false gods" (Chapter One) and match them with one or more of the qualities of the One True God. These are the qualities that are lacking in you whenever you find yourself "bowing down" to that particular false god. For example, match the false god of "anxiety" with Peace or Trust, or Acceptance. There are many possible qualities to choose from. (See "Qualities of the One True God" on the next page.) As you do this activity, keep in mind the Lord's words to the children of Israel: "I have set before you today life and good, death and evil. . . . But if your heart turns away so that you do not hear, and are drawn away, and worship other gods and serve them, I announce to you today that you will surely perish. . . . Therefore, choose life, that both you and your descendants may live" (Deuteronomy 30:15, 17-19).

ACTIVITY: BECOME A SPIRITUAL ATHLETE

World class athletes will often visualize themselves going through the movements associated with their sport over and over again. Whether it is diving, figure skating, walking a balance beam or swinging a golf club, this kind of mental training can be quite valuable. Similarly, in spiritual development it can be useful to visualize ourselves going through the steps of the commandments. As you prepare for the events that will come before you this day or this week, visualize yourself identifying false gods and praying for the qualities that are lacking. Become a spiritual athlete.

ACTIVITY: TRANSFORM BLUNDERS INTO BLESSINGS

This activity is similar to the previous one, except it is related to those times when we have been unsuccessful in keeping one or more of the commandments. At such times we may be tempted to mentally return to the scene of the incident and rehearse our errors over and over again. Instead we can mentally revisit the situation and visualize ourselves handling it differently. This time see yourself keeping the commandment: identifying the false god and praying for the qualities that are lacking. Return to the scene of the blunder and transform it into a blessing.

ACTIVITY: PRAY TO BE WILLING TO PRAY

Sometimes the last thing that we want to do is to identify false gods and pray for the qualities that are lacking. At such times we can still pray to God and ask for the willingness to pray. Try this exercise at those times when you don't feel like praying, and see what happens!

QUALITIES OF THE ONE TRUE GOD

A SAMPLING

Love	Optimism	Peace
Kindness	Joy	Encouragement
Mercy	Faith	Respect
Courage	Chastity	Praise
Compassion	Humility	Rest
Humor	Contentment	Playfulness
Patience	Forgiveness	Innocence
Generosity	Tranquillity	Trust
Acceptance	Gentleness	Truthfulness
Confidentiality	Charity	Honesty
Strength	Wisdom	Appreciation
Action	Gratitude	Peace
Order	Assurance	Understanding

Remember the Sabbath day, to keep it holy.
Six days you shall labor and do all your work,
but the seventh day is the Sabbath of the Lord your God.
In it you shall do no work.

OLD TESTAMENT—EXODUS 20:8

 Come to Me all you who labor and are heavy laden,
and I will give you rest.

NEW TESTAMENT—MATTHEW 11:28

 O ye who believe! When the call is heard for prayer
on the Day of Congregation, haste unto remembrance
of Allah and leave your trading.

QUR'ĀN 62:9

 Still your mind in Me, still yourself in Me,
and without doubt you will be united with Me,
Lord of Love, dwelling in your heart.

BHAGAVAD GITA 12:8

 To be led by goodness is to be led by the Lord.
A person who comes into this state is then in heaven
and in the tranquillity of peace. This state
is what is meant by "the seventh day,"
and by the "Sabbath of Sabbaths."

ARCANA COELESTIA 9274:2

CHAPTER THREE

The Sabbath

Wait on the Lord. Be of good courage.
And He shall strengthen your heart.
—PSALM 27:14

Keeping the Sabbath

IN HEBREW, the word "*Shabbat*," or "Sabbath," means "rest." We all know how important it is to take a break and rest our body, mind and soul. Traditionally, the Sabbath has been seen as a holy day, a day to "rest from our labors," a day to turn to God, to read God's Word, and to join with others in a worship setting. For those of us who never seem to have enough time to get all of our work done, the discipline of a "Sabbath day" is essential. It is one day, at least, when we get a chance to rest from our labors and reconnect with God.

In the Old Testament a story is told about how God miraculously connects a heap of dry bones and brings them to life. At the time of the miracle, the children of Israel are described as feeling spiritually dead and disconnected from God. They cry out, "Our bones are dry; our hope is lost, and we ourselves are cut off." But God responds by saying, "O dry bones, hear the word of the Lord . . . I will put sinews on you, and bring flesh upon you." Indeed, God causes breath to enter the dry bones, and they stand on their feet—"an exceedingly great army." The story ends with the beautiful prophecy, "I will put My Spirit in you, and you shall live" (see Ezekiel 37:1-14). This is an ancient promise of how God can bring us back to spiritual life. No matter how disconnected and scattered we may feel; no matter how hopeless or "cut off" we may think we are, the Sabbath is given to us so that we may reconnect with God and have life.

Getting re-connected to God—and through God with others—is the essence of religion. In fact, the etymology of the word "religion" may be traced back to its Indo-European root *leig* meaning to "tie together or to bind."[1] This is also the root of the Latin verb *ligare* meaning "to bind together, to connect, or to unite." Just as *liga*ments connect bone to bone, religion helps us to reconnect (*re-ligare*) with God. A religious Sabbath, then, can transform us from a heap of dry, disconnected bones to living beings, connected to God and with one another. We emerge "covered with sinews and flesh" and filled with the breath of God's spirit.

We keep the Sabbath commandment at the literal level by setting aside time each week to reconnect with God, and to focus on that which is holy. The day of the week or the particular form of ritual that is used is not as important as regularly coming before God with a humble heart. It is a time to put aside our worldly concerns and to nourish our spirit. This is what is meant in the literal sense of the Word by the commandment "Remember the Sabbath day to keep it holy."

The manager of a fast-food restaurant writes:

I remember my childhood still. On Sundays the stores were closed. The mills were silent. People went to church and did things as a family. Some of my fondest memories are of Sunday dinners as a family. I also fondly recall that on Sundays we would visit family, friends or neighbors just for the sake of visiting. Friendships seemed more of a priority than they do now.

For this person, the "Sabbath" was a time to focus on God, family and friendships. It was a time when businesses were closed, and the world was still. It was a day when people did not earn or spend money. Instead, they spent their time with each other.

Another participant writes:

There was a time in my life when I worked seven days a week for ten or twelve hours a day. This was a common practice for more than fifteen years. I used the statement that "any day could be the Sabbath." It could be, but I was not putting that statement into practice. My children were growing up. I realized that I was not giving my children a day, much less God. I needed to "Remember the Sabbath." I started closing my business on Sundays.

1. Julius Pokorny, *Indogermanisches Etymologisches Woerterbuch* (Bern and Muenchen: Francke Verlag, 1959), 668.

The commandment about remembering the Sabbath day is given to remind us to focus on what is *internal* and *eternal*. It is given so that at least one day a week we may lift our eyes above the things of the earth and reflect on the things of heaven. This call to the remembrance of God and to the usefulness of the Sabbath day is beautifully expressed in the words of the prophet Isaiah:

> *If you turn your foot from [breaking] the Sabbath, so that you do not do your own will on My holy day; and if you call the things of the Sabbath a delight, and the Lord's holy day honorable, not doing as you please, or following your own desires, or speaking idle words, then you will find your joy in the Lord, and I will cause you to rise above the lofty things of the earth. I will feed you with the heritage of Jacob* (Isaiah 58:13-14).

The Sabbath, then, is a day of rest, and a time to reconnect with that which is holy. It is a time to reflect on God, heaven and the teachings of the Sacred Scriptures. It is a time to "rise above the lofty things of the earth."

Picking up sticks

The idea that a person was to "do no work on the Sabbath" was treated with greatest reverence in Old Testament times. In fact, *The Jewish Encyclopedia* lists 1,521 activities that were not permitted on the Sabbath day. These included plowing, reaping, sowing, spinning, knitting, knotting, unknotting, salting, writing, erasing, hammering, squeezing lemons, milking animals, wringing out a garment, washing one's head, combing one's hair, clapping one's hands, riding on an animal, tearing paper, carrying a child, setting a broken bone, plucking fruit, and even making mental calculations![2] While these activities were not specifically forbidden in the Sacred Scriptures, the religious leaders felt that it was their duty to define more precisely what was meant by the words, "The seventh day is the Sabbath of the Lord your God. *In it you shall do no work.*" Their concern is understandable, for in the Old Testament we read about a person who was put to death for picking up sticks on the Sabbath:

> *Now while the children of Israel were in the wilderness, they found a man gathering sticks on the Sabbath day. . . . Then the Lord said to Moses, "The man must surely be put to death; all the congregation shall stone him with stones outside the camp"* (Numbers 15:32-36).

2. *The Jewish Encyclopedia*, Vol. 10 (New York: Funk and Wagnalls, 1910), 536.

With stories like this as a part of their cultural heritage, we can perhaps understand the fear that the Israelites experienced around the literal keeping of this commandment. No work meant just that; and any violation of the commandment was punishable by death. It was for this reason that the religious leaders of the day came up with long lists of things that constituted "working on the Sabbath." They wanted to be sure that no one came close to breaking this commandment. So "picking up sticks" became just one of many activities that were forbidden on that day.

But what does this Scriptural teaching mean to us today? A "stick" is that which is separated from a tree. It is lifeless and dead. Jesus said, "If anyone does not abide in Me, he is cast out as a branch and is withered; and they gather them and throw them into the fire, and they are burned. If you abide in Me, and my words abide in you, you will ask what you desire, and it shall be done for you" (John 15:6-7). This is the essence of the Sabbath commandment—to remain "connected" to God, even as a branch must remain connected to a tree. When we are connected to God we bear fruit effortlessly, as if from ourselves, just as the branch of a tree bears fruit as if from itself. Again, "If you abide in Me and My words abide in you, you will ask what you desire, and it shall be done for you. By this My Father is glorified, that you bear much fruit; so you will be My disciples" (John 15:7, 8).

The person who was put to death for picking up sticks on the Sabbath represents each of us when we have separated ourselves from the Divine, not taking time to abide in God, and not allowing God's words to abide in us. Instead, we are perpetually restless and without peace. We do not believe that God will accomplish all things in His time. Instead, we seize every opportunity we can to do more things and to accomplish greater results. Many years ago people were forbidden to squeeze lemons on the Sabbath. But today we often feel compelled to squeeze in a few extra hours of work here and there. Like the person who was caught picking up sticks on the Sabbath, there is something within each of us that will not rest in God nor trust entirely in the Divine.

In the following journal entry a young father who is experiencing many problems at work has great difficulty entering the Sabbath state. Spiritually, it might be said that he is "picking up sticks" on the Sabbath. He writes:

On Sunday my mind was buzzing with thoughts about work. There were so many problems to sort out, so many misunderstandings. I kept thinking that if I could just come up with a solution, my mind would be at rest. I tried to get

60

my wife to talk with me about it, but she didn't want to. She said, "This is Sunday. How about if we don't talk about work today?"

That was a hard one! How could I just stop talking about work? My work was driving me, consuming me. It was everything to me. Suddenly, I realized that this is what is meant by a "false god." Right then I decided that I would do more than not talk about work—I wouldn't even think about it.

After church we made plans to go to Peace Valley Park, have a picnic, and enjoy our children. I gave it my best shot, but it wasn't easy. All through the day, whether I was in a paddleboat with the kids, or playing ball with them, or just strolling by the lake, my mind kept wandering back to my work and the problems that I had to solve. I tried not to pay attention to any thoughts associated with my work, but it was difficult.

When we got home I felt tired, exhausted, and sad. Sadness was the dominant emotion. I didn't know why. I had managed to say nothing about work all day, but that in itself hadn't brought a great deal of happiness. As I sat there on the couch, sinking into my sadness, it occurred to me that my Sabbath had not been a day of rest, and that I had not kept the Sabbath holy. My work had become an all-powerful false god, and in that moment I remembered to pray. So I prayed for peace; I prayed for joy; I prayed to be able to totally focus on my family; I prayed for clarity about my concerns at work; and as I prayed, the words of Scripture came to mind: "Come to Me all you who labor and are heavy laden . . . and you will find rest for your souls."

This father had been trying to accomplish all things by himself. He felt sad and tired. But when he remembered to pray, the message that he needed to hear came in the words of Scripture, "Come to Me all you who labor and are heavy laden . . . and you will find rest for your souls." This father is not alone in his effort to "pick up sticks" on the Sabbath. Whenever we try to accomplish a little more or solve another problem without trusting in God, we, too, "pick up sticks." This man kept thinking that if he could just come up with a solution, his mind would be at rest. The truth is really quite the opposite: if only he would remember to "rest in God," the solution would come.

The Scriptures of all the great religions urge us to remember the Sabbath—to rest from our labors and receive spiritual nourishment. In the *Qur'ān* it is written, "On the

Day of Congregation, haste unto remembrance of Allah and leave your trading" (62:9). In the Sacred Scriptures of India we read, "Those who surrender to God . . . attain supreme peace" (*Bhagavad Gita* 5:12). Whether it occurs in the Jewish, Christian, Muslim or Indian Scriptures, the "call to remembrance" is always the same: "Come to Me . . . and you will find rest for your souls" (Matthew 11:28). "Come to Me alone for shelter" (*Bhagavad Gita* 18:16). "Even the worst sinner who comes to Me . . . shall obtain everlasting peace" (*Bhagavad Gita* 5:10-12). This state of interior rest and inner peace is the "Sabbath" in us. It is not only a day of the week, but also a state of mind when we rest in God, trust in God's leading, and strive to do God's will.

You shall kindle no fire on the Sabbath

As we have pointed out, the religious leaders of Old Testament times were greatly concerned about the question, "What kind of work constitutes a violation of the Sabbath commandment?" While most of the restrictions that were mentioned by the religious leaders do not appear in the Old Testament, or in other Sacred Scriptures, one restriction—a highly significant one—does occur. It reads, "You shall kindle no fire throughout your habitations on the Sabbath" (Exodus 35:3). Even today, in orthodox homes, electric lights are not turned on during the Sabbath because the spark of electricity is considered "kindling a fire." Similarly, cars are not driven because the ignition of the sparkplugs is also considered "kindling a fire."

While such scrupulous attention to keeping the literal sense of the commandments is commendable, it is important to remember that the Sacred Scriptures also contain a deeper meaning. The words, "You shall kindle no fire on the Sabbath," are a promise as well as a prohibition. They speak to us of a time when we shall experience true Sabbath rest, a time free from the burning, raging fires of anger, hatred, lust, fear, anxiety or greed. These are the "fires" that will no longer rage, flare up, nor even be kindled in us. In the Buddhist Scriptures, fire is also a symbol for selfish passion and burning hatred: "There is no fire like passion, no ill like hatred . . . there is no happiness higher than tranquillity" (*Dhammapada* 14:6).

In this commandment we begin to realize that "hell-fire" is something that we bring on ourselves by piling up hurt feelings, justifying our anger, feeding the fires of revenge, and striving—even at the expense of others—to fulfill our selfish ambitions. We become like so many old rags, full of volatile chemicals, that have been heaped up in a corner. Eventually, when the rags reach a kindling point, they spontaneously ignite. It is called "spontaneous combustion." As long as we cling to our hurts, or spend time worrying about our unfulfilled ambitions, our volatile nature will continue to fume in dark corners, ready to flare up at any moment. We will find ourselves "burnt up" about many things, and eventually we may feel "burnt out." There will be no "Sabbath" in our life. This is why God invites us to "Remember the Sabbath day." It is a call to quiet our inner dialogue, to still the incessant chatter in our minds, and to cease from all internal fuming.

In the following journal entry a father is driving a van through a snowstorm while his children are "horsing around" in the back seats. As his anger mounts, he recognizes his need to "Remember the Sabbath." He writes:

We were coming back from Boston late at night with four kids in the back seats of the van. The snow had been falling steadily, and the road conditions were getting worse as we entered the mountainous region of western Massachusetts.

The kids (who were oblivious to all of this) continued to poke each other, squeal, laugh and horse around in the back seats. As the snow continued to fall, and the traffic started to slow down, I could feel the tension mounting in my body. I was worried about what the road conditions would be like further ahead, and whether we would have to pull off the road and spend the night somewhere. I was aware that we had three more hours of driving ahead of us before we would be home, and I just didn't know how much further we could go.

I asked the kids to be quiet. I told them that I was dealing with dangerous road conditions, and that I had to stay focused on driving. When they didn't listen to my request, I began to speak more loudly, with anger in my voice. I was very worried about having an accident on the slippery turnpike, and extremely upset that the kids were not listening to me. I was getting ready to explode when I remembered that this was a perfect opportunity to "keep the commandments." So I identified the false god of anger, and prayed for the peace of the Sabbath state. Taking my focus off of the kids and the noise they were making, I concentrated on driving through the storm, while waiting on the Lord.

A few moments later I found myself suddenly aware of the beauty of the evening. The tall pine trees on the sides of the road were magically decorated with snow in one of the loveliest winter scenes imaginable. The snowflakes streamed softly and steadily into my headlights and onto the windshield as the wipers rhythmically wiped them away. I became aware of the love song that was playing on the radio, and of my wife beside me in the front seat. I felt as though I had been given this incredible gift of peace, beauty and tranquillity—all because I had simply refused to go with the negative thoughts and emotions. A little later the kids had fallen asleep, the road conditions had improved, and we continued our late-night journey through Massachusetts and into New York, in a beautiful Sabbath state.

Instead of "kindling a fire" and exploding at his children, this father was able to recognize the false god of anger, pray for the opposite quality and wait on the Lord. As a result, a way was opened for the Lord's kingdom to flow in with all its beauty, serenity, and power. This kingdom is available to each of us at every moment whenever we recognize the false god that is ruling over us, pray for the quality that is lacking, and then enter the stillness of the Sabbath state. It is in this state—when the fires of selfish desire are quieted—that we wait for the coming of the Lord's kingdom: "Thy kingdom come."

In the following journal entry a prisoner decides to let go of his rage, and to experience, instead, the peace of God:

Our task this week is to Remember the Sabbath—take a break—let go and let God. Chill. Inner peace. Something everyone longs for. Yesterday a guy who owed me two bucks reneged for the fourth week in a row. I was so incensed that my whole body shook.

Later, as I attempted to find solace, this week's lesson, Remember the Sabbath, came to mind. I realized that I had been doing myself physical and emotional harm—and for what? It wasn't worth all that, and I felt blessed when I was able to just let go of my rage. My inner turmoil was quelled. I just said, "Whatever." It was like the first three commandments came back to slap me silly, or awaken me to reality. For what does it profit a man to gain the whole world, but lose his soul?

Tonight I'll pray for guidance to control my temper and not react like an animal when I can't get my way.

This is a dramatic example of what can happen when we choose not to kindle a fire on the Sabbath. Notice how this prisoner describes his feelings of rage: "*I was so incensed that my whole body shook.*" Rather than allow himself to be "burnt up" and consumed with anger, he chose to rise above it, or as he put it, to *chill*—to Remember the Sabbath day and to keep it holy.

Doing good on the Sabbath

The Sabbath commandment clearly states that on this day we shall "do no work." As we have already mentioned, this restriction was given elaborate detail by the religious leaders of Old Testament times—even to the forbidding of tearing paper, squeezing lemons and making mental calculations! In keeping with the spirit of this commandment, the question arises, "Is there any kind of work that *is* lawful on the Sabbath?" According to the New Testament, there is. Jesus said, "What man is there among you who has one sheep, and if it falls into a pit on the Sabbath, will not lay hold of it and lift it out? Of how much more value, then, is a man than a sheep? Therefore *it is lawful to do good on the Sabbath*" (Matthew 12:11, 12; emphasis added).

This teaching, revolutionary in its day, is now widely known and practiced. But it must be understood at a deeper level. For "doing good on the Sabbath" does not mean merely taking time out to do kind deeds for others. Rather, it is about allowing God to act into us and through us—it is about doing *God's* will rather than our own. When we are laboring from God rather than from ourselves, we will find that our work will be invigorating rather than exhausting. Our spirits will be uplifted, and we will feel as though we are soaring on high. Although we may feel a need for physical rest after long periods of physical and mental exertion, our spirits will feel refreshed and vibrant. It does not matter whether we are arranging flowers, digging ditches, leading a company, vacuuming the rug, preparing a legal brief, running a pre-school, or coaching an athletic team. A course participant writes:

We have a huge lawn to mow, and while doing it (mostly on Sundays) I usually feel resentful because my kids are not helping. When I finish mowing, my back is usually killing me and I am stiff all over.

But yesterday I decided to mow the lawn without resentment or anger. Instead, I focused on the job, felt grateful for the beautiful lawn, the mower, and thought about God's love for all of His children. When I finished the job I was amazed. My back felt fine, and I was not stiff or tired. I actually felt energized and refreshed. Now that's what I call a Sabbath!

As this journal entry illustrates, the type of work we engage in does not matter. What does matter is the love and affection that move us, the force that motivates us, the feelings that drive us. Whenever our motivation is to gain the approval of others, to control others, to enhance our reputation, to be praised and admired, or merely to accumulate wealth and possessions, we are operating from a self-centered motivation, and it will not sustain us. Such labor will be experienced as difficult and heavy, rather than as easy and light. We will become exhausted, and eventually we will "burn out."

This is also true of good-hearted volunteers who have a difficult time saying "No" when asked to do an extra job or lend a helping hand. They may believe that the Kingdom of Heaven is a kingdom of useful service, and their goal may be to serve others with no thought of themselves. Sadly, however, they can become so caught up in the idea of "being useful" that they can no longer discern whether their useful service is truly useful, or whether it is just compulsive busy-ness. In fact, the idea of "being useful" may have become a false god for them—a cruel taskmaster that drives them relentlessly to the point of exhaustion. The following journal entry is from a kindly grandmother who actively participates in the life of her community, but realizes that she may be over-extending herself. Faced with the challenge of saying "No" to her friends, she writes:

I recently had the experience of several people begging me (and bugging me) to help out as a volunteer, no matter how many ways I said I would rather not. Most of my friends were working hard on those very projects, so I felt a lot of guilt about saying "No." When I work on projects that I don't want to work on, I get exhausted or even sick, and have no time left to do things I really love to do, like sew, practice the piano, and take part in spiritual growth groups like this one. These are the things that I love to do, and I find that doing them gives me energy, rather than depleting my energy. They restore my soul—which is what the Sabbath is supposed to do.

The Sabbath, then, is given to us to restore our souls. It is a time when we truly rest in God and allow ourselves to be moved by God's will rather than our own. The good that we then do is truly good, because it is not motivated by our fears, our desire for personal gain, our wish to control others, or the need for approval. When these selfish motives are put aside, the way is opened for God to act into and through us. This is what is meant by "doing good on the Sabbath."

Stilling our minds

As we enter more deeply into this commandment, we begin to realize that the Sabbath *"day"* is not only a day of the week; it is also *a state of mind*. It is a sacred, holy time when we deliberately empty ourselves of all selfish ambition, all discontent, all thought of self and world. We simply wait on the Lord, stilling our minds in humble recognition of that great spiritual truth—that everything that is good, and everything that is true, comes from God. As it is written, "I am the vine, you are the branches. He who abides in Me and I in him, bears much fruit; for without Me you can do nothing" (John 15:5).

In this state of humility we recognize that without God our lives are meaningless. No matter how vast our plans and ambitions, if our intent is to exalt our selves rather than to glorify God, all our efforts will be hollow and empty. Therefore, before undertaking any endeavor, we humbly acknowledge that without God we are like the earth as it is described in the opening words of the Old Testament: "And the earth was without form, and void; and darkness was upon the face of the deep" (Genesis 1:2).

This time of emptiness is also the point when we are able to allow God to become active in our lives. To the degree that our own plans, ideas, concerns and thoughts are put to rest, the light of God begins to illumine our minds: "And the Spirit of God was hovering over the face of the waters. Then God said, 'Let there be light' and there was light" (Genesis 1:3-4). Notice how beautifully this Old Testament teaching coincides with the the first words of Jesus' Sermon on the Mount: "Blessed are the poor in spirit, for theirs is the Kingdom of Heaven" (Matthew 5:3). When we are truly empty of selfish desire, we are fully open to receive the Kingdom of Heaven. In Buddhism this is referred to as emptying the boat: "Empty this boat, O *Bhikkhu*! Emptied by you it will move swiftly. Cutting out lust and hatred, to *Nirvana* you will thereby go" *(Dhammapada* 25:10).[3]

This time of supreme stillness is also one of profound emptiness. We experience a sense of "nothingness," and for a time we are content just to "be." We do not have to do, or plan, or think. We may notice thoughts and feelings as they come to us, but we just let them pass by as we go deeper and deeper into a state of internal rest, calmness, and tranquillity. Eventually our minds are stilled, and we experience the peace of the Sabbath state. As we read in the Old Testament, "Be still, and know that I am God" (Psalm 46:10).

In the following journal entry a woman feels overwhelmed by the many upsets in her life. She responds by choosing to take a Sabbath break. She is not giving up or dropping out. Rather, she is making a conscious decision to give God the opportunity to restore her soul:

> *A few weeks ago I was headed for depression—so many concerns, so many responsibilities, so much to do. I felt overloaded. It was just stuff that had accumulated over a long period of time. I felt run-down and only wanted to sleep. I cried a lot, and I knew I needed to do something. So I decided to take a Sabbath break. I canceled or shifted all appointments for the following two weeks. I took on only minimal responsibilities. If anyone called asking me to do volunteer work, I simply said, "I'm sorry, I'm on a sabbatical."*
>
> *I used this "sabbatical" as a time for rest—rest for my body, mind and soul. I slept; I took vitamins regularly; I ate lightly; I allowed no conversation on upsetting topics; I filled my mind with Scripture and uplifting music; and I prayed. I stayed home and just enjoyed being quiet. I entered the stillness of the Sabbath state.*
>
> *I began to notice things I hadn't for a long time—the early morning songbirds heralding in the new day, and the pleasant summer breezes. I enjoyed breathing deeply in the open air. I worked in my garden and planted flowers. My external life circumstances with all the upsets were still there, but I had changed. I felt peaceful, calm. I felt joy and appreciation—even for the upsets. In fact, they*

---

3. *Bhikkhu* is a term of endearment which means "beloved" or "dear one." *Nirvana* is the Buddhist equivalent for the Kingdom of Heaven—a state of supreme enlightenment beyond the intellect. It can only be reached when self-will is extinguished. The Sanskrit words "*Nir*" meaning "out" and "*vana*" meaning "to blow" suggest that the flame of self-will must be "blown out" before we can receive the Kingdom of Heaven.

were no longer upsets, just challenges and opportunities. The Sabbath break transformed my internal world. I now feel God's presence in the smallest details of my life. I am grateful. My Lord has restored my soul.

This woman experienced the magnificence of a Sabbath break which restored her soul. Her external circumstances did not change, but she chose to still her mind, recognize her spiritual poverty, and move closer to God. Rather than trying to accomplish everything by herself, she simply rested in God, and in the assurance of Sacred Scripture. In quieting her mind she was able to enter the stillness of the Sabbath state. As it is written, "The Lord is my shepherd; I shall not want. He makes me to lie down in green pastures; He leads me beside the still waters. He restores my soul" (Psalm 23:1-3). It was in this stillness that her heart was strengthened and her soul restored. This is the point when God enters and gives us a new understanding of our situation and a new will to go forward. *Thy kingdom come; Thy will be done.*

In the preceding journal entry a woman chose to take a two-week sabbatical so that she might restore her soul. Sometimes, however, our "sabbaticals" might be only a few days long, a few hours long, or even a matter of minutes. In the following e-mail entry a minister describes how a sabbatical break of less than an hour helped him to be reconciled with his wife:

After my wife and I had a huge fight I decided that I wanted to smooth everything over. So I told her that I was sorry, that I didn't really mean to get upset, and so on. I could see that she wasn't buying it. She had that "Nice try, but no sale" expression on her face. I could almost hear her saying, "Go get rid of your anger first, and then we can talk."

I didn't like it when she rejected my offer to make amends, but I realized that she was right. In all honesty, I was still upset and angry, but I just didn't want to live with the unpleasant feelings. I thought that if I apologized it would take care of everything. But my wife saw right through that. So I decided to take a little Sabbath break. I took a walk, and prayed, and waited for the emotions to settle and for the Sabbath to come.

I don't remember the exact moment when the Sabbath came, but it did. Somewhere between the back door of my house and the path leading down to the creek, the unpleasant feelings subsided. I simply felt no anger, and I was no longer upset.

So I approached my wife again. She could see the difference, even before I spoke. I didn't need to say very much—just a few words—and everything was cleared up. She just reached out and touched my hand, and I knew in that moment that God was present, bringing us together again.

This is an example of the sort of miracle that can take place whenever we choose to still our minds and rest in God. Something wonderful happened between this minister's initial feeling of anger, the peace that he experienced on his walk down to the creek, and the positive response that he later gave to his wife. When he made a conscious effort to remember the Sabbath, God was able to remove the unpleasant feelings and replace them with genuine feelings of love for his wife.

For the most part, God's great work of reformation and regeneration goes on in secret, in a realm far beyond our conscious control or reasoning ability. It is like the beating of our hearts and the healing of our bodies. Nevertheless, we still have a part to play in the process. By reading and meditating on Sacred Scripture, we can receive spiritual nourishment in much the same way that our bodies receive physical nourishment from healthy food. Just as food is miraculously transformed into energy for our bodies, the words of Sacred Scripture are miraculously transformed into ongoing guidance and direction for our lives. To illustrate, consider the following journal entry from a twenty-year-old college student. She was struggling with the question of whether or not it would be wise for her to interrupt her education in order to do service work in a developing country. She writes:

When Sarah first told me that she had decided to go to Ghana I was so impressed. I thought it would be such a wonderful opportunity for her. However, when she later asked me if I might want to accompany her, I felt pretty sure that I'd never have the courage to do something like that. I knew that it would be an incredible experience, but I also knew there would be many difficulties. I kept thinking about things like disease and malaria and how scary it would be to drink the tap water.

Around this same time I received a great financial offer from the college I liked the most, and it seemed so appealing. I could just move on to college and not have to worry about traveling all the way to Ghana, spending a chunk of my life in a strange place, or getting sick. I took out a sheet of paper and began writing pros and cons. As I wrote, I realized that everything that was affecting my decision related to things other people had said. I prayed that the Lord would help me listen to the still small voice and help me choose whether or not to go.

That night before I went to bed, I decided to open the Word and read one chapter. The part of the Word I opened up to was the story about Caleb and Joshua who went into the Promised Land and brought back a big bunch of grapes. Although they did see some "giants" there, they said that it was a good land, flowing with milk and honey. When I woke up in the morning, I found myself humming the song we sing at church, "Go up and take this land . . . this land is flowing with milk and honey."

I realized that I had been like the children of Israel who were afraid of the "giants" in the land. I had been focusing on the problems rather than on the blessings. Well, I have made my decision. I am going to Ghana. I know there may be some "giants" in the land, but I know that the Lord will be with us. And I'm looking forward to those grapes!

This young college student decided that she would go directly to God for guidance about a difficult decision in her life. She wanted to hear God's "still small voice." And it came to her by reading and meditating on the Sacred Scriptures of her religious tradition. There are various forms of meditation and other time-honored traditions that can help people tune in to the "still small voice." However, we do not have to be reading the Word, meditating, or engaged in formal prayer in order to tune in to this voice. We can enter this state at any time and in the midst of any situation. The important thing is to be internally "waiting on the Lord"—to be open, receptive, and emptied of selfish desire. We might be washing the dishes, working in the garden, driving across town, or taking a walk from the back porch down to the creek. The external activity is really not the important thing. The part that matters is what is happening to us *on the inside* as our minds are stilled, and as we patiently wait on the Lord.

It must be emphasized that the "still small *voice*" may not be an audible message at all. It may simply be "the voice of conscience"—the eternal truths of the Ten Commandments speaking to us with majesty and power. At other times the "still small voice" may come to us as a gentle assurance, a sense of calm, an inner stillness, a slight lifting of a negative state, a renewal of hope, or a feeling of internal joy. Perhaps a passage of Sacred Scripture, a melody from a beloved hymn, or a memory of some kindness extended to us will arise in our consciousness. It may not come immediately, but it will surely come—sometimes at a time when we least expect it. "Watch, therefore, for you do not know what hour your Lord is coming" (Matthew 24:42).

"Stilling the mind" and listening for the "still small voice" are essential steps in our spiritual development. Through these spiritual practices we learn to subdue the burning fires of our self-will, and wait for the coming of the Lord's kingdom. That kingdom comes to us as the Spirit of God moving upon the still waters of our mind, calling to remembrance some comforting and guiding truth from Sacred Scripture. The Spirit of God begins to move upon the face of the waters, stirring something deep within us. There is a new insight, the dawning of hope, a reassurance of God's presence, and a gentle reminder that it is time to go forward.

Going forward

While it is absolutely essential for us to "still our minds" and "wait upon the Lord," these spiritual practices are not our final goal. For example, if a mother feels agitated and upset with a willfully disobedient child, and she prays for Compassion, Patience or Understanding, her prayer is not the end of the matter. Although it is commendable that she recognizes her agitation and prays for certain qualities, she still must *do something* about the situation with her child. In other words, prayer is only a means to an end—not an end in itself.

It is clear, then, that prayer must be followed by action. Before engaging in a serious operation, a surgeon's hands may be folded in prayer, and the surgeon's eyes may be closed. But the surgeon cannot rely solely on prayer—especially if the patient's life is at stake, and if time is running out. The surgeon must finish the prayer, and get started on the operation with hands unfolded, and eyes fully open. Similarly, athletes may "lift their eyes to the Lord" before an event; but once the game begins, their eyes must be open and their minds focused. It is not that we are to cease praying, but that we are to carry the essence of our prayers into a life of action. Prayer precedes; action follows. Though we are to "pray without ceasing," the time comes for each of us when we must "take arms against a sea of troubles and by opposing end them."[4]

---

4. William Shakespeare, *The Tragedy of Hamlet*, Act 3, scene 1, lines 59-60. These words are from Hamlet's soliloquy, "To be, or not to be—that is the question./Whether 'tis nobler in the mind to suffer/The slings and arrows of outrageous fortune, / or to *take arms against a sea of troubles / And by opposing end them*"(emphasis added). Hamlet's inability to act was considered his "tragic flaw." He remained the contemplative scholar rather than becoming a decisive man of action.

This spiritual lesson appears in all Sacred Scripture in a variety of ways. In the Old Testament, for example, when the children of Israel were being pursued by the Egyptians, they came up against a seemingly impossible situation. With the impassable Red Sea in front of them and the Egyptians gaining rapidly from behind, they were trapped. It was at this point that Moses said to them, "Stand still and see the salvation of the Lord." He assured them that the Lord would fight for them. This might be compared to those times in our lives when we are called to stand still—to simply quiet our minds and to *pray*. Then, in the very next verse, the Lord says to Moses, "Why do you cry to Me? Tell the children of Israel to go forward" (Exodus 14:13-15). This was the time to *act*!

Similarly, at the end of the Gospel of Luke, Jesus gave this final command to the disciples: "Behold, I send the Promise of My Father upon you; but *tarry in the city of Jerusalem until you are endued with power from on high*" (Luke 24:49; emphasis added). To "tarry in the city of Jerusalem" means to go into the stillness of prayer, looking to the Lord and meditating on God's Word. This "tarrying in Jerusalem," this time of prayer, always precedes the reception of "power from on high"—the power that will enable us to go forward in the Spirit of the Lord.

The idea of "standing still," "tarrying in Jerusalem," or "stilling our minds in God," is expressed variously in different religions, but the central point is always the same. In the *Qur'ān* we read, "Allah has sent down Tranquillity into the hearts of the Believers so that He may help them with powerful help. . . . He sent down Tranquillity to them; and He rewarded them with speedy Victory" (48:4, 18). It is significant that tranquillity —the stilling of the mind—precedes the reception of "power from on high." The tranquillity of the heart precedes the victory of the spirit.

The Buddhists, in describing this same process, use the analogy of the bow and the arrow. For them, deep meditation is symbolized by the drawing back of the bow. It is a time of gathering strength through stilling the mind. The further back one draws the bow (the deeper one goes into the quieter and more profound depths of meditation), the further forward the arrow will fly when it is released (the greater will be one's service to others). As it is written in the *Bhagavad Gita*:

> *Still your mind in Me, still yourself in Me,*
> *And without doubt you will be united with Me,*
> *Lord of Love, dwelling in your heart* (12:8).

73

In an ancient series of pictures, the Zen Buddhists describe this "stilling of the mind" or "waiting on the Lord" as the ninth stage of enlightenment. It is called "returning to the Source." In the tenth and final stage—the point just after the complete stilling of the mind—there is a picture of a man "entering the marketplace with helping hands." Here too, in Zen Buddhism, we can see that "waiting on the Lord" must precede going forward into a life of useful service.[5] At the end of the *Bhagavad Gita*, in his last utterance, Arjuna says to Sri Krishna:

> *You have dispelled my doubts and delusions, and made me ready to fight this battle. My faith is firm now, and I will do your will* (18:73).

The assignment: Remember the Sabbath

In this commandment we are invited to remember the Sabbath and to keep it holy. It is a time to rest our body, renew our mind, and restore our soul. It is a time for us to re-connect (*re-ligare*) with God through reading and meditating on Sacred Scripture. It is also a time to re-connect with others so that we might support one another in our mutual resolve to live according to the Divine commandments. Most deeply, the Sabbath is the state of mind in which our self-will becomes passive so that God's will may become active within us. As we are moved by some beloved truth from Sacred Scripture, behold! there is light in our consciousness, a renewal of hope, a strengthening of the heart; and it is time to go forward into a life of useful service. This is the Sabbath day. "This is the day that the Lord has made; let us rejoice and be glad in it" (Psalm 118:24).

5. Wilson Van Dusen, *Returning to the Source* (Moab, Utah: Real People Press, 1996), 243.

Assignment

Remember the Sabbath day/ Keep it holy

Rest your body; quiet your mind; restore your soul.
Read, listen to, and meditate on Sacred Scripture.
Listen for the "still small voice" . . . then, go forward.

In your journal, record your experience of keeping this commandment.

SUGGESTIONS FOR FURTHER REFLECTION AND APPLICATION

MEDITATION: "THY KINGDOM COME; THY WILL BE DONE"

While the opening words of the Lord's Prayer remind us that there is One True God ("Our Father"), and the next section tells how we are to address God ("Hallowed be Thy name"), this commandment helps us to focus on receiving what God is giving us ("Thy kingdom come") and on using it in our daily lives ("Thy will be done"). Try using the words, "Thy kingdom come; Thy will be done" as a meditation as you practice the spiritual discipline of keeping this commandment. Set aside a few minutes each day to stay your mind on the simple words, "Thy kingdom come; Thy will be done." As you do so, remember that the Sabbath is a state of mind we enter whenever we put aside our own will so that God's will may be done. This is how we "keep it holy."

JOURNAL REFLECTION

Describe early memories related to "keeping the Sabbath." What form did it take in your life when you were young? What does the Sabbath mean to you today? How do you keep the Sabbath at the present time? Describe a perfect Sabbath.

ACTIVITY: PRAYER JOURNALING

Take five minutes to write a prayer to God in your journal. Pay attention to your opening and closing words. *Please do this now before going on to the next activity.*

ACTIVITY: AN ANSWER TO PRAYER

Now take five minutes and write out a response to your prayer. Do it as if God were speaking to you. Again, pay attention to your opening and closing words.

ACTIVITY: LISTENING TO GOD

A seminar participant writes, "I remember as a kid always rushing into a room with adults and interrupting them with my loud chatter. Grandad used to say, 'Enter a room with ears open and mouth closed.' Sometimes we need to do that in prayer."

As this participant reminds us, prayer involves more than just speaking to God. It also involves listening for God's response. One of the keys to listening is being quiet. "The Lord is in His holy temple, let all the earth keep silence before Him" (Habakkuk 2:20). We can become spiritually "quiet" by clearing our minds of all earthly and worldly concerns, and by practicing what the Hindu Scriptures call "sitting in evenness."[6] As you do this in the coming week, practice listening for the Word of God—some truth or some teaching from Sacred Scripture. As it flows into your mind, meditate on it, and ask God to show you how this truth might be put to use in your life. As ideas come to you, write them down in your journal.

REFLECTION:

In the early days of the American railroad there was a familiar sign at many railroad crossings. It said, "Stop, Look, and Listen." It was a warning to stop, look both ways for an approaching train, and listen carefully to be sure that no train was coming. When you were sure that there was no danger, you could cross the tracks. As you practice this commandment, it might be helpful to remember the sign at the railroad crossing.

6. The Sanskrit word for "sitting in evenness" is "*samasate.*" As it is written, "He who knows this [the Sacred Scriptures] sits in evenness" (*Rig Veda* 1. 164:9).

STOP!
Stop bowing down to false gods.

LOOK!
Look to the Lord in prayer.

LISTEN!
Listen for God's response.

A NOTE ABOUT DANGEROUS CROSSINGS

Ancient wisdom teaches that when we are in a negative state, we can't trust the emotions we are experiencing or the thoughts that are coming to mind at that time. An evil tree cannot bear good fruit. At times like these it is wise to remain passive, letting emotions and thoughts rumble by like a passing freight train. We can still go about our normal business, noticing the emotions we are experiencing and the thoughts that are passing through our minds, but not acting on them. It is a time to remain prayerful, quieting our self-will, and allowing God's will to become active within us. This is what is meant in the Lord's Prayer by the words, "Thy kingdom come" (standing still in prayer/waiting for the Lord), and "Thy will be done" (going forward in the power and strength of the Lord).

Honor your father and your mother, that your days may be long upon the land which the Lord your God is giving you.
OLD TESTAMENT—EXODUS 20:12

 God has commanded, "Honor your father and your mother";
and, "He who speaks evil of father or mother, let him surely die."
NEW TESTAMENT—MATTHEW 15:4

 Be kind to parents. Whether one or both of them attains old age with thee, say not to them a word of contempt, nor repel them, but address them in terms of honor. . . . Say: "My Lord! Have mercy on them both as they did care for me when I was little."
QUR'ĀN 17: 23, 24

 I am the Father and Mother of this universe, and its Grandfather too;
I am its entire support, I am the sum of all knowledge,
the purifier, and the syllable Om;
I am the Sacred Scriptures.
BHAGAVAD GITA 9:17

 In the celestial sense, by "father" is meant our Lord Jesus Christ, and by "mother," the communion of saints, or His church throughout the whole world.
TRUE CHRISTIAN RELIGION 307

CHAPTER FOUR

Our Spiritual Inheritance

When I was a boy of fourteen, my father was so ignorant,
I could hardly stand to have the old man around. But when I got to be
twenty-one, I was astonished at how much he had learned in seven years.
—MARK TWAIN

Two Tables of Stone

THE TEN COMMANDMENTS were written on two tablets of stone. The first of these tablets, or "tables," is traditionally regarded as "God's table," because it focuses primarily on our relationship with God. The essence of this relationship is summarized in the first three commandments. In the first commandment we identified false gods—whatever interfered with our worship of the One True God. In the next commandment, we were to pray for the quality that was lacking: we were not to take the Lord's name (God's qualities) in vain. This brought us to the commandment in which we were to remember the Sabbath day and keep it holy. In this commandment we were to be still, reconnect with the Lord, and then go forward by doing God's will, not our own. These commandments, taken together, are called "God's table" because they are primarily about our relationship with God.

The second table focuses primarily on our relationship with our neighbor. These two tables of the law correspond to the two great commandments:

The first of all the commandments is: "Hear, O Israel, the Lord our God, the Lord is one. And you shall love the Lord your God with all your heart, with all your soul, with all your mind, and with all your strength." This is the first commandment. And the second, like it, is this: "You shall love your neighbor as yourself." There is no other commandment greater than these (Mark 12:29-30).[1]

As we explore the more interior levels and applications of this commandment, we will see how "honoring father and mother" wondrously connects the two tables of stone and brings together the two great commandments—love to God, and love to the neighbor. But first it is essential to focus our attention on keeping this commandment at the literal level.

Re-seeing our parents

For many people, honoring father and mother is quite easy. It calls to mind many warm and cherished memories. A seminar participant, now in her seventies, writes:

I am grateful to the Lord for the parents He gave me. My father was moral, industrious, and often loads of fun. He had a vibrant enthusiasm for life. You couldn't rain on my dad's parade because he enjoyed the rain as much as the sunshine. I think my own cheerful attitude is because of his example. There were six of us kids and our family was poor, but Dad was very creative about home improvements and other things. He made a dirty clothes chute that allowed us the fun of aiming and firing clothes into various bins in the basement below.

Once, on a family car trip to Wisconsin, with the car radiator boiling over and six hungry kids in the back seat, dad turned a can of cold baked beans into a

---

1. In the Old Testament we read, "You shall love the Lord your God with all your heart, with all your soul, and with all your strength" (Deuteronomy 6:5). Jesus, however, added the significant phrase "*with all your mind*" (Mark 12:29), suggesting that the Decalogue is meant to be understood deeply—that is, with *all our mind*. Keeping the commandments is not merely a mechanical matter in which we dutifully "keep a contract with Jehovah"; rather, it is striving to *understand* God's will as fully as we can, and then living according to that understanding with all our strength. In our efforts to understand rightly and to live well, we draw near to God and allow God to draw near to us. We enter a reciprocal, covenantal relationship. This is not just a matter of blind belief, or faith without action. It involves a total effort of heart and soul, mind and strength.

hot lunch! He did it by placing the can on the manifold of the engine under the hood of the car. When we stopped for lunch, and to let the car cool down, the beans were piping hot. It was a celebration and another wonderful memory. Dad's precious and rare capacity to enjoy life made him a living example to us all.

For this person it was relatively easy to recall a pleasant experience with a parent she loved and honored. For others, however, the process of honoring father and mother is somewhat more difficult. And for some, it seems to be just about impossible. A female prisoner writes:

I cannot do this assignment. I hate my parents. Sure they told me that they loved me, but they never did anything to show it. Forcing me to think of their good qualities and asking me to honor them only makes me remember all the bad stuff I am trying to forget. I really believe that if I allow myself to start thinking about my parents in this way I will go insane. Sure I would like to honor my parents, and maybe someday I will get there. But right now there is just too much pain. I have to work through the pain. So please don't push me.

This person, like many others, carries deep emotional wounds, and these wounds are real. Some people carry such traumatic memories from childhood—especially in cases of serious abuse—that it may be necessary for them to seek professional help. They will need to enter into the difficult process of revisiting and being healed of childhood traumas as a first step in working on this commandment. In this seminar, we do not encourage participants to re-open or dwell on the memory of their childhood wounds, or to speak about their perceptions of how their parents may have mistreated them. Although this may be very appropriate in some therapeutic settings, we urge participants to strive to raise their thinking above any resentments they may feel towards their parents. We ask them to focus their attention on any honorable qualities in their parents that they can remember. A young college student writes:

I am very thankful that the task this week is to honor my father and mother. Since I had a talk with my sister three weeks ago, I have not had very many warm thoughts about my mother or family. It may be necessary at times to reflect on the problems which you see in your family, but I am upset about the effects of this discussion with my sister. Obviously we took comfort in each other's observations because they confirmed our own. But it would have been wonderful if someone else had been there telling us to remember how much Mom and Dad love us—despite all their faults.

So, I am thankful that this seminar came at a time when I needed to change my thoughts and when I was ready. I have begun to think about my Mom's positive qualities: her laughter, humor, sweetness, beauty, independence of mind, strength of thought, and special personality. She really is a sparkly gem.

I never felt ready to do this before. But tonight I came home from the seminar with an open heart. My parents were there, and we had a great talk about my childhood. They told me I was a good kid—something special. I got happy inside. They told me how I loved life, and they pointed out many of my positive qualities. They described me as a happy, fearless, special, gorgeous, alive, loving-to-run-around-without-diapers child, whom they both loved very much.

God bless my mother and father. Let me bring them joy (more than grief). They have given me a great gift by telling me about a child they loved and honored. Praise the Lord of all who will bring us joy—great joy beyond all we could imagine or manufacture ourselves.

It was amazing to me how easily the negative mood that had been with me for the past three weeks (ever since that conversation with my sister) lifted—merely by thinking well of my parents and appreciating them. What an unexpected joy! I pray that my good feelings and my focus on my parents' positive qualities will continue.

Keeping our focus on our parents' good qualities means that we strive to *re-see* our parents in the way that God sees them. In honoring their God-given qualities, we not only honor our parents, but we also honor God who is the source of these qualities. At the same time we can accept these qualities as a part of our own spiritual inheritance—qualities that come to us from God through our earthly parents. In a remarkable way, re-seeing and accepting our parents, and seeing their God-given qualities, helps us to accept ourselves, and ultimately to accept God. The following journal entry illustrates how someone can still see good qualities in his father, even after years of being rejected by him:

In the Jewish culture one of the saddest customs is that of "disowning" someone who disgraces the family in some way. My father, a Jewish atheist, spontaneously practiced this custom when he discovered that I had chosen not only to "hook up with Jesus" (as he put it) but even worse, to become a Christian minister. Deeply hurt by what he considered my "betrayal," he refused to talk to me for the last ten years of his life. I was "off his list," "cut off," "dead." Although I regularly tried to re-establish contact with him, my father had become a wall of stone.

One day, after ten years of silence on my father's part, I heard that he was in the hospital. I decided that I would make an unannounced visit—just show up in his room and see what would happen. It had been several years since my father had last seen me, and I had grown a beard (something he had never seen me wearing). I was also about thirty pounds lighter and ten years older, so I didn't look much like the son he had "disowned." When I arrived at the hospital room, he was sitting in a chair, quietly looking out the window. I was struck by his quietness, his gentle nature, his ability to enjoy the gift of reflection, to think deeply. I sat down in the chair beside him, and trying to disguise my voice, I said, "Hello, how are you?"

He didn't recognize me. Thinking that I was probably a social worker from the hospital staff, my father proceeded to give me a generous philosophical discourse about life and the way to happiness. I listened quietly for a long while, genuinely enjoying my father's words.

About forty-five minutes into the conversation my father said something about life being difficult, but that we just had to put up with it because it would all be over soon. It was then that I remembered one of his favorite expressions— one that he had learned from an Italian friend. "Oh, yes," I said, "Qu'esta cuccaagna deve finire?" (which is a sarcastic Italian idiom meaning, "When is this 'sweet life' going to come to an end?"). When I spoke these words my father's eyes widened with recognition as he said, "Raymond, are you my Raymond?"

"Yes, Dad," I replied.

We hugged with deep affection, and while we hugged he spontaneously said, "I have always loved you."

It was a beautiful moment—one that I will never forget. It was as if the Red Sea had parted for an instant in time, and my father and I stood there together on dry land.

But the sea did not stay parted for long. An instant later my father broke the embrace, backed-off and said, "But I'm still mad at you."

"I understand, Dad," I said.

*"You **don't** understand," he replied. "You turned against what I considered sacred."*

I knew that Dad had always been an atheist, but I had no idea that he had considered anything "sacred." So I said, "What was that, Dad? What did you consider sacred?"

"My hatred of religion!" he said, and we both laughed out loud.

* * *

As I look back on this experience, I recall the glimpse that I was given of my father's essential qualities: his quiet, reflective spirit; his undying love (no matter how deeply he felt I had hurt him); and that wondrous moment of forgiveness when the Red Sea of hurt and hard-heartedness parted, and I learned that love can never die.

I know that in deciding to become a minister I deeply embarrassed my father, and, in his eyes, dishonored him and dismissed everything he tried to teach me. At the same time, I believe that beneath his atheism was a love of truth, and that beneath his hatred of religion was a love for sincerity, a love for honesty, and a love for a way of life that was free from hypocrisy. I can now see that these were my father's good qualities; and I pray that I may continue to honor these qualities as they manifest themselves in my own nature and in my life.

This journal entry illustrates that it is possible to look beyond how our parents may have treated or mistreated us, to the love that has always been there. Instead of focusing on our hurt, we can focus on the concern they have had for us, and the hopes they have had for our future, regardless of how appropriate or inappropriate their child-rearing practices may have been.

Whenever we present this seminar we emphasize that learning to honor our father and mother is a crucial step in our spiritual development. *If this step is omitted or bypassed, it is extremely difficult to make any further spiritual progress.* Our childhood wounds, which we cling to like sacred scars, will discolor and distort our current relationships, causing us to misperceive reality and overreact to present circumstances. So we urge participants to enter deeply into this commandment, to make the effort to re-see their parents, and to focus on their parents' good qualities. To the extent that we are willing to re-see our parents (who are our first "neighbors"), we will be able to understand and move beyond any blockages that we might be experiencing in our relationships with others. We will then be ready for the second table of the Ten Commandments, where the focus shifts from loving God with all our heart, soul, mind, and strength, to loving our neighbor as ourselves.

A commandment with a promise

To the extent that we succeed in honoring our parents, we are promised a great reward: "Honor your father and your mother, *that your days may be long upon the land which the Lord your God is giving you.*" Taken literally, this seems to say that if we treat our parents well, God will reward us with long life—our "days will be long." But when we read this at a deeper, more spiritual level, the message is even more profound! We know that the "Promised Land" is not a geographical place. Rather, it is a state of mind, a loving attitude that flows into us from God and out of us to others. Therefore, the promise that "our days may be long upon the land which the Lord our God is giving us" is not just about physical longevity; more deeply, it promises that the spiritual practice of honoring father and mother will bring us into longer periods of loving-kindness and wise discernment. Each day of our lives will be blessed by the heat of God's love and the light of God's wisdom. Increasingly, the spiritual sun of God's love and wisdom will fill our days, until we approach a time when that sun will never set: "There shall be no night there . . . for the Lord God gives them light" (Revelation 22:5). "If a thousand suns were to blaze forth all at once in the sky, the brightness of that light might resemble a little the splendor of God" (*Bhagavad Gita* 11:12).

Conversely, as our days in the Promised Land become longer and longer, states of coldness (absence of love) and times of darkness (absence of wisdom) will become shorter and shorter. These negative states will occur less frequently, with less intensity, and with shorter duration. In other words, we will spend less time dwelling on our resentments, less time harboring grudges, and less time revisiting situations in which we felt mistreated, misunderstood, unfairly criticized, abused or neglected. As our "days" are lengthened our "nights" are shortened, and we gradually come into a state of mind which the Sacred Scriptures of India refer to as "the end of sorrows" (*Bhagavad Gita* 2:64, 65). In that state of mind we spend more time counting our blessings ("honoring father and mother"), and less time nursing our hurts—whether real or imagined. In this regard, consider the following journal entry in which a daughter realizes that underneath her mother's apparent criticism of her was genuine concern for her welfare:

This commandment, "Honor your father and mother," has opened the way for a miracle to take place in my life. Several years ago I was in this seminar and I was asked to identify those good qualities that God has given to each of my parents. Although my father had been harsh, I could readily list numerous good qualities. When it came to my mother I went blank. This surprised me. I thought it would be easy. I stayed with it and came up with a list of my mother's good qualities; but still, I felt detached from my list. So I prayed.

What I came to understand was that there was a ten-year-old child inside of my forty-year-old body who was still angry with my mother and claiming that, "Mom liked my sister best."

Wow! What a realization! My sister had been very ill as an infant and nearly died. My mother did give her a lot of attention growing up, but that did not mean that my mother did not love me just as much. My adult mind understood this, and I couldn't believe I had carried these thoughts and feelings of rejection (along with anger towards my mother) for all of those years.

Even after this realization I still felt angry. As I went deeper, something else came to mind. Once, as a child, my father had whipped me and my mother didn't stop him. I had worked this through with my father. I knew he loved me, and that he had just lost control. But I was still angry with my mother for not protecting me.

I made an airline reservation and flew to her home to see her. We talked about my childhood. As I looked into the old, wrinkled face with the soft brown eyes, I asked, "Mom why didn't you stop him?" With her reply, all of my anger melted. She said, "Didn't you know? I was afraid, too."

We hugged as if for the first time. I thought, "This is it. Now I can accept my mother for who she is." We began a committed relationship. For the past four years we have kept in touch by phone and letters each week. Each year I travel to her home to visit for a week.

This, however, was not the end of my realizations. Recently I realized that although I understood and accepted my mother, I was still seeking my mother's approval and trying to "win her love." I saw that all of the love I felt for her was tainted by my need for her approval, and I wanted to be free of it. I wanted to just love her with no strings attached. I wanted to love her just because I love her. So this time I invited her to come to my home.

She was hesitant, but I was determined. I told her I missed her in my life and wanted my children to be with her, and for her to be with my children. She had undergone heart surgery a few years back, so I knew it would be a great effort for her. We worked through all the barriers one by one, and she did come to visit for one week.

This time when she said things like, "Why do you have so many children?" "You work too hard," "Why don't you use your degrees and have your own career?" I did not get hurt or "hooked." This time I looked at her and said, "Mom, you really love me, don't you?" She said, "Of course I do. Why else would I say these things?" For the first time in my life I could hear through those words that she loved me and really cared about my happiness. I finally understood how much she does love and care about me. What a gift.

It was a wonderful week. My children had the opportunity to witness me honoring my mother, and they were kind to her as well. When she left to fly home I cried, because I knew I would miss her in my daily life. It was as if I were just getting to know my mother for the first time.

The commandment, "Honor father and mother," is transforming my life. Practicing this commandment is healing a thirty-year wound and allowing me to grow up. God's promises are real. In keeping this commandment my days are long and full of joy in the Promised Land.

Through keeping this commandment, this individual was able to overcome long standing feelings of anger and rejection. She was able to recognize a false god that might be called "the need for approval." As she began to realize that she was being ruled by the thoughts and feelings of a ten-year-old child, she experienced an awakening of genuine love for her mother.

She also realized that *underneath* her mother's criticism—or what she perceived as criticism—was genuine concern and love. This kind of awareness is crucial for our spiritual development. In the *Rise Above It* seminar we refer to this as "untwisting" or "corkscrewing back" our misunderstandings, misperceptions and distortions of our parents' motives so that we might see the *original goodness* behind our parents' actions. For example, if we have seen "anger" in our parents, we might try to re-see it as stemming from "determination" or "a great concern for our welfare." If we have seen "stubbornness" or "inflexibility," we might try to re-see it as originating in qualities of "strength" or "conviction." This process might take real effort, but it contains the possibility of setting us free from negatively charged memories, and it can open the way for compassion to grow within us.

In this commandment, we are not asked to dismiss our parents' past behaviors as trivial or insignificant. Nor are we asked to ignore current injustices which might need attention. However, we are encouraged to see any negative behavior or trait in our parents as a distortion or perversion of some original good quality in them. We are also asked to search for and to focus on anything that might be worthy of honor in our parents. As we strive to do this, we will experience the promise that is contained in this commandment: our days will be long upon the land which God is giving us.

It should be noted that God is giving us this land *right now*. Above the clouds of gloom, above the despair, above the hurt, discouragement and misunderstanding, the sun is always shining. We just have to rise above the clouds to the place where God dwells. It is a place where we can see things more clearly and from a heavenly perspective. We begin to see the larger pattern of our lives; we gain a new perspective on our own histories and our parents' histories as well; and we come to see that each of us is made "in the image and likeness of God." To the extent that we are able to do this, we will come to understand that this is indeed a commandment with a promise, and we will experience the joy of living in the Promised Land.

"Mom always said . . ."

Honoring our parents is an essential step in our spiritual development. But how are we going to do this—especially if we feel that they have hurt us? As we have pointed out, it is necessary to re-see our parents through the eyes of love and compassion. What were their best qualities? What acts of kindness can we remember? What words of wisdom did they pass on to us? In this commandment we are invited to reflect on the positive aspects of our upbringing, to appreciate the good things that our parents did for us, and to recall words of wisdom that they passed on to us. A young African speaks of a time when he hated his parents for going against his wishes to be part of a gang. But later, when he came to see the value of his parents' viewpoint, he appreciated their wisdom and their concern for his welfare. He writes:

> When I was growing up I used to believe mostly in friends, and not in God. My friends became my "false gods." I even hated my parents and my brothers when they tried to tell me about my friends and the wrong things they were doing. My friends and I used to gather every day and discuss things that were not building anything [constructive], but instead thinking, "Where can we get the money to buy some beers?" So every time we would gather on Fridays and put some money together so that we could have some beer to drink. We drank from the evening until the morning, and the next day we would go around and tease other people because we felt strong in a group. We would go over and fight those enemies of ours, and I would end up being injured. This continued to happen until I was told by my family that if you don't separate with these friends you will end up in jail or die. I then realized, as I looked at myself in the mirror, that my face and head were full of scars which I was not born with. I had been following a false god—my group of bad friends—and not honoring my parents.

Our African friend realized that if he had honored his parents he could have avoided a great deal of trouble. In the following journal entry an American prisoner expresses a similar feeling. He says, "One thing my parents asked of me was not to get into trouble." Even though he is in prison, he realizes that it is not too late to honor his parents. He does this by remembering their words and trying to live up to their high hopes for him. Standing up in class, in the presence of thirty other prisoners, he read aloud the following excerpt from his journal:

To me this commandment means to respect, obey, and love your parents. One thing my parents asked of me was not to get into trouble. Well, this is hard to do when you're around people with different personalities. This can be a big problem if you are trying to stay out of trouble. Well today I had a run-in with a guy about turning off the coffee pot. Yes, the coffee pot. Now what happened was very stupid on my part, but this is what happened. The guy had just gotten the last drop of hot water out of the coffee pot. I walked up and said, "Why don't you turn the pot off?" He said he was about to turn the pot off. Me not giving him a choice, I turned the pot off. Now here comes the bang. He told me, "The pot won't burn up in thirty seconds." Me being already on the edge, I flew in his face, and as I approached him some of his coffee spilled from his cup, from the knock of my hand. Now some words were exchanged and almost a little violence, because I drew back my hand. He moved out of the way and just walked over to the rail. After about twenty minutes he came up to me to apologize about what happened, but I didn't apologize to him.

Now I ask myself, "Are you honoring your father and mother?" Well, I know the answer to that question and that's "No." Well, I must honor my father and mother and show some respect, so I would like to apologize to that guy. [The prisoner was reading this journal excerpt aloud to the entire class. At this point he looked up and spoke directly to an inmate on the other side of the room. "Eddy," he said, "I want to say I'm sorry for the hot temper." There was spontaneous applause from the entire class.]

Honoring our parents means that we appreciate them, see their value as human beings, recognize their good qualities, and respect them for the wisdom they tried to pass on to us. As we have seen in the journal entry about "the coffee pot incident," this is not only a matter of looking back at our childhood with nostalgia and honoring our parents with words of praise. It is also a matter of honoring our parents in the here-and-now by the actions of our lives, and by living up to their high hopes for us. When the prisoner decided to "show some respect" for a fellow inmate, he honored his parents in the profoundest way.

In the next journal entry, a young man who grew up in a crime-ridden, drug-infested city honors his mother for the wisdom she passed on to him—wisdom which helped him rise above his surroundings. He writes:

Being one of five children growing up in a single parent home has its advantages. I can say that the strict policies and my mom's way of handling us is the major contributing factor to the fact that I'm alive and well today.

One saying of mom's that came from her mom was, "You always reap what you sow." Mom used the saying so effectively that it always remains in my mind just about as well as the Lord's Prayer. I mean whenever the question of right or wrong would come to mind, I would try to do the right thing because I knew that at some point in life, in some form, or in some fashion, I would see the situation again, and I would reap what I had sown. I can say that this one saying kept me from being killed or from killing anyone in my life.

I grew up in the inner city with its housing projects and dope-filled neighborhoods and high crime rate. It is definitely true here that "you reap what you sow." Although mom made this as clear as possible, I learned the truth of her words through experience. A prime example of this was back in my youth days when I was in seventh grade. Some of my buddies (or delinquents as mom called them) and I had decided to go down to the arcade. We had just stepped off the subway when an old man, dressed in rags approached us. "Hey, bro," he said. "Let me have some change, man. I'm trying to scrape together a meal and I am a little short."

My friends and I began to make fun of the guy. "Man, I ain't giving you my money to go buy no Thunderbird," I said, laughing so hard that my side hurt. "Get away from us you stinking bum," one of my other friends said. We went away laughing and having a ball while the old man moved on. I noticed, though, that someone else gave the man some money, and not just change either. And I saw the old man go into a restaurant for a meal.

I felt kind of bad about the whole thing. I didn't even want to give the old man a little change to help him get something to eat. I tried to forget about it as we continued to walk the noisy streets to the arcade.

When we got to the arcade we began to spend money without caution. We must have spent six or seven hours there, and when our money was almost gone it was time to go home. As we got to the train station I reached into my coat pocket for my subway tokens, but only had two quarters left, and I needed four quarters for the subway. I looked over at my friends and they were holding their mouths and laughing at me. "Cut it out," I said. "Give me fifty cents so I can catch the train. No one did, because they had also spent all their money but had saved enough to get home. So here I was stuck with fifty cents when the train was a dollar.

How would I get home? It was late and there was probably only about two more trains running. I looked around to see if there were any friendly people that might lend me fifty cents. There wasn't. As a matter of fact the station was deserted. Then all of a sudden I heard some laughter. When I looked over my shoulder I saw the old man that had asked me for some change earlier. He and a couple of other old men were coming toward the turnstile as if they were about to catch the train.

"Hey, young buck," he said slowly. "What's wrong? Why are you standing here this late?" I didn't know what to say. Then the saying came to mind. I could hear mom's voice clearly saying, "Thomas, you'll always reap what you sow."

"Come here, young buck," the old man said. I walked over to him, told him that I needed fifty cents, and boy, did the old drunk bum (as I thought earlier) drop some serious knowledge on me. Then he summed up his little speech by smiling and saying, "Young man, you reap what you sow." He handed me fifty cents. I took the money, gave my thanks, and walked away, amazed at what had happened.

From that day forward I've always kept the saying in mind and always tried to sow good as much as possible. Even today the saying is alive and couldn't be more true. Mom knew how valuable the saying was when she stressed its importance to us. I appreciate her and honor her for that, but more importantly, I praise and honor the Author of the saying. I've already made up my mind that this saying will be the one that I make known to my kids as being one of the most important sayings if not the most important saying in life.

These journal entries show how we can honor our parents not only by how we speak about them, but also by living according to the wisdom they have passed on to us. As we stay focused on the good and true things our parents tried to pass on to us, we will be spending less time dishonoring our parents (either secretly in our minds, or openly as we speak to others) and more time honoring them by the words we speak, and the things we do. Focusing on our parents' good qualities, kind deeds, and true words is not about *denying* reality; rather, it is about rising into a higher reality where we can re-see our parents, honor their wisdom, and appreciate the spiritual inheritance we receive through them.

Our "spiritual allies"

Appreciating our earthly parents opens the way to a deeper understanding of this commandment. At this deeper level we are asked to honor our heavenly Parent—who is the origin of all good qualities—and to appreciate all that our heavenly Father has done for us to bring us to this point in our spiritual development. As we do this, we begin to understand and appreciate how perfectly God has been leading us at every moment of our lives, especially through our reverent study of and meditation on the Sacred Scriptures. We are familiar with the time-honored teaching that God speaks to us "through the Word." This is perhaps God's most direct influence on us. In going to the Word reverently, in listening for the voice of our Father attentively, and in striving to live according to what we believe God is telling us, we honor our Father in heaven. As it is written in the New Testament, "In the beginning was the Word, and the Word was with God, and the Word was God" (John 1:1).[2]

But this commandment also asks us to honor our "mother." In explaining this aspect of the commandment, Emanuel Swedenborg writes:

---

2. In the Sacred Scriptures of the Muslim faith we read, "Allah, most gracious! It is He who has taught the *Qur'ān*" (55:1, 2). Also, "This is the Book; in it is guidance sure, without doubt, to those who fear Allah" (2:2). In the *Bhagavad Gita* 9:17 we read: "I am the father and mother of the universe . . . the sum of all knowledge . . . I am the Sacred Scriptures." As Jesus said, "The flesh profits nothing. The words that I speak to you are spirit and they are life" (John 6:63). Swedenborg explains this idea—that God speaks to us through the Word—in the following manner: "The Word conjoins man with the Lord and opens heaven. The person who reads it from the Lord, and not from himself alone, is filled with the good of love and the truths of wisdom; his will with the good of love, and his understanding with the truths of wisdom. In this way man has life by means of the Word" (*Doctrine of the Sacred Scripture* 3).

Honoring father and mother means venerating and loving God and the church. In this sense, father means God, who is the Father of all, and mother means the church. . . because, as a mother on earth nourishes her children with natural food, so the church nourishes her children with spiritual food (True Christian Religion 306).

We should note that when Swedenborg defines our heavenly mother as being "the church," he is not referring to a physical building or to a specific organization of individuals. The word "church" actually comes from the Greek word *ecclesia* which means "to be called out" or "gathered together." It was first used in ancient Greece merely to designate an assembly of citizens summoned together for legislative or other purposes. According to Biblical scholars,

The Protestant doctrine of the church is that the church may exist without a visible form, because it is both visible and invisible. The invisible church is composed of all who are united to Christ. It is not an external organization. Its members are known to God, though they cannot always be infallibly detected by the human eye.[3]

This is similar to Swedenborg's teaching that the church is "the communion of saints, or the Lord's Church throughout the whole world." Swedenborg refers to this spiritual fellowship of true believers as the "Church of the Lord," and says that it is "the Holy City, New Jerusalem, coming down out of heaven from God, prepared as a bride adorned for her husband" (*True Christian Religion* 307; Revelation 21:2).

With this definition of the "church" in mind, we can begin to see that our spiritual "mother," whom we are to honor, includes countless persons who have impacted our lives and deepened our spiritual journeys. Whether we refer to them as "guardian angels," or "invisible saints," it is important to acknowledge and appreciate all of our spiritual allies—both earthly and heavenly—some of whom we may have never seen. Helen Keller writes:

When I review my life, it seems to me that my most precious obligations are to those whom I have never seen. My dearest intimacies are those of the mind; my most loyal and helpful friends are those of the spirit. As I wander through the dark, encountering difficulties, I am aware of encouraging voices that murmur from the spirit realm.[4]

94

3. John D. Davis, *Dictionary of the Bible* (Baker Book House: Grand Rapids, Michigan, 1980), 146.
4. *Light in My Darkness*, 135.

The Sacred Scriptures of all religions testify that we are supported at every step of our spiritual journey by a vast network of unseen allies—bands of angels and spiritual friends—whose responsibility it is to guard, encourage, inspire and watch over us. As it is written in the Old Testament: "The Lord shall give His angels charge over you, to keep you in all your ways" (Psalm 91:11). Similarly, we read in the Sacred Scriptures of the Islamic faith, "But verily, over you are appointed angels to protect you, kind and honorable" (*Qur'ān* 82:10).[5]

The "communion of saints" is not limited to our spiritual associates in the other world. This term also refers to all people who have nurtured us with the milk of human kindness, anointed us with the oil of healing love, and inspired us with the wine of spiritual truth at various times in our lives. They may be the people in our family, in our neighborhood, in our peer group, or at the school we attended while growing up. They may be people in our church, temple, synagogue or support group. The "saints" and "angels" in our life might include a beloved aunt or uncle who gave us special attention, a kindly school bus driver who greeted us with a smile each morning, or the owner of the neighborhood grocery store who called us by name and let us buy candy on credit. Maybe it was an inspiring lecturer, or a coach who helped us develop confidence, or a friend who took time to listen to us and support us at a low time in our life. These are the people who have nurtured us spiritually. These are the "Good Samaritans" who poured oil (love, compassion) and wine (truth, inspiration) on our wounds when we desperately needed spiritual help. These are the people who constitute "the communion of saints"—the Lord's Church throughout the whole world.

One seminar participant described the "communion of saints" as all those people who have been "spirit lifters, consolers, motivators and positive role models" in our lives. To acknowledge their influence in our spiritual development, and to appreciate what they have done for us, is to "honor our mother." In the following journal excerpt a prisoner honors those people who have formed "the communion of saints" in his life:

> *I'd surely like to take this time to recall the teachers who taught me in school: Ms. H., Ms. C., Mr. Z., Ms. F. and the others who laced their lessons with love and caring. I'd also like to thank my Dad for his understanding, providing and love. He never struck one of his children; his memory is with me always.*

---

5. For a thorough discussion of the invisible influences of angels in our lives, see *Angels in Action: What Swedenborg Saw and Heard*, by Robert H. Kirven (Chrysalis Books: West Chester, PA, 1994), 3-16, 84-96; also *A Book of Angels: Reflections on Angels Past and Present and True Stories of How They Touch Our Lives*, by Sophy Burnham (New York: Ballantine Books, 1990), 79-161.

Mom, you never did see the bad in people, and I thought you were blind. You always encouraged, never criticized, and tried to instill in me the difference between right and wrong. You always felt I was destined to become something. You were a free and open person, and you continue to be with me in my heart. I'd also like to thank all the people I've had the privilege to have come in contact with, whether good or bad. Also, to all the authors across the world, I'd like to show my appreciation. To the Author of all, I would like to say thank You for Your protection and endless vigil.

Divine distractions

As we enter more deeply into an understanding of the commandment, "Honor your father and your mother," we begin to realize how wondrously God has been leading us and protecting us all along. From the moment of our birth our heavenly Father has operated secretly and in wonderful ways to distract us from our negativity, to deliver us from evil, and to lead us toward all that is good. In the following example, a female prisoner writes about her anger, and how God distracted her from it in a miraculous way:

(5:30 p.m.) Today I experienced a negative situation. I immediately got angry and started being defensive. However, something caused me to remember that I have this assignment to do, so instead of striking back I am just going to get all prayed up and read a few Scriptures in my Bible. There's nothing in the Good Book to cause me any distress or pain.

(11:15 p.m.) I am back in my cell again and writing in this journal. All my angry feelings are gone. God has a way of pulling you on toward Him when He knows you're trying. After I wrote my first entry earlier, I was called to the chaplain's office. When I got there I was asked if I would be willing to sing the song called, "He's Working it Out for You" at evening church service. I had not planned to attend church service tonight. However, I was living in my assignment. Therefore I agreed to sing, and all was well with my soul afterwards. I want to thank God for the marvelous ways He helps and never hinders.

Notice that this "Divine distraction" began shortly after the upset. She writes "Something caused me to remember I have this assignment to do." So often in our lives, what appears to be an irritating interruption at the moment, turns out, in retrospect, to be part of God's gentle leading—a Divine distraction, intended for our eternal well-being. Recognizing that God is always leading us in mysterious, miraculous ways, and that there are no interruptions, is a mighty step forward in our spiritual development. As this female prisoner says, "God has a way of pulling you on toward Him when He knows you are trying."

In the following example a nineteen-year-old college student, struggling with a dating relationship, shares an unusual story in which a series of Divine distractions helped her to rise above a complaining attitude. She writes:

Yesterday was a beautiful sunny day. I sat outside with my parents, hoping that they could give me a wiser perspective on a relationship with a guy I'm dating. I started out just wanting to explain some reasons why I'd been feeling confused. However, as I spoke to them, I started getting really worked up about little details, and I just kept thinking, "This is all so hard! Why do relationships have to be so difficult?" The more I complained, the more anxious and confused I became.

As I was speaking, I looked up and saw a wild turkey standing right by our chairs. (This docile little turkey had been hanging around our house.) I tried to ignore him so I could get on with my venting, but he started doing funny things. He buried his whole head in the feathers on his back, making himself look headless. Then he'd pop his head in and out. He almost seemed to be mocking my seriousness. How could I complain about my boyfriend with the turkey doing that? But, like a mother deeply engrossed in a phone conversation while her child tugs at her skirt, I ignored the giggle tugging at my throat. A few minutes later a woman walked right through our lawn walking her dog and wearing the flashiest, funniest stretch pants I've ever seen! But for some reason I felt like I was supposed to remain serious, even though all these humorous things were going on around me. I didn't want to laugh—I just wanted to complain! I guess my heavenly Father was using these "Divine distractions" to gently nudge me out of my complaints.

A friend once told us that he wanted to produce a movie that would demonstrate the innumerable ways that God secretly leads us by apparently "random" distractions. He described a scenario that would take place in a restaurant where two friends were eating lunch. One of the friends would actually be an angel whose assignment was to protect the other person; but the angel would only be able to do this discretely, through a series of distractions. For example, the angel would know that a murderer was just outside the restaurant window getting ready to shoot the person that the angel was protecting. Knowing this, the angel would say, "Well, it's been a great meal. If we hurry, we can make it to the ballgame on time!" They would then get up and leave the restaurant just before the gunman had a chance to shoot. And so the movie would continue, through a series of "Divine distractions," until everyone would get the point that, as Emanuel Swedenborg says, "Withdrawal from evil is effected by the Lord in a thousand most secret ways" (*Divine Providence* 276:10).[6]

In this context, consider the following story:

> *A little boy was playing with his school-mates on some heath-land when he spied a big red butterfly. He pulled off his cap and flung it at the creature, but missed; the butterfly hovered a little, and fluttered away. The boy followed excitedly until it settled. Again he threw his cap, but again the butterfly opened its crimson wings and flew away.*
>
> *So the boy continued chasing it round and about the heath. Ever it led on, and ever the boy followed, but he could not take it for his own.*
>
> *Suddenly he heard a cry from a little girl. "That is Effie," he thought. "She must have hurt herself. Oh bother! I will have just one more shot." He threw his cap again, but missed the butterfly as before.*
>
> *Effie gave another cry. She was evidently in trouble. Well, he would give up the butterfly after all, and see what was the matter with her. She had caught her dress in a bramble, but seemed more frightened than hurt. He stooped and carefully removed the prickles. She was glad and smiled, and rubbed a sore place on her bare arm.*
>
> *He thought sadly, "The butterfly will have gone now, I have lost it."*
>
> *"Oh look!" exclaimed Effie, clapping her hands with delight. The butterfly had settled on his shoulder.*[7]

6. Thanks to Jonathan Rose for this illustration.
7. Brian Kingslake, *Angel Stories* (Evesham, England: Arthur James Limited, 1982), 5.

This story illustrates how God works to give us the desires of our heart, but often does so through a series of Divine distractions—distractions that may help us experience, however briefly, the kingdom of God. Whether it takes place through a turkey doing funny things on our lawn, or the call of a child in need of help, God comes to us in unexpected ways to distract us from our concerns, worries and frustrations, and to guide us into the paths of peace.

In the following example the peace of God comes into a worried father's life in an unexpected way:

> *Three weeks ago our neighbor found a stray kitten and asked me if I would like to have it. It was about two weeks old and about as cute as kittens can get. Normally I am not a "cat person" and would have said, "No." But when I picked him up and held him, my heart softened and I said, "Yes, we'll take care of him."*
>
> *I have been out of work for a while now and concerned about how I am going to support my family. We are all feeling the stress of the situation. Finances are very limited, so paying fifteen dollars for powdered kitty formula was not very practical. And yet it seemed like the right thing to be doing.*
>
> *The kitten is five weeks old now and has brought incredible peace to my heart. It snuggles up into my arm and sucks down its bottle of warm milk, just like a baby; then it goes purring off to sleep. Sometimes, while I am working at the computer, it crawls up my leg and snuggles into my lap, resting quietly and bringing peace during a difficult time in my life.*

Truly, it can be said that the invisible hand of Providence is present everywhere, at all times, protecting us and guiding us like a mother who takes the hand of a little child and gently leads it away from danger. This unceasing providence and protection is in the tiniest and seemingly most insignificant details of our lives. As Emanuel Swedenborg says, "The Divine Providence is in the least details of all things, according to the Lord's words, that not even a hair falls from the head without the will of God" (*Arcana Coelestia* 6494). To the extent that we can believe and appreciate this, we can honor our "mother"—the vast network of saints, angels, prison chaplains, friends, ordinary people, and sometimes even turkeys, butterflies and kittens through whom God leads, guides, and protects us continually.

Assignment: Honor your father and mother

This commandment asks us to do precisely what it says: "Honor your father and your mother." It asks us to conduct ourselves in ways that would bring honor to our parents, and to appreciate the people who have nurtured us in our spiritual development. These are the people who have been important influences in our life. Pay them a visit; send them a letter, fax or e-mail; make a telephone call. Find some way to express your appreciation for the ways they have supported and nurtured you. Also, in your prayers be sure to thank your heavenly Father for all He has done and continues to do for you. Let *appreciation, gratitude, and thanksgiving* be the center of your prayers and your predominant attitude as you go about your daily affairs. As you do this, notice how your "days upon the land" (states of happiness) become longer and more heavenly, as they are filled with greater love, greater wisdom, greater vitality and greater peace. Realize that this is a foretaste of the "Promised Land" that God is giving you, even now.

Assignment

Honor your father and mother

Dwell in the land of appreciation, gratitude, and thanksgiving. Appreciate God, your parents, and others.

In your journal, record your experience of keeping this commandment.

SUGGESTIONS FOR FURTHER REFLECTION AND APPLICATION

MEDITATION: "AS IN HEAVEN, SO UPON THE EARTH"
The meditation for this commandment shifts our focus from that which is in heaven (loving God—the first table of stone) towards that which is upon earth (loving the neighbor—the second table of stone). Interestingly, the corresponding part of the Lord's Prayer is properly translated, "As in heaven, so upon the earth."[8] Try using the words, "As in heaven, so upon the earth" as a meditation as you practice the spiritual discipline of keeping this commandment. Set aside a few minutes each day to stay your mind on the simple words, "As in heaven, so upon the earth," remembering as you do so that we are to honor God (our "Father in heaven") and all those who have nurtured us on our spiritual journey (our "Mother on earth").

ACTIVITY: EXPRESS APPRECIATION
At the natural level: Express appreciation and gratitude to your biological parents or care-givers—those who raised you and cared for you when you were young.

At the spiritual level: Express appreciation and gratitude for your particular support group (religious or otherwise)—those who encourage you to live according to your highest principles and beliefs.

At the highest level: Express appreciation and gratitude to God (Honor your Father) and to all those people who have supported and are supporting you on your spiritual journey (Honor your Mother).

REFLECTION:
Recall any "words of wisdom" that a parent or care-giver passed on to you—something that "Mom always said," "Dad always said," or "Grandma always said." Was it a poem, a proverb, a famous saying, a passage of Scripture, or perhaps something that Mom or Dad or Grandma made up themselves? How have these words of wisdom affected your life? Can you think of a particular time when these words helped you to rise above, or make it through, a particularly difficult circumstance?

---

8. Jay Green, *The Interlinear Hebrew Greek Bible*, Vol. 4 (Lafayette, Indiana: Associated Publishers and Authors, 1981), 12. The word order in the original Greek is as follows: *hos* (as) *en* (in) *ourano* (heaven) *kai* (also) *epi* (on) *tays* (the) *gays* (earth). *As in heaven, also on the earth.* (i.e. As above/So below.)

ACTIVITY: THANK-YOU

Send a thank-you note to someone this week—someone who has helped you or inspired you on your journey. Thank them for their influence in your life.

ACTIVITY: GRATITUDE

Take five minutes to "count your blessings." List them in your journal. For example, "_____ is a blessing in my life." The list might include friends, authors, artists, doctors, teachers, children, relatives, pets, foods, hobbies, etc.

ACTIVITY: FAMILY CREST

Make a family crest. In the upper left section, draw a symbol of a positive quality in your father. In the upper right section, draw a symbol of a positive quality in your mother. In the bottom section, draw a symbol of how these two qualities come together in you.

Here are some examples:

Anna remembered her father as being good at paying attention to detail and at fixing things. She drew a toolbox to represent this. She remembered her mother as being resourceful—able to create treasures from so little. She drew a treasure chest to represent this. Then, in the bottom section of the Family Crest, she drew a quilt to represent how these two qualities of "love for detail" and "creating beauty" were combined in her.

Joseph remembered his father as being quite studious. He drew a book to represent this. He remembered his mother as being radiant with life. He drew a shining sun to represent this. Then in the bottom section of the Family Crest he drew a classroom in which he was sitting on a desk teaching students. He saw his father's studious nature and his mother's fun-loving nature combined in him as a love of teaching and of making learning fun.

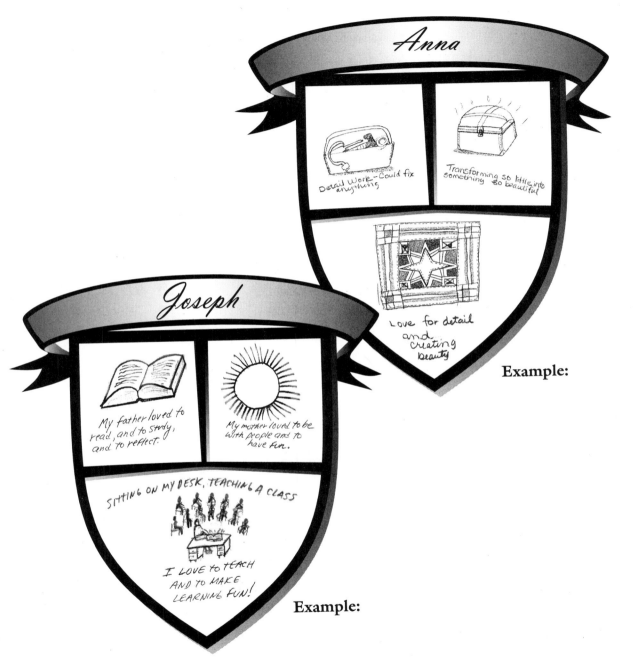

Example:

Example:

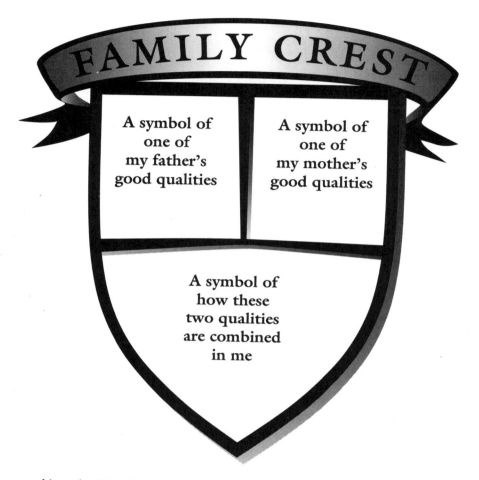

When making the Family Crest, it is important to separate our negatively charged memories from the essential good qualities that exist within each of our parents. Sometimes these qualities, which were originally good, get distorted as they take on life. As we pointed out in this chapter, what may appear as "anger" in our parents might be re-seen as having originated in them as "determination" or even a "great concern for our welfare." What may appear to be "stubborn" and "inflexible" might be re-seen as being "principled" or "strong." Striving to re-see our parents for their underlying good qualities can connect us to our own good qualities and ultimately to our spiritual inheritance.

You shall not murder.

OLD TESTAMENT—EXODUS 20:13

 He who hates his brother is a murderer.

NEW TESTAMENT—1 JOHN 3:15

 Whosoever slays a soul...shall be as if he had
slain mankind altogether; and whosoever gives life to a soul,
shall be as if he had given life to mankind altogether.

QUR'ĀN 5:35

 Right action is to abstain from taking life.

THE NOBLE EIGHTFOLD PATH OF BUDDHISM

 If a person shuns an evil as a sin,
he comes into the good opposite to the evil.
The good opposite to the evil which is meant by murder
is the good of love towards the neighbor.

THE DOCTRINE OF LIFE 70

CHAPTER FIVE

Do Not Murder / Be a Life Giver

Him I call a Brahmin who is free from anger.
—WORDS OF THE BUDDHA
THE DHAMMAPADA 26:9,18

Crime and Punishment

ON AN EXCEPTIONALLY *hot evening early in July, a young man came out of the garret in which he lodged in S. Place and walked slowly, as though in hesitation, towards K. bridge.* These are the opening words of Fyodor Dostoevsky's great novel, *Crime and Punishment.* It is the story of a brilliant young college student named Raskolnikov. "For sometime past," writes Dostoevsky, the young student "had been in an overstrained irritable condition. . . . He had become completely absorbed in himself and isolated from his fellows." And he adds, "There was accumulated hatred and contempt in the young man's heart." The reader soon discovers that Raskolnikov is on his way for a "rehearsal" of his "hideous dream"—the carefully planned murder of his landlady. The opening paragraphs of this novel reveal the strain and torment taking place within Raskolnikov's mind. Clearly, even though "the crime" has not yet taken place, the punishment has already begun.[1]

Raskolnikov's cold-blooded crime is referred to as "pre-meditated murder"—a murder that is carefully planned out before the actual crime. It is distinguished from a "crime of passion" which might happen in the heat of the moment, or "involuntary manslaughter" which is an accidental killing. Just as the English language has a variety

---

1. Fyodor Dostoevsky, *Crime and Punishment* (New York: Barnes and Noble, 1994), 1-3.

of terms to describe the various levels, degrees, and situations in which the loss of life occurs, so too does the Hebrew language. The Old Testament speaks about the "cities of refuge" that were set up to shelter those who accidentally killed someone:

> *Whoever kills ["nakah"] his neighbor unintentionally, not having hated him in the past—as when a man goes to the woods with his neighbor to cut timber, and his hand swings a stroke with the ax to cut down the tree, and the head slips from the handle and strikes his neighbor so that he dies—he shall flee to one of these cities and live (Deuteronomy 19:4-5).*

In this example, the Hebrew word "*nakah*" is used to describe the accidental killing of a person—a killing that was not based on "having hated the person in the past." Another term for "killing" that occurs in the Hebrew language is "*shachat.*" It refers to the act of killing animals sacrificially, as when the children of Israel were told to "kill the passover lamb" or to "kill the goat of the sin offering." However, when the situation involves the brutal act of taking human life with premeditated malice, the word that is often used is "*ratzach*," meaning not only "to murder," but more precisely to "rip apart," "dash down," and "break into pieces." Through its sound and through its meaning, this strong word calls to mind images of the most violent kind of crime in which human bodies are literally "torn apart." When this commandment was given on Mt. Sinai and was brought down to the children of Israel, what they heard was "You shall not "*ratzach*" (Exodus 20:13). It is no wonder, then, that modern scholars have decided to translate this commandment as "You shall not murder ("*ratzach*"), rather than simply, and more generally, "You shall not kill." It is as though God is saying to each of us, "You shall not be a cruel and malicious person; you shall not take a person's life, rip it apart, and dash it to pieces."

In the *Rise Above It* seminar we do not focus on the social/ethical aspects of this commandment. In other words, we do not discuss whether or not it is wrong to kill an intruder, or if killing is justified in times of war. Neither do we discuss killing in self-defense, the death penalty, abortion, suicide or euthanasia. While these are important questions and deserve our serious consideration, the focus of this seminar is on observing and rooting out "the accumulated hatred and contempt" in our own hearts. While laws and punishments are necessary for the preservation of order in this world, it is a law of spiritual justice that we are not punished *for* our crimes; rather, we are punished *by* our crimes. Crime and punishment are inseparable companions. To the extent that we harbor hatred for others, we hurt and murder ourselves. In the Buddhist and Hindu traditions, this might be called "the law of instant *karma*"! Conversely, as soon as we identify and remove hatred and contempt, "love for the neighbor" rushes in with healing in its wings.

This seminar, therefore, is not about finding "answers" to the social or ethical dilemmas of our day. Rather, it is about fearlessly and rigorously identifying the crimes we commit in our own lives, examining them in the light of spiritual truth, and turning away from all that is unloving, untrue, and ignoble in our own hearts. As we strive to live according to the highest, noblest teachings of our respective religious traditions,[2] our consciousness will be raised above our selfish wills, and we will be given to see more clearly how to be and what to do in any particular situation. This is what it means to "Rise Above It."

Physical murder

This commandment says, "Do not murder." In the following journal entry a prisoner describes the slowly mounting anger that finally led to the physical murder of his wife. He writes:

> *Today would have been my fifteenth wedding anniversary. My wife believed in physically punishing our son—to excess. I could not tolerate seeing anyone beat my son. The chasm between us grew as we went tit-for-tat. Knowing that I would go to prison for life, when she made her last threat to beat him, I killed her. A large part of myself and many others died with her.*

When we do not know how to deal with our anger, and we allow it to mount to the point where it controls us, murder can happen. A thirty-year-old mother shares her feelings about serving a life sentence for a murder that she claims she did not commit:

> *Today I broke the commandment against murder. I broke it by letting an old wound re-open. Tomorrow is Mother's Day and I won't see my children. I have a lot of hate in my heart for the ones who sent me to prison on a false conviction,*

---

2. Swedenborg writes: "God has provided that there should be precepts in every religion like those in the Decalogue: that God should be worshipped; His name not be profaned; a holy day be observed; parents be honored; that murder, adultery, and theft not be committed; and false witness not be spoken. A nation that regards these precepts as Divine and lives according to them in religion's name is saved." *Angelic Wisdom about Divine Providence* 254:2.

and I have hate in my heart for the man who murdered my daughter. Everyone tells me to forgive, but how do I forgive a man that took my child's life and didn't stop there? He took me from my other three children. I tell myself that I must pray harder, and I do. But on holidays, birthdays and sometimes just on ordinary days, my wound re-opens, and I find myself hating even more. I believe that if I had a gun in my hand and was standing in front of this man, I would actually shoot him. At least then I would be in here for something I really did.

In these journal entries from people imprisoned for murder, we find that at the root of murder lies resentment, bitterness, anger, hatred, and revenge—emotions opposite to those that we associate with the Kingdom of Heaven. In these personal testimonies, we find that anger breeds anger, hatred breeds hatred, and murder breeds murder.

Initially, individuals may be able to restrain themselves—and not act from anger—for a variety of reasons. A prisoner who has been provoked might not strike back for fear that it might mean losing a chance for parole. A teacher might not strike a child for fear that it might hurt her reputation or cause her to lose her job. A jilted lover may decide not to carry through on a murderous plan of revenge for fear that it might lead to arrest and incarceration. Whatever the reason, the first step in dealing with our anger is one of self-restraint. It is simply a matter of not allowing pent-up hatred or rage to burst forth on the physical level. Our teeth may be clenched, and our hands may become white-knuckled fists—but we refuse to lash out at others.

As we grow in our self-awareness, we begin to realize that true control of our external, physical actions begins by controlling them at an internal level—perhaps with the simple decision to keep the commandments because God has said so. Society's **external controls** may help to prevent angry, vengeful people from taking the law into their own hands and acting impulsively and irrationally. However, we must gradually develop ***internal controls*** based not only on societal sanctions and civil law, but more importantly, on Divine Law.

In the following journal entry a prisoner describes the murderous feelings he experienced when another inmate called him a derogatory name:

Today in the chow hall, during a misunderstanding, a fellow inmate called me a name I can't mention here. It was a tense moment, and I saw friends getting *ready to jump into it. My ire boiled. I was almost at the point of no return, when I realized that this problem was **his** problem, and I should not make it mine too. So instead of letting myself be ruled by anger, I let him have it—the problem, that is. I simply walked away from it and did not let the false god of murderous anger control me. Praise God for giving us this commandment.*

The self-restraint shown here becomes even more meaningful when we realize that it was motivated by a desire to obey the commandments of God. This prisoner resisted the impulse to lash out at another inmate—not merely to avoid a fight, or to protect his prison record—but because he realized that "being ruled by the false god of murderous anger" was against the commandments of God. Although he was "at the point of no return," he remembered the commandments, and decided to simply let the other prisoner have it —"the problem, that is."

The many levels of murder

Murder can take place on many levels. This is well illustrated in a traditional Jewish story about a man who had spread malicious rumors about the local rabbi. Feeling guilty about what he had done, the man went to the rabbi and asked what he could do to make amends. The rabbi told him to bring him a pillow. The man did so, and the rabbi told him to go to the top of a hill, tear open the pillow, and let the feathers blow away in the wind. The man followed the rabbi's instructions. He went to the top of the hill, ripped open the pillow, shook out all the feathers, and watched them drift away in every direction. Returning to the rabbi, he said, "Is that all?" "Not quite," said the rabbi. "Now you must go and collect the feathers." The man replied, "Why, that would be impossible. They have blown away in every direction." The rabbi looked at him and said, "Yes, that is true. And it is the same with the malicious rumors that you have told. They cannot be reclaimed, for they have been spread abroad in every direction."

This story indicates one of the ways that we can commit murder—by murdering the reputation of others, tearing down their good name, and "ripping them apart" through malicious gossip. This is called, quite simply, "character assassination." As one seminar participant put it, "There are words that cut deeper than any knife. There are words that bruise and maim one's spirit." It is for this reason the Old Testament sternly warns, "You shall not go about as a talebearer [gossipmonger] among your people" (Leviticus 19:16).

In the following journal entry a seventy-year-old African speaks of the many people he has "murdered" by his thoughts and words. He writes:

> *This is an assignment that touched my heart most. I've got a feeling that right now I am working against this commandment, and I need everybody's prayers right now. I know that I have committed murder in my heart many times. In my mind I can see the people I have murdered by my thoughts and by my words, and I must confess that they would fill many graveyards.*

Perhaps, at times, we too have been "character assassins" and have gone about as "gossipmongers," murdering the reputations of others. Perhaps there are times when we find ourselves "cutting down" and "tearing apart" the things people say and do, "piercing them" with words that are sharper than knives. Perhaps, if we are honest with ourselves, we can identify with our African friend, and confess that the people we have spiritually murdered "would fill many graveyards."

An American banking executive offers this insight from his journal:

> *I have come to realize that I often enjoy creating a common enemy, an anonymous "them," and then I rally the troops to join me in a bash party. Frequently the murdered enemy isn't any real person—just a broad "THEM." At first glance this seemed to me to be an exception to the commandment against murdering because, after all, it was a "nobody," a "nothing." But then I realized that what I was doing was really mass murder! I was guilty of an "ism"—"them-ism"—killing all with a broad brush, like racism. We do it in church when the people who prefer a more "traditional" service condemn the "happy-clappy" people, or when the "happy-clappies" condemn the "pillar huggers."*
>
> *At work we get into bashing all the idiots at the other company who compete against us. Maybe there is one "good guy" whom we might know personally. We say that he is all right because he agrees with us. But we feel free to murder all the rest.*

This individual has "caught himself" in the act of mass murder! It is so tempting to engage in gossip sessions, and to allow ourselves to be swept up in the critical atmosphere that sets in when "mob mentality" begins to rule. This is especially true for us when we have been hurt, mistreated or misunderstood. When our words have been twisted, and when false things have been said about us, we may notice that a spirit of revenge arises within, and we want to strike back—either directly through words that hurt and kill, or indirectly through gossip, slander and backbiting.

In the following journal entry a female prisoner feels devastated because a man with whom she had shared much of her life has refused to accept her phone call. In identifying her feelings of anger and revenge, the realization comes to her that planning how she would "get even" was like "planning a murder." She writes:

> I tried to reach my "friend" on the phone tonight. I had been trying to reach him for days. Then, when I finally reached him, the operator said he refused the charges and hung up the phone. A million thoughts went through my mind. I shared some of the best years of my life with this man. I had been thinking about him every day for weeks. How dare he not accept my phone call!
>
> I said to myself, "You can get even. When you get out, have nothing to do with him. Ignore him and allow him to feel the hurt and pain that you felt." But my task for the week again comes to mind. To think thoughts of getting even was like planning a murder.
>
> I prayed about what had happened. I asked God to remove such a thought from me. I remembered that at one time this man and I had real unity, and that maybe we would have unity again in the future. I thought about his good qualities and the things I love about him. I fell asleep praying.
>
> Today is a brand new day. Apparently I slept very well. I awoke this morning with a refreshed spirit.

In the following journal entry another prisoner describes how remembering the commandment "You shall not murder" helped him to let go of his anger and respond differently in a tense situation:

> I had a problem that occurred this past week. I felt that I was about to break this commandment, but by the grace of God I didn't. A young man stepped on my foot and I was awaiting an apology, but he ignored the fact that he stepped on me. So I said to him, "You smashed my foot." He said, "I didn't see you,"

*but the way he looked made me very mad. He looked as if he didn't care. So I told him he needed to be more observant of his surroundings. And he said I should be more considerate. I couldn't believe it. He steps on **my** foot, but **I** should be more considerate!*

I was thinking at that moment of blasting him, when there standing in front of me in the chow line was Joe Peters (from the commandments class). All at once I remembered my task. So I let the anger subside and I apologized to him. I feel that God used Joe Peters to get me to remember this important commandment. I did not let anger rule over me and make me do something I would regret.

Spiritual murder

A classic and heart-wrenching example of a murder that is both physical and spiritual at the same time is given in Shakespeare's play, *Julius Caesar*. Bleeding to death from physical stab wounds, Caesar looks up and discovers that his best friend, Brutus, has become one of the conspirators who are betraying him. Caesar then utters those famous words, "*Et tu Brute?*" (*Even you, Brutus?*). Later, at the funeral oration, Marc Antony speaks eloquently about the pain of betrayal, calling it "the unkindest cut of all":

> *This is the unkindest cut of all,*
> *For when the noble Caesar saw him stab,*
> *Ingratitude, more strong than traitors' arms,*
> *Quite vanquished him. Then burst his mighty heart.*[3]

It wasn't so much the stabbing that pierced so deeply; rather it was the sharp and painful sense of betrayal. This is not just Shakespearean drama. This is real life. Recently, a friend told us how he felt when his wife ridiculed him in public. He said, "It felt as though she had taken out a knife and plunged it into my gut."

As we practice self-examination in the light of this commandment, we might ask ourselves whether we have "stabbed anyone in the back" lately. Do our words have a sarcastic and cutting edge? (The word "sarcasm" comes from a Greek word meaning to cut and tear flesh.) Do we "shoot down" other peoples' ideas, like shooting down birds

3. William Shakespeare, *The Tragedy of Julius Caesar*, Act 3, scene 1, line 77; Act 3, scene 2, lines 187-190.

in flight? Do we discourage the efforts of others, dash their hopes, and shatter their dreams? As people leave our presence, do they feel inspired, encouraged, uplifted and filled with life? Or do they leave our presence feeling wounded, discouraged and downcast? As we listen to ourselves speaking to others, or about others, does the tone of our voice sound kind or unkind?

An aspiring young person says, "I want to do something good for the world; I want my life to make a difference," and the discouraging response comes back, "You are just one person. It will never happen. Just forget it." A small child, trying to help her mother clear the dinner table, drops a dish, and, without saying a word, the mother glares at her disapprovingly with a "piercing look." Next time, the child quietly slips away from the table and doesn't even try to help. Something in this little girl's spirit has been murdered. A father, furious with his son for deceiving him, says, "You are deceitful! How can I ever trust you? You will never be any good. You'll never amount to anything." Something in this boy's spirit is being murdered.

The Sacred Scriptures are quite direct in their warnings about this human tendency. In the Islamic Scriptures, for example, we are sternly warned to avoid saying anything either directly, or by innuendo, that would be harmful to others. And we are specifically admonished to examine the motives behind our words, even if "the tale is true," for "the taint is in the motive." As it is written, "Woe to the man or woman who deals in scandal, in word or act, or by insults or suggestions. Woe to the backbiter, even if his tale is true, for the taint is in the motive." The passage continues with a stern warning about what will happen to those who engage in this form of spiritual murder: "The Fire of Wrath will envelop them and wither up their hearts and minds" (*Qur'ān* 104: Introduction).

In the following journal entry "spiritual murder" takes place in the most unlikely of settings—during a meeting of church deacons. It is another indication that the commandments were given for all of mankind, and that no one is exempt—not even church leaders:

> *On Tuesday I was attending our regular deacons' meeting. We were discussing some very sensitive issues, and we were not all in agreement. As I sat there I found myself caught up in the highly critical atmosphere, and saying very critical things about my fellow Christians. It was a shock when I realized that we "church leaders" were acting as if we had never heard of the commandment "Thou shalt not murder."*

As temperatures and feelings rose to critical points, I reminded this body of deacons that we were doing the Lord's work, and in so doing we must follow His laws and commandments. I pointed out that there was more than one way to break the commandment against murder. I said that when we slander, criticize, or make fun of others, we commit murder by destroying that person's character.

I think these comments shifted the tone of the meeting, and we were able to continue on in a more Christian spirit. It works to remember the commandments!

In whatever life situation we find ourselves, whether in church, in prison, at the office, or around the kitchen table, we need to monitor carefully the thoughts coming in, select only those that are useful, and express them in ways that do no harm. In the sacred texts of India we read, "Him I call a *Brahmin* who does not hurt by body, speech, or mind, who is controlled in these three things" *(Dhammapada 26:9)*.

The commandment against murder, as we have seen, goes beyond the physical plane. As we consider it more deeply, we can see that this commandment invites us to examine not only our physical actions, but also our thoughts and feelings. This is why Jesus deepened this commandment, saying,

You have heard that it was said to those of old, "You shall not murder," and whoever murders will be in danger of the judgment. But I say to you that whoever is angry with his brother without a cause shall be in danger of the judgment. And whoever says to his brother, "Raca [You worthless fellow]!" shall be in danger of the council. But whoever says, "You fool!" shall be in danger of hell fire (Matthew 5:21, 22).

To illustrate, consider the following journal entry from a father who learns a deeper lesson about what it means to murder:

The phone was ringing this morning. It kept ringing and ringing. It was 7:00 a.m. on a Saturday morning and I really didn't want to get out of bed. On about the sixth ring I jumped out of bed and dashed for the phone. The person had already hung up. "It must have been Jason," I thought. "He asked if he could go to his friend's house last night, but didn't ask for permission to stay over. Now he is calling at 7:00 a.m., waking up the whole house, and asking me to come pick him up. He really has his nerve. He's so selfish. I can't believe how inconsiderate . . ."

Just then, quick as a flash, I remembered my assignment for this week: "Do not murder; be a life giver."

I caught myself in the middle of a stream of critical thoughts towards my son, and just stopped them immediately. Just as quickly, for some strange reason, this new thought—completely foreign to anything I would ever think—came flowing in. In essence, it was about how I would feel if our children didn't follow the vegetarian life-style we have raised them in. I have always said that I would be terribly disappointed if they chose to be meat-eaters as adults, especially since I believe that killing animals and eating their flesh is wrong. But the new thought that came in was accompanied by the kindest, most widely embracing feelings I could ever imagine. It would be all right if they didn't choose to be vegetarians. I had the opportunity as their parent to expose them to this way of life, but ultimately they must decide for themselves.

I found out later that the phone call wasn't even from my son! He came home on time last night like he was supposed to, and went to bed like he was supposed to—and there I was murdering an innocent person! Please forgive me, son. I'm the guy who doesn't like killing animals, but I should be more aware of how I murder you with my critical thoughts.

The words return, "You shall not murder, and whoever murders will be in danger of the judgment, but I say to you that whoever is angry with his brother without a cause shall be in danger of the judgment." The phrase "without a cause" (omitted in some early New Testament manuscripts) is sometimes a stumbling block for people. Some have relied on it as an "escape clause" to justify their feelings of hatred, revenge and murder. People sometimes feel that they "have a right" to be angry. They speak about "righteous indignation," "heavenly zeal," and "justifiable anger"—but these terms may often be used to rationalize self-righteousness and false interpretations of other people's actions.[4] Take, for example, the following journal entry in which a man's initial response of self-righteousness was a form of spiritual murder:

This weekend I drove through an intersection, and someone on the cross street went through the red light. I stopped fast and the other vehicle missed us by a few feet. This fulfilled the most literal level of the commandment—but there is more.

---

4. This topic will be given more attention in Chapter Eight.

I had some critical thoughts. My friend and I had a few things to say about the "diminished mental functioning" of the other driver. One thing that stands out in my memory is my comment: "The nerve of him honking at US!" It's easy to justify criticism when it's so glaringly obvious that the other person has broken a rule, done the wrong thing, or threatened my life.

We pulled over for a few minutes to get over the scare, and to remember that we are in the Lord's hands no matter what. It was a hard thing for me. When I was seven, my mother and two sisters died in an auto accident that happened in almost the same way.

This journal entry involves strong emotions evoked at the time of a near fatal car accident. It also involves deep-seated emotions from childhood—the tragic loss of this person's mother and two sisters. We can understand his upset and why he might say, "The nerve of him honking at US!" But notice how this journal entry continues, and how the process of self-examination deepens:

Later it occurred to me that, if that other person had suddenly discovered himself going through a red light—for whatever reason—maybe leaning on the horn wasn't rude or arrogant. Maybe it was the only thing left that might do some good. Swedenborg says that angels put a good interpretation on everything that other people do. This situation reminded me that a good interpretation is always possible.

Although this individual had what might be called "every right to be upset," he realized that it did not justify committing spiritual murder. Rather than focusing on criticizing the other driver, he chose a higher path. He chose to be "like the angels" and put a good interpretation on what had happened.

Is it kind? Is it true? Is it useful?

We may not all be angels yet, but we can strive to be like them. When we speak to others, or about others, we can observe what comes out of our mouths. As Jesus said, "Not what goes into the mouth defiles a person, but what comes out of the mouth" (Matthew 15:11).

There is perhaps no clearer indication of our essential character than what we say to or about others. In the words of an old German proverb, "A man is seldom better than his conversation."[5] This idea—that every word we speak reflects the condition of our soul—is taught plainly in the New Testament. As Jesus said to the Pharisees, "Out of the abundance of the heart the mouth speaks. A good man out of the good treasure of his heart brings forth good things, and an evil man out of the evil treasure brings forth evil things" (Matthew 12:34-35). The Pharisees, however, were not listening. Instead, they proceeded to put an evil interpretation on everything that Jesus did. For example, when Jesus cast out demons, they said that this was done through Beelzebub, the ruler of the demons; and when Jesus healed a man's withered hand, they were filled with contempt and condemnation. Instead of rejoicing that a man was healed, they complained that Jesus was "working" on the Sabbath.

In truth, it was not Jesus they were condemning, but rather themselves, for Jesus goes on to say,

I say to you that for every idle word men may speak, they will give account of it in the day of judgment. For by your words you will be justified, and by your words you will be condemned (Matthew 12:36-37).

It's not what goes into the mouth that matters—it's what comes out. By our words we will be justified, and by our words we will be condemned. When we speak about other people, the tone of our voice and the words that we choose may reveal more about ourselves than about others. Our words become a statement of who *we* are. They reveal the desires of our heart. "For out of the abundance of the heart the mouth speaks." The external actions of our lives (what we say and do) come from our internal thoughts and feelings. Paying close attention to what we are saying, and how we are saying it, helps us to better understand where we are in spirit and who we are as people.

As we have pointed out, the first step in spiritual development is to identify false gods, and, as we have seen, murderous anger can certainly be one of them. Therefore, we need to identify it at its earliest uprising—like an unwanted weed just putting forth its first shoot. Then we need to pray for the quality that is lacking—patience, mercy, forgiveness, courage—whatever seems necessary at the time. As our prayer carries us into the stillness of the Sabbath state, we will find that loving feelings will arise within us, noble thoughts will come to mind, and sometimes we will be given the words to speak.

---

5. Quoted by John Marks Templeton in *Worldwide Laws of Life: 200 Eternal Spiritual Principles* (Philadelphia: Templeton Foundation, 1997), 366.

Even when our message may be difficult for the recipient to hear, our delivery will be so filled with God's love and compassion that it will be received well and with with less resistance than we may have expected. Consider, for example, the following journal entry from a young father:

I am learning that I can say things matter-of-factly, even kindly and cheerfully, from a heart of love. I do not have to thunder threats and penalties. For example, I went into my son's room at 7:00 a.m. and asked him to pick up his baseball cards. A half hour later they were still not picked up. So rather than just ignore my feelings, or murder both my son and myself with anger, I said a quiet prayer, then simply reminded him once again.

It worked! That's all it took. No big hassle. He did it right away. Oh, how wonderful this feels. I have to get rid of this murderous feeling that keeps telling me, "You have to get really angry in order to make your kids listen."

This father learned that he could speak to his son kindly without using anger or harsh criticism to get his son to cooperate. Like this father, we also need to learn and to practice healthy patterns of communication. Therefore, *in this commandment you will be asked to say nothing critical to or about anyone for one week.*

We realize that for some people this may seem difficult at first—if not impossible. "But I am a mother," someone says. "It's my responsibility to criticize my children." Another person says, "Look, I am a quality control specialist. It's my job to be critical. That is what I get paid to do!" And someone else says, "I am a teacher. I have to grade papers and correct homework. Isn't that being critical?" In response to these legitimate questions, we say that that there is a difference between a surgeon's scalpel, which is used to help and heal a patient, and an assassin's knife which is intended to hurt and murder. For this reason, we ask participants to focus their attention on *their internal attitude* before they speak, to think carefully about the words they choose, and to carefully consider the manner in which they will deliver them. In order to assist in this process, we ask participants to imagine three "gates"[6] (or questions) through which their words will pass before they are spoken: Is it kind? Is it true? Is it useful?

These gates also include considerations of time, place and tactfulness. We need to exercise wise discretion in choosing the best timing and conditions, so that our words

---

6. Adapted from an Arab proverb which teaches that "The words of the tongue should have three gatekeepers."

Is it kind?   Is it true?   Is it useful?

will be received affirmatively and with the least resistance. Correcting a child in the presence of peers, for example, could be devastating. What we say may be true, but the embarrassment that we cause the child may be neither kind nor useful. The same words of correction, however, could be spoken with much greater effectiveness in a private setting. In the following example, a parent arranges a private meeting with a teacher in order to discuss a difficult matter:

Mid-term grades came out this week, and again one teacher gave my son an unsatisfactory mark on the report. Again, as in three other quarters, she said that he had not turned in the required work assignments, and that this resulted in a zero mark for those days. I have had this problem with this one teacher before and have confronted her on several occasions. In the past I lost my cool and became very critical.

As I wrote the note requesting a meeting with her I wanted to be very critical. But then I remembered our assignment for this week. I took a few minutes and said a prayer asking for guidance and a clear perspective. After this prayer I was able to finish the note without being critical. I chose my words carefully, making sure they were kind, true, and useful. The note resulted in a conversation with this teacher, and a solution was reached without any critical remarks from either the teacher or myself. It's amazing what's opening up for me in terms of healthy communication, just by keeping this commandment.

The words we choose, in any particular situation, can have a powerful effect on all of our relationships. When spoken *kindly*, from a heart of love; when spoken *truly*, with honesty and sincerity; and when spoken tactfully, at a time and in a manner that will be most *usefully* received, our words will open many doors—not only in this world, but in the next world as well: "For a man's heart determines his speech. A good man's speech reveals the rich treasures within him" (Matthew 12:34-35).[7] As Emanuel Swedenborg says, "The angels can know from a single word that comes forth from the thought the quality of the person's spirit" (*Arcana Coelestia* 6623).

Loving the neighbor

The Ten Commandments are perfectly ordered so that the keeping of one commandment leads on to the keeping of the next one. In the previous commandment we expressed gratitude and appreciation to our "communion of saints"—those people who have inspired and nurtured us on our spiritual journey. It now becomes our turn to inspire and nurture others on their journey. We can offer encouragement and comfort. We can be life givers to others and become a living part of the "communion of saints."

Though we may not, as yet, be able to fully forgive those who have hurt us deeply, we can still shun murderous thoughts and feelings; we can still rise above our mechanical tendency to criticize; we can still strive to see what is good in others; we can still encourage others to further develop their innate goodness, and, in so doing we can indeed think well of others. In the *Qur'ān* we read, "It may be that Allah will grant love and friendship between you and those whom ye now hold as enemies. For Allah has power over all things; and Allah is oft-forgiving, and most merciful" (60:7).

We can become life givers not only by our words, not only by our deeds, but even by our thoughts. When Jesus taught the disciples to love their neighbors, He also instructed them to love their enemies, to bless those who cursed them, to do good to those who hated them, and to pray for those who spitefully used them and persecuted them (Matthew 5:43-44). In other words, they were not only to *do well* to friends and enemies; they were also to *think well* of friends and enemies. In Aramaic, the original language that Jesus spoke, the word "neighbor" (*karebak*) refers to the person we are thinking about at the moment.[8] *This means that whoever comes to mind is our neighbor,*

7. This translation is from *The Book* (Wheaton, Illinois: Tyndale House Publishers, 1986), 950.
8. See *Enlightenment from the Aramaic: Selected Passages from the Khabouris Manuscript, An Ancient Text of the Syriac New Testament* (The Yonan Codex Foundation: Atlanta, 1970), 17. We thank Dan MacDougald, director of the Laws of Living Institute (Albany, Georgia), for this information.

for—in spiritual reality—this is the closest person to us! Our neighbors, who are to be loved, are not only those who "cross our path," but also those who "cross our mind."

This is a great challenge. In fact, for many of us, giving up life-long habits of criticism—whether verbal or mental—may feel like we are giving up our very lives. Rabbi Joseph Telushkin, a lecturer on the "ethics of speech," routinely asks his audiences to raise their hands if they think they can manage to go through twenty-four hours without saying anything unkind to or about people. Most people do not raise their hands. He then says,

> *If you cannot go for twenty-four hours without drinking liquor, you are addicted to alcohol. If you cannot go through twenty-four hours without smoking, you are addicted to nicotine. Similarly, if you cannot go for twenty-four hours without saying unkind words to others, then you have lost control over your tongue.*[9]

Learning to love our neighbor can begin by simply choosing to control our tongue. When we choose to say nothing unkind to or about others, we open the way for God to flow in with loving thoughts and kind words. As Emanuel Swedenborg writes, "The good opposite to the evil which is meant by murder is the good of love towards the neighbor" (*The Doctrine of Life* 70).

The assignment: Be a life giver

This commandment asks us to go forth and be a life giver rather than a murderer. For most of us, letting our words be kind, true, and useful (saying nothing critical or unkind for one week) will be a difficult assignment. Therefore, we will need special nourishment to sustain us. Just as physical bread is a basic symbol of earthly nourishment, the "bread" which comes down from heaven (God's goodness) is a symbol of spiritual nutrition. Through meditation, through prayer, through reading and reflecting on Sacred Scripture, and by keeping this commandment, we can become aware of the heavenly bread that God is giving us at every moment. Truly, this is "the bread which comes down from heaven" (John 6:58) and gives life to the world.

9. Rabbi Joseph Telushkin, "Words that Hurt, Words that Heal: How to Choose Words Wisely and Well," from a speech given at the Center for Constructive Alternatives at Hillsdale College, September, 1995. Re-printed in *Imprimis* (Hillsdale College, Hillsdale, Michigan) Vol. 24, no.1 (January, 1996): 1.

Assignment

Do not murder/Be a life giver

**Say nothing critical to or about anyone.
Let your words be kind, true, and useful.**

In your journal, record your experience of keeping this commandment.

SUGGESTIONS FOR FURTHER REFLECTION AND APPLICATION

MEDITATION: "GIVE US THIS DAY OUR DAILY BREAD"
The petition, "Give us this day our daily bread" is a prayer for spiritual nourishment. Every benevolent emotion and noble thought that comes to us is our "daily bread." As you practice keeping this commandment try using the words, "Give us this day our daily bread" as a meditation. Set aside a few minutes each day to stay your mind on the simple words, "Give us this day our daily bread," remembering as you do so that just as physical bread sustains our physical life, God's love sustains our spiritual life.

ACTIVITY: PASSING BREAD
In a group setting, pass around a small loaf of whole grain bread. Each person in turn breaks off a piece and says, "This week I choose to be a life giver by _____." The person then eats the piece of bread (a symbol of receiving God's goodness into his/her life) and then passes the remainder of the loaf to the next person (a symbol for allowing God's goodness to pass through him/her to others).

ACTIVITY: INSTANT REPLAY
If you catch yourself getting into a heated discussion, speaking harshly or gossiping, do an "instant replay." This means that you stop what you are doing, and say something like, "I'm sorry; let me start over." As you do so, remember to speak consciously, to choose a pleasant tone of voice, and to select words that are kind, true, and useful.

ACTIVITY: STAR CHARTS

The purpose of this activity is to become aware of how often and in what circumstances we break and/or keep this commandment. We keep track of our behavior on a "Star Chart." You will need to purchase gummed stars to place on your chart, or just hand draw them (see next page). We recommend the gummed stars, because they are fun to use, and they add a nice effect.

On the Star Chart, each day of the week is broken into three sections: morning, afternoon, and evening. If you successfully manage to make it through a section of the day keeping all of your words kind, true, and useful, give yourself a star for that portion of the day. If you fail, or have a close call, note it briefly on your chart and record the experience in your journal. At the end of the week, notice any patterns. If you find that you are unable to keep this commandment for an entire morning, afternoon or evening, don't give up! Try breaking the day into smaller sections—even by hours—so that you may experience success. Each new section can become a new beginning—a new chance to create new habits.

JOURNAL REFLECTION

In your journal, write about your Star Chart in relation to this commandment. How were you a "life giver" this week? What is one thing you learned about yourself this week?

STAR CHART

The following is a sample of how you might use the Star Chart in order to keep an accurate record of your spiritual progress.

	MORNING	AFTERNOON	EVENING
MON	Criticized other drivers on the way to work	Complained about a fellow worker	Yelled at the kids
TUE	Criticized other drivers on the way to work	★	★
WED	★	★	Complained about the boss
THU	★	★	Criticized my wife
FRI	Criticized other drivers on the way to work.	★	Criticized a driver on the way home from work
SAT	Complained about no one helping with chores	Criticized my wife	★
SUN	Criticized other drivers on the way to church	★	★

Note: This particular chart starts on a Monday and continues for one week; but it could start on any day and continue for as long as necessary. Note that the day is divided into three segments. These can be further divided into smaller segments such as early morning, late morning, etc. Charting our behavior can help us identify areas of our life, and times of the day, when we tend to be most critical. On the next page is a blank Star Chart that you may use or photocopy in order to do this assignment.

STAR CHART

	MORNING	AFTERNOON	EVENING
MON			
TUE			
WED			
THU			
FRI			
SAT			
SUN			

You shall not commit adultery.

OLD TESTAMENT—EXODUS 20:14

 You have heard that it was said to those of old,
"Do not commit adultery."
But I say to you that whoever looks at a woman to lust for her
has already committed adultery with her in his heart.

NEW TESTAMENT—MATTHEW 5:27-28

 And come not near to adultery.
Lo! it is an abomination and an evil way.

QUR'ĀN 17:34

 Right action is to abstain from sexual lust.

THE NOBLE EIGHTFOLD PATH OF BUDDHISM

 True marriage love, from its Divine origin,
is celestial, spiritual, holy, pure and clean.

CONJUGIAL LOVE 64

CHAPTER SIX

Do Not Commit Adultery / Honor Marriage

Create in me a clean heart, O God.
—PSALM 51:10

Sacred Fire

ALL RELIGIONS TEACH that marriage is a sacred and holy covenant. In its ideal form it is the most intimate, fulfilling, and ennobling of all human relationships. It is within the marriage bond that two human beings have the opportunity to practice what is taught in all religions—to treat one another with respect, courtesy and honor; to love and care for each other; and to do each other every good. In brief, it is an opportunity to practice the Golden Rule: "Whatever you want men to do to you, do also to them, for this is the Law and the Prophets" (Matthew 7:12). As Confucius says, "Do not do to others what you do not want them to do to you" (Analects 15:23).

Anyone who has been married, or who has been intimately acquainted with married partners, knows that a true marriage relationship is living and organic. Although it has its times and seasons, it also promises lasting happiness and inmost tranquillity. Consider for example, the following teaching from the Sacred Scriptures of India:

> In that family where the husband is pleased with the wife, and the wife pleased with the husband, happiness will assuredly be lasting. . . . The husband who wedded her with Sacred Texts always gives happiness to his wife, both in season and out, in this world and the next (Laws of Manu III:60; V:153).

In the Sacred Scriptures of the Islamic faith, marriage is seen as a holy bond, ordained by Allah and given as a sign of His love. This is made clear in the thirtieth chapter of the *Qur'ān* where seven "Signs of Allah" are recorded. The first sign is the miraculous creation of human beings from the dust of the ground. The second sign is the gift of marriage:

> *And among His signs is this, that He created for you mates from among yourselves, that you may dwell in tranquillity with them, and He has put love and mercy between your hearts* (30:21).[1]

In the Old Testament, God's first blessing is upon a marriage: "And God created man in His own image . . . male and female He created them. *Then God blessed them*, and God said to them, 'Be fruitful and multiply'" (Genesis 1:27-28; emphasis added). God's original plan provides that one man and one woman live together as husband and wife and experience the holy blessings of wedded love.

The Sacred Scriptures of India declare that the marriage ceremony is "the Vedic sacrament," and is equal to a man's initiation into Vedic teachings. After the marriage ceremony, the performance of household duties is equivalent to "the daily worship of the sacred fire" at the Holy Temple (*Laws of Manu* II:67). It should be pointed out, however, that this "sacred fire"—a beautiful phrase that captures the essence of marriage—is also a spiritual refinery. The discipline, self-restraint and selfless love that are to be practiced within the marriage covenant are essential for our spiritual development. Just as silver and gold are purified in the heat of the refiner's fire, the sacred relationship called "marriage" helps us to purge away whatever is crude and selfish in us until nothing is left but that which is clean, pure and precious. Emanuel Swedenborg writes, "True marriage love between one man and one wife is the precious treasure of life, and the repository of the Christian religion" (*Conjugial Love* 457). And in the New Testament it is written, "I counsel you to buy from Me gold refined in the fire" (Revelation 3:18).

In an earlier chapter we spoke about an Old Testament law that said, "You shall not kindle a fire on the Sabbath." We said that this referred to the fire of self-will—the burning, unquenchable "hell-fire" of hatred, greed, lust and selfish passion. But there

---

1. In the Islamic faith, marriage is not an option; it is an essential aspect of the religious path. Among the traditional sayings of the Holy Prophet (Muhammad) were these: "O you young men! Whoever is able to marry should marry, for that will help him to lower his gaze and guard his modesty." "Marriage is my spiritual path. Whoever keeps away from it is not from me." "When a man marries, he has half fulfilled his religion." (From an Internet article written by Professor Abdur I. Doi, Director of the Center for Islamic Legal Studies, Ahmadu Bello University, Zaire, Nigeria.)

is another kind of fire—a fire that cleanses and purifies. It is the fire of God's love. When this heavenly fire is kindled within the hearts of those who are falling in love, it burns brightly in their lives and within their marriage. This is sacred fire, "a perpetual fire that shall never go out" (Leviticus 6: 13).

The marriage relationship, then, contains the possibility for the greatest happiness and the greatest tranquillity that human beings can experience. It is also a spiritual crucible—a Divinely ordained relationship which can bring out the very best in a man and a woman. The holy bond of marriage is not intended to confine or limit us. Rather, it is intended to set us free from the tyranny of selfish desire, to help us rise above the promptings of our unregenerate will, and to awaken our nobler nature. Because it is God's greatest gift to mankind, it is not to be violated in any way. That is why the words, "You shall not commit adultery" are inscribed not only on a tablet of stone, but also on the human heart.

Defining adultery

Though the Divinely spoken words, "You shall not commit adultery," have been written on the human heart, their origin and importance seem to have been forgotten. As a result, many people are confused about adultery, and are uncertain about the place of sexuality in human relationships. Several questions arise:

Isn't sex a basic drive that needs to be satisfied, just like hunger and thirst?

Isn't sexual expression one of our inherent freedoms?

Isn't sexuality a wonderful way of expressing our unique individuality and of bonding with another human being?

What's wrong with sexuality outside of marriage as long as everyone involved agrees to it?

Why should I deprive myself of extra-marital passions when they give me so much life, vitality and happiness?

Wasn't this commandment given merely to keep society in order?

Haven't we evolved beyond the restrictions of this commandment?

These questions reveal some of the confusion and misunderstanding associated with this commandment. In this chapter we will try to give a full account of the many ways that this commandment applies to each of us, whether married or unmarried, widowed or divorced. We will try to show that the words, "You shall not commit adultery," contain the fullness of God's love, compassion and forgiveness—if we will only choose to hear.

Technically speaking, physical adultery refers to voluntary sexual intercourse outside of the marriage covenant. The English word "adultery" comes from the Latin word "*adulterare*" which means "to make impure" or "to pollute" by adding extraneous or improper ingredients. It is to make something that is pure, impure; to make something that is clean, unclean. Sometimes a product is advertised as being "pure and *unadulterated.*" This means that the product is in its original, pure state. Nothing has been mixed in or added to it.

When we carry this idea into the realm of marriage, it is expressed in the Ten Commandments as, "You shall not commit adultery." This refers not only to committing physical adultery, but also to "willing and doing obscene things, and thinking and speaking impure things" (Swedenborg, *True Christian Religion* 313). As Jesus said,

> *You have heard that it was said of old, "You shall not commit adultery." But I say unto you that whoever looks upon a woman to lust for her has already committed adultery with her in his heart* (Matthew 5:27-28).

When we speak about "a dirty old man," or about people who have "dirty thoughts," tell "dirty jokes" or have "dirty minds," our association is almost always with the perversion of sexuality and the defilement of marriage. Such people may not openly commit physical adultery, but their minds have become polluted and filthy. In their thoughts, and by their words they have taken that which is pure—the idea of marriage—and made it impure.

More deeply, we commit "spiritual adultery" whenever we "mix together" our selfish motives with truth from God's Word—whenever we misrepresent Scripture to justify our thoughts, words and actions. One way this happens is when we use Scripture to condemn others rather than to examine our own hearts and minds. In this chapter we will look at the various levels of the commandment against adultery and give examples of the possible ways that we can violate it in our everyday lives. Nevertheless, God says to each of us, "Return to Me . . . for I am married to you" (Jeremiah 3:7, 14).

Adultery in contemporary culture

In today's world we are often surrounded with images of men and women in seductive, alluring poses. Sexualized advertising is used to sell soda, soap, cars, toothpaste, fitness equipment, medicine and any number of other things not normally associated with sexuality. Clothing styles, the lyrics of popular music, the plots of novels and the content of many movies are often designed or produced in ways that stimulate our sexual appetites. Young people, perhaps more than ever before, find themselves in situations where chastity is regarded as an old-fashioned notion, and where sexual activity is seen as a key to social success, fulfillment and happiness. It is as if people have forgotten the time-honored teaching, "You shall not commit adultery."

Jesus' warning two thousand years ago—that whoever looks at a woman lustfully has already committed adultery with her in his heart—still rings true today. This applies equally to men and women. Therefore, we must be aware of the wide variety of ways in which we can dishonor marriage. This can happen, for example, by watching extramarital passions on TV or at the movies; by lingering on the pages of a magazine with sexually provocative advertising; by gazing at the figure of an attractive man or woman in a way that arouses sexual feelings; or by engaging in any mental fantasy that violates this commandment. When "channel surfing" on TV, for example, or flipping through the pages of a magazine, we are not responsible for what flashes across our sight, or across our consciousness, but we are responsible for what stations we select, what magazines we choose to read, what images we choose to absorb, and where we allow our mind to linger. In Goethe's famous play, *Faust*, the hero's downfall comes when he says to the passing moment, "*Verweile, du bist so schoen*" (Linger, you are so beautiful).[2]

In the following example, a happily married, middle-aged administrator finds himself struggling against the desire to let his thoughts linger on the sight of a seductively dressed woman. He writes:

I believe that God made women pleasant to look upon, just as the other things of creation. But I have come to the conclusion that Satan made some of the clothes that women wear today. It is easy to let your thoughts wander, seeing some of the outfits being worn by women today. While shopping at one of the local malls there was this attractive young woman that came out of one of the stores and started walking up the mall right in front of us. This young woman

2. In this classic scene Faust says to the devil, "Let's make a deal. If ever I say to the passing moment / 'Linger a while! Thou art so fair!' / Then you may cast me into fetters, / I will gladly perish then and there!" Johann Wolfgang von Goethe, *Faust*, Part I, lines 174-178.

had a light-weight see-through mini-dress. Every man in the area was probably lusting after her. I thought of the commandment and our assignment. I prayed for the strength to fight the temptation and I am proud to say I found that strength in Christ. I was able to continue my relationship with my Lord without interruption.

A thirty-year-old prisoner, struggling against the temptation to look at a pornographic magazine, relies on his Islamic faith:

I've gone a whole week resisting the urge to pick up a skin book. It does cross my mind, but I cut it off just like someone would turn off a switch. So I know that you can keep this commandment. I've been into the religion of Al-Islam for a few years, and what really is attractive to me is the self-discipline. "Thou shalt not commit adultery" is one of their commandments, too. The Islam religion taught me to look at women in a whole different kind of way—far from the way I was used to looking at them. It gave me more respect for females.

This prisoner learned from his religion that it is possible to look at a woman respectfully rather than lustfully. "Say to the believing men that they should lower their gaze and guard their modesty: this will make for greater purity" (*Qur'ān* 24:30). As we shall see, the practice of this kind of spiritual self-discipline is absolutely essential if we are to resist the onslaughts of adulterous messages in contemporary culture.

Early warning signs

Adulterous feelings can begin as quickly as a passing glance, and emotions can be kindled that are difficult to quench. This is especially true when a husband or wife who feels unappreciated at home finds affection, attention, and a sense of worth in a relationship outside of the marriage. An individual may reason: "My spouse can't be Mr. Perfect or Mrs. Perfect. It's unrealistic to expect one person to fulfill all my needs." Such a person may use their longing to be comforted, understood, and appreciated as a way of justifying a relationship in which unmet needs may finally be satisfied. The relationship may begin as a "polite" flirtation, exchanging favors, perhaps an occasional hug that lingers a bit longer than it should, a luncheon date, a walk in the park, a longing gaze, a "deep discussion" about things that one's spouse is too busy for or just not interested in. These are powder-keg situations that run the risk of exploding into full-blown affairs, complete with the agony, pain, sorrow and tragedy that ensue when people play with "unholy fire."

This level of adultery is often so subtle that we hardly notice that it is happening. It can also apply to a single person. In the following journal entry a young, unmarried woman with a profound respect for marriage finds herself slipping into adultery. It is a moving and instructive account of how our apparently innocent desires can become— almost imperceptibly—adulterous longings. She writes:

> *Our church likes to be "welcoming." That's one of the reasons I wanted to reach out to Larry. Because he was a newcomer I wanted to get to know him and his needs.*
>
> *After one of the church services, everyone was invited to an open house at the pastor's home. During the ten minute drive, I was thinking about Larry, turning over in my mind his nice qualities, and hoping that he would be there. When I pulled into the driveway and shut off the car, I sat there for a moment, waiting for people to come to the house. I was busily entertaining thoughts of how nice it would be to be with Larry, what a nice person he seemed to be, and how much I loved the conversation that we had had—about family, church, etc.—good, healthy stuff. I was thinking about how I could make contact with him and "include him in the church events." I was thinking about how I could connect with Larry in a "very loving, selfless way."*

At this point it is difficult to detect anything that might be labeled "adulterous." There is an apparently innocent desire to reach out to a newcomer and include him in church events. The young woman is simply sitting in her car thinking of Larry in "a very loving, selfless way." However, something begins to shift. She writes:

> *I began to think about Carol, his estranged wife. I knew they were having problems. I remember thinking that I never saw them sitting together in church, and I remember hoping that they wouldn't be able to work out their problems. It wasn't that I felt any hostility toward Carol—I just didn't want her in the picture. I can distinctly remember thinking, "Well maybe things won't work out with Carol." I also remember that there was a certain pleasure accompanying that thought. "Oh wouldn't that be nice!" I said to myself.*

At the same time I felt as though some darker force were controlling me. Suddenly I had a breathtaking realization. The thought came, "If I am capable of thinking this about a marriage, I am capable of doing anything to get what I want! Would I really do anything?" It was a frightening, eye-opening experience to discover how low I could go, even to the point of hoping that someone's marriage wouldn't work out.

Even though she was raised in an environment where marriage was honored, this young woman was able to see that she was not "immune" to adultery—that even she could suddenly find herself wishing for the destruction of someone's marriage. Horror-stricken at the scandal going on in her own mind, the thought came to her that she needed to pray:

Praying for their marriage, and focusing on that, immediately relieved me of the hateful, selfish, adulterous thoughts. I had an immediate sense of release from the evil sphere that I had been in. I never experienced the power of prayer like that before, and I saw clearly how prayer changes me, not other people. As soon as I started to pray about their marriage I began to feel loving toward both of them as human beings, and I didn't see Larry as anything but Carol's husband.

This is an example of how an innocent desire, in this case the desire "to include a newcomer in church events," can gradually turn into something far less innocent—the hope that someone's marriage won't work out. Fortunately, this person recognized the early warning signs and asked God for help.

Often, however, we do not "read the writing on the wall," or see the warning signs until it is too late. Consider the story of Amy and Jim who had been married for seven years and had two children. Jim traveled a great deal because of his job, and Amy had been terribly lonely. When a girlfriend said, "You can't expect Jim to fulfill all your needs," Amy felt that there was some truth to this. Soon afterwards she met a man who would "listen" to her and who "understood" her. As this new relationship deepened and the time they spent together lengthened, the warning signs were not heeded and the "friendship" became an adulterous affair.

Amy began to realize that she couldn't live in this deceit for the rest of her life. Rather than blame her husband's absence for her behavior, she decided to take responsibility for her actions. She broke off the affair and prayed for the strength and humility to ask her husband for forgiveness. It was the hardest and most painful thing they had ever been through. Nevertheless, they both agreed to try to put their marriage back together. They went for marriage counseling and began praying together. They resolved to honestly look at their relationship and tenderly open their hearts to one another. They listened to each other. They knew they had a long road ahead, and that it would take hard work to rekindle the love and trust they once had for each other. But they also knew that it was worth the effort—a journey worth taking.

Just for a moment let's roll back the hands of time and take a look at Amy's life one year earlier when she first became attracted to another man. Although it would have been difficult to tell her husband about her attraction at that time, it would have been easier than telling him about her active adultery. Or suppose we could roll back the clock four years to the time when Amy first began to sense that something was missing in their marriage. How much easier it could have been for her to come to Jim *at that time* with an expression of her love for him, to tell him how much she enjoyed his company, how much she longed to do things together with him, and how much she missed him when he was away.

Hopefully, Jim would have understood her words as an expression of her tender love for him and her care for their marriage. Perhaps he, too, would have realized that their marriage needed attention. Maybe Jim would have told her how much he loved her, how much he cared for their marriage, and how much he missed her when he was away. Perhaps they could have worked out a way to spend more time together, even if it meant that she would accompany him on some of his trips, or that he would make fewer trips, or even that he would find a new job. Perhaps this could have been a time to open their hearts to one another and to God. When we bring this kind of courage, honesty, and openness to the marriage relationship, it is possible to detect early warning signs and prevent the pain and suffering of a broken relationship.

Unfortunately, many people do not see the early warning signs. As one seminar participant writes, "If I had realized how many people were going to be wounded by my affair, I never would have gotten involved." Consider the following journal entry:

> *Five years ago I met Cynthia. We worked in the same office building. It began with friendly, casual conversation; and one day I asked her if she wanted to have lunch with me. At the time my wife and I had been married for fourteen*

years. It had been an O.K. marriage. It started out great, and we had two kids. But we didn't communicate anymore, and over the years our sexuality had really gone downhill. I had accepted the situation, but I was not happy. And I was often depressed.

When I met Cynthia it was hard to believe that this bright, attractive woman seemed interested in me. One thing led to another, until I began to realize that this new relationship was awakening feelings in me that I thought had long been dead. It was as though Cynthia was bringing me back to life. My depression lifted and I felt as though a whole new world was opening up for me. I decided to divorce my wife and marry Cynthia.

I did.

Right now, five years later, the magic is gone again, and I am right back where I was before I met Cynthia. I realize that the answer is not a new relationship. I need help.

As this journal entry illustrates, attraction to another person is almost always a sign that something is missing in a marriage.[3] This is not to say that married partners cannot experience true friendships with other people. But it is important that such friendships remain orderly and not trespass the commandment against adultery. Ultimately, each of us must judge for ourselves whether or not a friendship is "crossing the line," and slipping into an adulterous attraction. Observing early warning signs can remind us that it may be time to stop and look at our marriage, listen deeply to each other, discuss unmet needs, pray for guidance, and work towards a more fulfilling relationship.

Unmet needs

Most of us would agree that preparation for marriage is essential and should begin long before the time when we exchange our wedding vows. Ideally, such preparation would begin by growing up in a warm and loving family, where parents truly love each other and provide an example of healthy communication. Additionally, we would live in a society where true marriage love is respected, honored and encouraged.

---

3. Sometimes attraction to another person does not necessarily mean that there is something missing in our marriage. A seminar participant writes: "*For me, attraction to someone other than my husband was not a sign that something was missing in my marriage. It was a sign that there was something sick and wrong in me.*" This aspect of attraction will be discussed in more detail later in the chapter.

Unfortunately, this is more often the ideal than the reality. Many people have been raised in families that have been torn apart by abuse, addiction, and divorce. They may have been raised in an environment where "individual freedom" was valued more highly than commitment to a growing relationship. Even in those situations where parents "stuck it out for the sake of the children," the married partners may never have learned how to resolve their conflicts or communicate in healthy ways. Though they may have begun their marital relationship as lovers, they may never have learned how to be friends. This is understandable, because few of us grow up in a perfect environment. As a result, people often begin a marriage relationship with a wide range of unmet needs and unrealistic expectations.

In the 1960's and 1970's, social theorists began to speak about a "new paradigm" for enriching the marriage relationship. It was called "open marriage." These theorists taught that one person cannot possibly satisfy all of another's needs. They said that it was wrong to believe that merely being married to someone would bring an individual happiness, security and comfort for ever and ever. Challenging the time-honored notion of sexual fidelity as a marital ideal, champions of this popular theory claimed that extra-marital liaisons could actually make the marriage relationship "more vital" and "more fulfilling." In brief, they argued that the traditional "closed marriage," because it was too narrow and too stifling, had failed. They suggested, therefore, that it was "only natural to wish to expand the circle of [one's] love, to develop additional relationships in an open way, with or without sex."[4]

The social theorists were not all wrong. They stressed the importance of being "non-possessive," "non-judgmental," and "open"—all of which are important in a marriage. But the "new religion" of open, non-possessive love, *apart from the commandments of God*, did not work. A deep, open relationship outside of marriage—with or without sex—with all the glitter and excitement that it promised, turned out to be "fools' gold." Lives were shattered, and families were broken, as thousands of people went off to seek their romantic fortunes and find fulfillment in this illusory paradise.

In 1986, a group of individuals in Boston, Massachusetts, published the first edition of *Sex and Love Addicts Anonymous*. It was an organized attempt to declare that the addiction to sex and romantic love was just as strong, just as destructive, and perhaps more illusory than any other drug, for it masqueraded so well as "the real thing." Members of this organization testify with one voice that their sexual and romantic

4. Nena O'Neil and George O'Neil, *Open Marriage: A New Life Style for Couples* (New York: M. Evans and Co., 1972), 257.

obsessions were all unsatisfactory attempts to fill a void that only God can fill. One member, describing himself as a "sex and love addict," writes:

> *I finally have a way to explain why and how I have had such unsatisfactory relationships. Because I am an addict. I have looked to lovers and sexual partners to fill a void in me that cannot be filled by another person. The void was in part a spiritual void: I only knew how to experience love in a sexual context, and since my hunger was for a spiritual kind of love, sexual and romantic love was never quite enough . . . to fill my great spiritual void.*[5]

This person came to understand that sexual and romantic love was never quite enough to fill what he called a "great spiritual void." Referring to this feeling of emptiness as a "nameless, bottomless void," a seminar participant writes:

> *I grew up with an alcoholic father and was intimately acquainted with addictive behavior. Searching back through my life, I came to realize that my addictive patterns began when I was a teenager. I kept trying to fill the nameless, bottomless void that I had been left with when my parents divorced. I had many crushes on people as a child; several boyfriends as a young woman; and then I married. To my horror, two and a half years into my marriage, I felt the void again, and found myself attracted to another man. I never told anyone about it until months after "the fever broke," when I confessed it to a trusted friend. That was the first time I felt attracted to a man outside of my marriage; but there were many more to come. In short, I was married to a good man, and yet I kept falling in love with others.*

> *We had enjoyed a strong, loving marriage for fifteen years when it happened one last time—the worst. It became a deep obsession. I was in full-blown addiction. Mercifully, I was allowed to "wake up" enough to know what was happening before I committed actual physical adultery. I silently screamed for help and found that God's help had been at my side all along. My life began to change.*

> *The year that followed my awakening was a year of withdrawal from addiction. It was the most painful time of my life. I worked a twelve-step program daily. I turned my life over to the care of God daily. The pain was unmanageable, but I kept walking. Then one day I felt my will loosen up and let go. It was*

---

5. *Sex and Love Addicts Anonymous* (Boston: The Augustine Fellowship, 1986), 190.

terrifying. It was like jumping off a cliff so high that I couldn't see the bottom, and then finding myself borne up on a warm, supportive wind. It was a "born again" experience, and I haven't looked back since that day.

Now there is only one reality in my life, and that is God. The blessings on my marriage are too many to count.

Quite simply, the shift that took place in these people's lives came when they recognized that only God could fill the aching void in their hearts. Material possessions could not do it; honor, fame and the approval of others could not do it; drugs and alcohol could not do it; not even sex and romantic love, with all of their towering promises, could fill that special place in the human soul that is reserved for God alone. The miracle is, however, that when we do allow God to enter our hearts and minds, *simply by keeping the commandments*, we experience the joy that fills that void, and miraculously, we discover that our needs are amply met. We begin to realize that true love in marriage is not need-based, but rather abundance-filled. It is not about "falling in love." It is about being filled with life, and rising in love. As it is written in the Sacred Scriptures, "I have come that they might have life, and that they may have it more abundantly" (John 10:10). "Thy Lord is most bountiful" (*Qur'ān* 96:3).

Emotional seduction

Emotional seduction is one of the subtler forms of adultery. Whether it is self-righteousness, self-pity, anger, greed or some other alluring emotion, we must be aware of its seductive power. We need to notice how an undesirable emotion can entice us, and then arouse us—even to the point where we relinquish self-control. We know that when we open ourselves to inappropriate sexual feelings we are playing with fire, and that if we entertain these feelings long enough, we will reach the point of no return and get burnt. The same holds true for other negative or inappropriate emotions. Therefore, we must exercise extreme caution whenever we are tempted to flirt with, linger on, or succumb to a seductive emotion. Consider the following examples:

- *You have just read a letter with some bad news in it. You feel the hurt and the self-pity coming over you as you toss the letter on the table. You can feel the seductive, alluring pull as this emotion settles in deeper and deeper. Feeling numb and paralyzed, you crawl into bed with your self-pity, embrace it totally, and escape into the oblivion of sleep.*

• *A person whom you counted on let you down. You feel hurt and disappointed. A number of possible responses go through your mind, and each in its own way has a certain allurement. While contemplating a possible course of action, you find yourself in the kitchen in front of the open refrigerator eyeing the leftover chocolate cake. It looks especially enticing. You think "just a finger-full of icing would be nice." Three slices later you are still upset and feeling even worse.*

• *Your spouse made a decision without consulting you. You feel resentment coming on, wanting to embrace you. You struggle to shrug it off, but it is insistent, compelling, alluring. Finally you give in to the resentment which has been building, and you explode at your spouse. In the end, after you have released all your pent-up anger, you feel emotionally drained. You are spent.*[6]

Each of us could add many examples to this list. The allurement of a negative emotion might seduce us into writing an angry letter filled with self-defense and retaliation. It might entice us into calling a friend so that we might find "relief" in bitterly complaining about the person who hurt us so much. It may suggest that we have a strong drink, or take a sedative, or find some other way to escape the pain. It may suggest that the best way to manage our anger is to "let it all out," regardless of who gets hurt. In this context, consider the following journal entry from an e-mail participant who writes about an angry outburst towards her daughter:

I thought this was one commandment I could breeze through, since I was a virgin when I got married, and have never committed adultery or ever wanted to in twenty-seven years of marriage. Unfortunately, when we got on the subject of committing adultery with negative emotions, I found I failed the test and am guilty every day of my life. Such lame excuses I think of for going with anger, depression, resentment, etc. Always a good reason I have. "WOW it was great to get THAT anger out of my system—probably now I won't get cancer because I'm so cleaned out!"—Never mind that a little girl is hurting badly from my outburst. "Oh, the world doesn't appreciate me! Everyone ignores my wonderful talents and offerings!" I can go on about that one for a whole day. This is a tough one.

6. When the seductress Delilah sought to find the secret of Samson's strength, she "pestered him daily with her words and pressed him so that his soul was vexed to death" (Judges 16:16). Seductive emotions can be powerful and persistent; a particular negative emotion may stalk us all day long until we finally give in.

As this writer suggests, resisting the allurement of a negative emotion can be difficult. Whenever we succumb to the allurement of a negative emotion, we have returned to the "house of bondage." The emotion "rules over us," and we become its slave, doing exactly what it wants us to do. We have become, once again, "slaves in Egypt." Therefore, whenever we feel that we are succumbing, weakening, giving in, it is vital that we take a firm stand in the teachings of Sacred Scripture. Consider, for example, the story of Joseph as it is told in the Old Testament. We read:

> And Joseph was handsome in form and appearance. Now it came to pass after these things that his master's wife cast longing eyes on Joseph, and said, "Lie with me." But he refused and said, . . . "You are his wife. How can I do this great wickedness, and sin against God?" (Genesis 39:6-9).

Although we know little of Joseph's inner struggle to fight against the seductive offer, we do know that he was able to stand firm and say, "You are his wife. How can I do this great wickedness, and sin against God?" The crucial aspect of Joseph's response is that he regarded adultery not only as a moral crime—an offense against the woman's husband—but more importantly, *he knew that adultery is a sin against God*. The situation is the same for each of us whenever we feel the seduction of some negative emotion. We can give in to the allurement, succumb to it completely and become "a slave in Egypt," or we can rise above it. Like Joseph, we can say, "No. This is a sin against God."

Catching ourselves "in the act"

In the New Testament a story is told about a woman who was caught in adultery. When her accusers brought her to Jesus, they said, "This woman was caught in adultery, in the very act. Now Moses, in the law, commanded us that such should be stoned. But what do you say?" (John 8:4, 5). It was indeed true that there was an Old Testament law which commanded that both the adulterer and the adulteress should be put to death (Leviticus 20:10), but Jesus wanted them to learn a deeper lesson. We read:

> So when they continued asking Him, He raised Himself up and said to them, "He who is without sin among you, let him throw a stone at her first." And again He stooped down and wrote on the ground. Then those who heard it, being convicted by their conscience, went out one by one, beginning with the oldest, even to the last. And Jesus was left alone, and the woman standing in the midst.

When Jesus had raised Himself up and saw no one but the woman, He said to her, "Woman, where are those accusers of yours? Has no one condemned you?"

She said, "No one, Lord." And Jesus said to her, "Neither do I condemn you; go and sin no more" (John 8:7-11).

A key to reading Sacred Scripture is to realize that the characters in the stories symbolize various aspects of ourselves. The stories are primarily about us—not about others. With this in mind, let us imagine that we are the woman who has been caught in the act of adultery. What does this mean? What do we do when we find ourselves in physical, mental, or spiritual adultery? How do we clean it up? How do we get back into order?

Let's take a look at what Jesus says, and how the woman responds, when she is brought to the temple for her trial. Jesus tells her quite simply, "Go and sin no more." This is probably the shortest marriage counseling session in all of recorded history! However, in order for the woman to really hear the love and wisdom within these words, she could not be defending and justifying herself. Whenever we feel surrounded by accusers our defensive nature blocks us from hearing what we need to hear. When the woman's "accusers" were no longer present, she could let down her defenses and listen to Jesus' message: "Neither do I condemn you; go and sin no more."

Now let's imagine that we are an "accuser" ready to stone the woman. We are angry and upset about what she has done. At the same time we know that Moses gave us a law which permitted us to stone to death those who commit adultery. So we feel justified about our intended action. In Sacred Scripture, the word "stone" usually symbolizes some truth such as "You shall love the Lord your God" (Exodus 20:3); or "Cherish the path to peace" (*Dhammapada* 20:13); or "Be chaste, not lustful, nor taking other lovers" (*Qur'ān* 4:25). These teachings are given to us for our benefit, so that we might lead happier lives, enjoy the blessings of married love, and become the fine people we are intended to be. These "stones" are rock-solid principles that we honor and love. When we stand upon these principles we cannot be moved. We become people of integrity; we are like "a wise man who built his house on the rock" (Matthew 7:24).

However, when we become "accusers," the stones that we hold in our hands no longer symbolize these same principles. The truths become falsified and the goodness within them is adulterated. This level of adultery is referred to as "profanation." This happens whenever we take true principles out of their holy context and use them to justify our actions, satisfy our lusts, exalt our pride, or condemn others. For example, the simple truth, "Love one another" (John 13:34) can be perverted and distorted to justify sexual promiscuity. Paul's words, "I know and am convinced by the Lord that there is nothing unclean" (Romans 14:14) can be used to justify an addiction to pornography. The beautiful teaching, "Judge not, that you be not judged" (Matthew 7:1) can be spoken to others to justify and mask our own sinful behavior. And in the case of the woman caught in adultery, her accusers use the commandment "You shall not commit adultery" as a stone of condemnation that will hit the woman hard, bruise, and even kill her. The commandment in itself is true, but when used apart from mercy, or to justify self-interest, it becomes a falsity.[7] In each of these examples the teachings have been twisted so that they are no longer in accord with the Spirit originally intended by God.

The message of this story is profound. Whenever we catch ourselves in the "act of adultery" or identified with a mob of angry accusers, we can pray for a clean heart and a firm spirit. We can lay down our stones of condemnation and create an altar of worship where we pray to God and ask for forgiveness: "Forgive us our debts, as we forgive our debtors." We can return to our Lord and hear the words of mercy and compassion, "Neither do I condemn you. Go and sin no more."

Beginning a new life

When two people meet and fall in love, they experience some of the purest and noblest feelings they have ever known. For many people it is a transcendent, mystical, "out of this world" experience which can only be described in religious terms. The beloved is referred to as one's "angel sent from above"; the relationship is said to be "made in heaven"; the lovers are totally "devoted" to each other, and would gladly "lay down their lives" for one another. Their love is "the pearl of great price," and it feels like they are in heaven. In the famous novel, *Little Women*, the heroine says, "I love my gallant captain with all my heart and soul and might, and never will desert him, while God lets us be together. O, mother, I never knew how much like heaven this world could be, when two people love and live with one another."[8]

---

7. Emanuel Swedenborg writes: "Truths without good are truths falsified. Such truths in themselves are falsities" (*Apocalypse Explained* 781:12). Also, "If truths are falsified to favor evil, this commingling is profanation" (*Arcana Coelestia* 9818:27). We have seen, for example, how basic values such as being non-judgmental, non-possessive, and open, can be falsified when used to justify sexual relationships outside of the marriage covenant.

8. Louisa May Alcott, *Little Women* (New York: Grosset and Dunlap, 1915), 354.

The religious experience called "falling in love" brings out the best in people. Lovers know that they would cross the deepest ocean, climb the tallest mountain, traverse the most barren desert, and confront any danger in order to be with the beloved. Their love inspires them to reach new heights of bravery and courage. A sixteenth century Italian scholar writes:

> *It is impossible that cowardice should ever again prevail in a man's heart where once the flame of love has entered; for one who loves . . . does not hesitate to risk his life a thousand times a day to prove himself worthy of her love; hence, if one could assemble an army of lovers that would fight in the presence of the ladies they love, that army would conquer the whole world.*[9]

There is much truth in the familiar expression, "love is blind." When people are truly in love, they see only the best in one another and are relatively blind to imperfections. To the extent that love opens their spiritual eyes, they see the beloved as the most wonderful person in all the world, and desire no other. During this time there is no thought of adultery, for they have found their "one true love."

But, as we said earlier, there are "times and seasons" in every relationship. In other words, even though we may have begun our marriage with the highest intentions, there may be times of serious disagreement, and times when we may wonder whether this relationship was truly "made in heaven."[10] Unless God is at the center of the relationship, and unless there is a mutual commitment to growth as individuals and as a couple, the marriage will not be able to withstand the challenges that will inevitably arise. It is during these times of trial that we especially need to remember the commandments and put them into practice.

When the Pharisees asked Jesus if it was lawful to divorce one's wife for any reason, Jesus took them back to God's original plan:

---

9. Baldesar Castiglione, *The Book of the Courtier*, translated by Charles S. Sigleton (New York: Doubleday & Company, 1959), 257.
10. While the Sacred Scriptures of all the world religions do allow for divorce—especially when adultery has been committed—the main thrust of this chapter is on forgiveness. It is our belief that when a husband and wife each prayerfully develop their own relationship with God and strive to nourish their relationship with each other, they will be able to deal with the stresses within the marriage and avoid the pitfalls that inevitably lead to a breakdown of the relationship. Unless both partners are willing to do whatever it takes to bring the relationship into order, even a "marriage made in heaven" can become a living hell. The decision to divorce should never be made without thoughtful consideration of the consequences and an exhaustive exploration of other alternatives—including separation. A time apart may provide a useful opportunity to work on personal issues before getting back together to work on the marriage relationship.

Have you not read that He who made them at the beginning "made them male and female," and said, "For this reason a man shall leave his father and mother and be joined to his wife, and the two shall become one flesh"? So then, they are no longer two but one flesh. Therefore what God has joined together, let not man separate (Matthew 19:4-6).

Not content with Jesus' answer, the Pharisees pressed the point, saying, "Why, then did Moses command to give a certificate of divorce and to put her away?" It was then that Jesus gave the following—and most significant—response:

Moses, because of the hardness of your hearts, permitted you to divorce your wives, but from the beginning it was not so (Matthew 19:4-6).

Jesus took them back to the original plan of creation, and the original plan for marriage. From the beginning there was no thought of divorce, for the hearts of the married pair were tender and forgiving. Because they were connected to God, their relationship was a heavenly one. Although disagreements might have arisen, hearts of flesh had not yet become hearts of stone. "Moses, because of the hardness of your hearts, permitted you to divorce your wives, but from the beginning it was not so." When God is present in a marriage relationship, there is no intent to deliberately hurt one another. And when we do things that cause pain to our beloved, we are quick to acknowledge our error, express our sorrow and make amends. Similarly, when we have been hurt by our spouse, we are quick to forgive, knowing that beyond whatever has happened, the sacred flame of love still burns brightly.

Whenever we are able to readily admit our faults and forgive each other, there is an opportunity for a new beginning in our relationship. It is as if David's prayer becomes a daily reality in our lives:

Create in me a clean heart, O God,
And renew a firm spirit within me (Psalm 51:10).

This beautiful prayer takes on even more meaning when we realize that David wrote this as a prayer of repentance after committing adultery with Bathsheba. David's prayer reminds us that no matter how far we have strayed, God's mercies are fresh every morning, and that if we ask, God can create within us a clean heart and a firm spirit. A ***clean heart*** is a heart which is being cleansed and purified from all that is hard and unforgiving. As it is written in the Old Testament, "I will give them one heart, and I will put a new spirit within them, and take away the stony heart out of their flesh, and give them a heart of flesh" (Ezekiel 11:19). A *firm spirit* is a steadfast resolve to resist the onslaughts of negative emotions. It helps us to stay focused on our marriage, feeding the sacred fire with forgiveness, tenderness, quiet times of prayer, and respectful attention to each other's needs. And, most importantly, it helps us to stay focused on God from whom all blessings flow—including the blessings of marriage.

The beginning of a marriage relationship is a foretaste of the greater joys that are in store for a husband and wife who can stay focused on each other's best qualities, love each other with all their hearts, do each other every good, and forgive each other continually. At the wedding feast in Cana of Galilee, Jesus performed the first of many miracles. He turned water into wine (John 2:1-11). Similarly, as the marriage relationship grows and develops, God turns the water of natural life into the wine of spiritual life. This is the miracle of marriage—the promise of a love that grows deeper, sweeter, richer and fuller every day. Like fine wine, it improves with age. Surely, for couples who love each other spiritually, and forgive each other daily, the best is yet to come. Today is just the beginning . . .

The assignment: Honor marriage

This week focus on honoring marriage. Avoid any discussions or joke-telling that may dishonor marriage; avoid provocative flirting. Just as you would avoid an adulterous relationship on the natural plane, avoid the allurement of negative emotions on the spiritual plane. Maintain your purity and your integrity; be faithful and true to God and (if married) to your spouse. Develop a "heart of flesh" by practicing forgiveness in your marriage and in other relationships. Ask God for forgiveness. Forgive others their trespasses. Do not commit adultery.

Assignment

Honor marriage

Do not commit adultery physically or spiritually.
Clean up relationships / Forgive.

In your journal, record your experience of keeping this commandment.

SUGGESTIONS FOR FURTHER REFLECTION AND APPLICATION

MEDITATION: "FORGIVE US OUR DEBTS, AS WE FORGIVE OUR DEBTORS"
Adultery is mixing what is pure with what is impure. This commandment helps us to focus on keeping our thoughts and affections pure and unadulterated. Just as David prayed for a "clean heart," examine yourself and see if there are areas in your life in which you need to ask for forgiveness or to forgive. As you practice keeping this commandment try using the words, "Forgive us our debts, as we forgive our debtors" as a meditation. Set aside a few minutes each day to stay your mind on the simple words, "Forgive us our debts, as we forgive our debtors," remembering as you do so to stay focused on honoring marriage—your marriage with your spouse, and your marriage with God.

JOURNAL REFLECTION
Read the story of the woman caught in adultery (John 8:3-11). Imagine that you are one of the accusers, with a large stone of condemnation in your hand, ready to commit murder. In your life, how have you separated truth from mercy? In what ways have you used truth to justify your anger or to condemn others? Reflect on the meaning of the words, *"He who is without sin among you, let him throw a stone at her first."*

JOURNAL REFLECTION

Now imagine that you are the woman caught in adultery. Search out one area in your life in which you can honestly acknowledge that you are not living according to the commandments. Ask God for forgiveness. Then, *"Go and sin no more."*

ACTIVITY: CLEANING UP THE PAST

Spend some time in quiet reflection. Light a candle. Bring to mind someone you have hurt recently or in the past, either intentionally or unintentionally. Again, ask for God's forgiveness. Then, if it is appropriate, visit the person, send a letter, or make a phone call apologizing for any hurt or pain you may have caused. (Note: Be careful that your willingness to make amends does not cause further problems—as, for example, by calling an "old flame," and upsetting that person's current relationship.) Finally, call to mind those people who may have hurt you and caused you pain. One by one, forgive them their debts. *"Blessed are the merciful, for they shall obtain mercy. Blessed are the pure in heart, for they shall see God"* (Matthew 5: 8-9).

REFLECTION / MEDITATION:

The Sacred Scriptures of all religions speak about the "heavenly marriage"—the marriage between the individual and God. In Isaiah, for example, God is called "Thy Maker, thy Husband" (54:5; King James Version). In the Arabic Scriptures we read, "I have breathed within thee a breath of My own Spirit, that thou mayest be My lover. Why hast thou forsaken Me and sought a beloved other than Me?" (*The Hidden Words of Baha'u'llah* 1:19). And in the Sacred Scriptures of India we read, "Whatever forms are produced in any wombs whatsoever. . . I am the Father who casts the seed" (*Bhagavad-Gita* 14:4). Spend time in reflection, meditation, and in reverent study of the Sacred Scriptures, opening yourself to receive "seed" (noble thoughts and loving affections) from "Thy Maker, thy Husband."

BECOMING ONE: THE INTERNAL MARRIAGE

Sometimes during a wedding ceremony a couple will light a "unity candle" to symbolize their mutual desire to unite their lives and become as one. The lighting of the candle also represents their commitment to look to God as the Source of their love, inspiration and direction. It is this mutual decision to open their hearts and minds to God and to each other that makes their marriage a sacred union.

But what if we are single, widowed or divorced. How can we honor marriage? In addressing this question we speak about an "internal marriage"—a marriage that takes place *within* each of us regardless of our marital status. It is the marriage of heart and mind, will and intellect, compassion and understanding, and—ultimately—our faith and our life. To the extent that we strive to express love for others through the truth that we know, this internal marriage continues to deepen within us. As it deepens, the love we feel becomes ennobled by truth, and the truth we understand becomes enriched by compassion. Gradually our beliefs are clarified in the holy waters of truth and made pure in the sacred fires of love, till they become one with our thoughts, words and deeds. It is this internal marriage—of our purified beliefs and our consecrated lives—that makes us capable of achieving a happy, contented, and growing relationship with another human being.

It is God's purpose to bring us to the altar of this internal marriage. In striving to unite love and truth in our thought, words, and deeds, we become strong, steady, and unwavering in our devotion to God and in our service to others: "As a flame in a windless place flickers not, so is the mind of one who attains union within" (*Bhagavad Gita* 6:19).

You shall not steal.

OLD TESTAMENT—EXODUS 20:15

 Let him who stole steal no longer, but rather let him labor,
working with his hands what is good,
that he may have something to give him who has need.

NEW TESTAMENT—EPHESIANS 4:28

 And the thief, male and female: cut off the hands of both.

QUR'ĀN 5:42

 The man who is united with the Divine, and knows the truth,
thinks, "I do nothing at all."

BHAGAVAD GITA 5:8

 The angels are indignant if anyone ascribes to them
anything of wisdom and intelligence; for they know that it would be
claiming to themselves what is not theirs, and thus incurring
the crime of spiritual theft.

ARCANA COELESTIA 4295:2

CHAPTER SEVEN

Do Not Steal / Be a Credit Giver

If a pickpocket meets a Holy Man, he will see only His pockets.
—HARI DASS BABA

To take what is not your own

HAVE YOU EVER stolen something? Have you ever been tempted to steal? Maybe it was money lying around the house, or a few dollars from your father's wallet or your mother's purse. It may have been a toy from a friend's house, or a pack of chewing gum from a candy store. Perhaps you advanced to larger, more expensive items. Whatever it was, no matter how large or how small, when *you took something that was not your own,* you violated the commandment against stealing. A man in his seventies reports his first memory of stealing:

> *I remember back to when I was about six years old. My grandfather owned a little grocery store, and used to keep change in a little tin box. My job was to take the tin box from the store to the house. One evening, while bringing it over, I snuck two quarters. I never told grandpa. He wouldn't have been too pleased!*

A nineteen-year-old course participant, raised in a small African village, remembers his youthful stealing and sees it as a "disease." He writes:

> *When I was younger I was just leaving my group and going to the fields near my home. We used to steal sweet cane and water melon. We even had a time*

table. We used to steal on Monday, Wednesday, and Friday at nine o'clock. We used to call each other by singing a song. So we just steal a lot of sweet cane and water melon and we eat it. The sweet cane and water melon that remained we would take and bury it at our homes so that we could eat it the next morning. This was my disease. Now I realize that this disease was controlling me, so I told myself, "I will work hard by planting the sweet cane and water melon so that afterwards I will have it in my garden." That was the solution of my disease.

The temptation to steal "forbidden fruit" is as old as the story of the Garden of Eden—and it applies to every culture. In the next example, an American college student is tempted to steal an orange at the home where she house-cleans:

There was a gorgeous orange in this refrigerator at the place I house-clean. I have been offered drinks, but not food. Normally, I would not take the orange because I was afraid that she would notice that it was gone. But this time I didn't take it because of the assignment.

I walked home thirsty and tired, wishing for an orange. When I got to my friend's house I told her about the orange. She gave me the best grapefruit I've ever eaten. That was a very rewarding feeling.

Many people do not steal simply because they might get caught, or because they do not want to hurt other people. In the above example, however, the young woman did not steal because it was against one of the the commandments. Unexpectedly, in place of the orange, she received a grapefruit—the best she had ever eaten!

There are indeed rewards along the way for all who strive to keep the commandments. These rewards may not always be as immediate or as tangible as the one we have just illustrated, but they are nevertheless there. These rewards include the inner freedom of having a clear conscience, the peace that comes from keeping promises, and the self-respect we experience when we live honorably and with integrity. These internal rewards are just a few examples of the many "fruits" that grow so abundantly in the Promised Land.

By contrast, when we choose to live contrary to Divine order, we must necessarily face the consequences—both externally and internally. In the following journal entry a man convicted of armed robbery recalls his first theft, and the pangs of conscience he felt at that time. Unfortunately, as he grew older he found ways to justify his criminal behavior. And yet, as he reflects upon his crime, he confesses that his conscience still bothers him:

> When I read this here commandment it takes me back to when I was about nine years old. It was the first time that I remember taking something that didn't belong to me (stealing). My conscience just wouldn't let me sleep in peace, so I confessed up to what I had done. But as I got older, I kind of found out a way of curving that guilty feeling that would always occur when I stole something.
>
> How did I do that? Well, I can remember one time when I stole $600 and that guilt feeling appeared in my mind. I told myself that the couple shouldn't have been so careless with that amount of money and that they deserved it, they had it coming, etc. But guess what? My conscience still bothers me.

Another prisoner experiences his guilt as a sense of remorse that "burns like fire":

> Truthfully, I have done a great wrong. I have stolen from a family I know nothing about. I did not actually rob these people of material things, but of life. It is hard for me to show emotion or remorse for these people, but deep inside it hurts and burns like fire. I have taken away one of their loved ones.

In actuality, this prisoner's remorse can be the beginning of a miraculous healing process. Whenever we are sincerely sorry for what we have done, ask God for forgiveness, and take responsibility for our actions, we can find our way back into order. We can experience, once again, the joys of the Promised Land. In giving us the simple commandment against stealing, God is inviting us to experience the happiness and the peace that comes when we refuse to take what is not our own. It is as if God is saying to each of us, "Don't steal; you are robbing yourself of so much happiness!"

Subtler forms of stealing

As we look at the wider applications of this commandment, we discover that stealing can take place in a variety of ways. For example, employers who pay low wages to their employees, and then demand an inordinate amount of work from them, are actually stealing from their workers. Such employers, who become wealthy by underpaying their employees, are taking what is not their own. Similarly, employees who cut corners, drag their feet, cheat on time cards, and do shoddy work, are also taking what is not their own. They are stealing from their employers the wages that they have not properly earned. A retired locomotive engineer writes:

In the middle of my career as a railroad man, when employees submitted their own hours of work, I had an experience with a conductor who wanted to put two more hours on his time card than we were actually entitled to. He was a very religious fellow who saw no harm in "stealing from the rich." He was a deacon in the church, and the minister of his congregation was with him at the time. They both thought that putting on the extra hours would be O.K. I still am shocked that they would interpret the Word of God in a way that would make it allowable to steal!

In the academic world, as in the business world, situations arise in which people are tempted to take what is not their own. For example, students who cheat on tests, and get grades that they do not deserve, are stealing from their classmates. They are taking something (a grade) that does not properly belong to them. In the long run they may also be stealing awards, honors, scholarships, and eventually jobs that really belong to those students who faithfully earned them.

One of the great concerns of the academic world is the problem of plagiarism. A twelve-year-old writes:

We had a big discussion about plagiarism at school. Our teacher said that we shouldn't copy other people's work. She said we could get ideas from books and write it in our own words, but we couldn't copy exactly from the book. The teacher said it's like stealing someone else's work that they worked hard on and you are copying it.

The word "plagiarism" comes from the Greek word "*plagios*" meaning "treacherous." It seems like a strong word, especially since some students are unaware that copying information from a book is a form of stealing. For others, however, who deliberately and deceitfully copy the work of others, "treachery" may accurately define what is happening. It takes place whenever researchers submit papers and publish articles disguised as their own work without giving proper credit to the original sources. In the academic world stealing other people's ideas and passing them off as one's own is called "intentional plagiarism." For those who engage in this kind of deceit there are strict penalties.

But plagiarism is not just a problem for the academic community. It can invade all professions. Artists, inventors, and other people who deal in the creation and promulgation of new concepts sometimes steal other people's ideas, and—without giving proper credit—attempt to pass them off as their own. That is why governments establish copyright, trademark, and patent laws—so that original ideas may be protected from being stolen. As the old saying goes, we must "give credit where credit is due." A prisoner, tempted to "take credit" for a poster he did not draw, decides to be a credit giver instead. He writes:

> *A friend and I were doing some posters for the prison health fair. On the day of the fair I was invited to go and serve refreshments to the "free world people" [non-prisoners] that were supposed to be present. The subject came up about the posters, and I was asked about who had done a certain one of the posters. My friend who had drawn that poster wasn't present at the time and the poster looked very good. I wanted to take the credit for it. But when I answered, I told the truth that he had done that particular one. I gave him the credit. I did not steal his compliments on a job well done.*

Young children are often proud of a picture they have traced or colored. They feel that the work is "their own," and they are pleased to take credit for what they have done. Similarly, young children can readily be forgiven when they take credit for information that they have copied from a book. We all begin by imitation. Also, since young people have not had the opportunity to fully develop their own ideas, it is understood that the ideas which they do present will not always be their own. As they grow up, however, and begin to assimilate the ideas and insights of others, they will gradually formulate their own ideas and opinions, develop their own style, and express themselves in unique ways. They will feel, more than ever, that their work is "original," "creative," and "their own."

Eventually, however, they will reach a time in their development when they begin to recognize that their finest ideas and their most creative expressions, no matter how well articulated or presented, are not "their own." Although it may seem to them that their work is self-derived, they know that it would be "spiritual plagiarism" to take credit for it. They understand that every brilliant idea they think, all the beautiful art they produce, and every loving deed they perform, is done—not by them—but by God acting into and through them.

This eternal truth is taught in all the great religions. In the Sacred Scriptures of India we read, "The man who is united with the Divine and knows the truth thinks, 'I do nothing at all'" (*Bhagavad Gita* 5:8). In the New Testament it is written, "Without Me, you can do nothing" (John 15:5); also, "A man can receive nothing unless it has been given to him from heaven" (John 3:27). The same wisdom comes to us through the Islamic Scriptures: "To Him belongs whatever is in the heavens and on the earth. . . . Ye have no good thing but [that which] is from Allah" (*Qur'ān* 16:52-53). And Emanuel Swedenborg writes, "The angels are indignant if anyone ascribes to them anything of wisdom and intelligence; for they know that it would be claiming to themselves what is not theirs, and thus incurring the crime of spiritual theft" (*Arcana Coelestia* 4295:2). It is for this reason that religious leaders have always said, "Give glory to God." We must be credit givers, not credit takers. As we read in the *Qur'ān*:

> *Give glory to Allah when ye reach eventide and when ye rise in the morning. Yea, to Him be praise in the heavens and on the earth; in the late afternoon and when the day begins to decline. . . . It is He who gives life to the earth* (30:17, 19).

Healthy and unhealthy pride

In this commandment we are asked to not take credit for the loving emotions we feel, the true thoughts we think, or the kind deeds that we do. We are to give credit to God. Though we may enjoy the fact that God gives us stewardship over the love, wisdom, and energy for useful service that come to us from "on high," we need to be watchful, lest we fall into the trap of attributing goodness and wisdom to ourselves. Otherwise we can easily develop an unhealthy feeling of pride in our accomplishments and a sense of superiority that robs us of the joy of loving others. As it is written, "Those with true knowledge are free from pride and conceit. They are gentle, forgiving, upright and pure" (*Bhagavad Gita* 13:7). If we do not examine ourselves in depth, and search out our own false gods, we may feel offended and taken aback by the "sinful" deeds of others. Unaware that the same tendencies exist in ourselves, and that we bow down to the same false gods that we see in others, we may feel self-righteous and proud. This kind of pride makes us feel superior to others; therefore, it must be overcome, for it is a thief and a robber. A father writes:

I awoke this morning to hear my thirteen-year-old daughter weeping loudly about how horrible she felt and how she was up all night with stomach pains. My inner response was that she was over-reacting and that she really didn't need to wake everyone else up just because she was sick. I was thinking, "She ought to be able to handle this better." And also, "I certainly would not act like that if I were sick."

I examined these thoughts in the light of the commandment on not stealing, and remembered what was said about pride. I was really surprised by the cold, unmerciful thoughts and feelings that arose within me in response to my daughter's pain. As soon as I saw the hardness of my heart, and my own self-righteousness, I began to soften. In fact, feelings of genuine sympathy began to arise in me. I realized how mistaken I had been, and how my self-righteousness had actually stolen from me the opportunity to feel genuine compassion for my daughter.

A grandmother notices prideful feelings arising while involved in a typing job:

My friend and I were each doing half of a typing job. As I started typing my half, the thought went passing slowly through my brain, "I bet I am doing this better than she is." I burst out laughing! The thought was totally irrational, especially since my friend is a terrific typist. I told the voice in my head to "Beat it!" The thought left at once.

However, a few hours later the same attitude was back in a different disguise:

A few hours later when I was practicing the piano in preparation for church service, the thought came sailing through my head, "I bet I play this music much better than the other pianists would." Again, it was a totally inappropriate, unbelievable remark. It was very clear that something prideful was trying to get planted in my head, but once again the soil was not going to receive that seed of pride. I took no pleasure in identifying with such self-righteous thoughts. Oh, give the glory to God!

As we have seen, feelings of superiority and self-righteousness are unhealthy for our spirits. This kind of pride is like dirty bathwater, and needs to be "tossed out the window." However, we need not "throw the baby out with the bath water." For there is healthy pride too. Healthy pride is based on the feeling that we, like all people, are children of God, made in God's image and likeness, and that through the power of God we are doing all we can to help make the world a better place. This has nothing to do with being better than others. *People with healthy pride measure themselves not by how far they rise above others, but rather by how far they can rise above their own selfishness so that they may give to others unselfishly*. At the same time they acknowledge that they can give nothing except what they have first been given by God. Such healthy pride is exhibited in the following journal entry written by an aspiring young actress:

> *There is a sanity in my life that I am not used to. I think it comes from working on these assignments. This week I was in a play. Pretty often when I felt I was doing a good job I thanked God. It helped to keep me balanced and to stay focused on the job at hand: the fact that we were doing the play so that we could bring joy to others. It helped me be more focused on others and less on my self. I felt that if I was reaching out to others there was more of a chance that I would do well in the show, that the Lord would work through me more, and that everyone would benefit. I still like to think that I have a talent, and that the Lord works through me in acting because it is something that I love. Although I like to think that I am good at it, I know in my heart that when I am at my best, it's all because of God and what God is doing through me. Praise God!*

The essence of humility

As we have pointed out, all faiths teach that "without God we can do nothing." The acknowledgement of this simple truth is fundamental to our spiritual progress. Without genuine humility, we will find ourselves caught in a never-ending cycle in which we get prideful, then humbled, then prideful again. Whenever we commit spiritual theft— taking credit for what belongs to God—we will necessarily go through spiritual temptations again and again more deeply, so that we might learn what it means to be truly humble. Although these spiritual temptations can be bitter and painful experiences, they are also a necessary and unavoidable aspect of our spiritual development. In the following journal entry a seminar participant shares his grief, and consequent experience of humility, after harshly criticizing his son:

> *Last week my ten-year-old daughter injured her shoulder. The doctor said that we would have to baby it a lot and let it heal slowly. Well tonight her little*

brother was upset with her and gave her a shove. He pushed her in such a way that she really hurt her shoulder. She was lying on the ground crying. I was instantly furious. I rushed after my son, grabbed him by the shirt collar, dragged him over to his sister, and said, "Look what you did! Look what you did to your sister!" I was so angry!

I can't say that this was a "Rise Above It" moment. I knew that I was not coming from a place of love. I saw that without God's help I have no ability to keep any of the commandments. We eventually worked things out, but I haven't yet recovered. I feel kind of hopeless, defenseless, and powerless. I've been totally humbled by this experience.

As this seminar participant experienced, it is during times like this that we are able to see that without God's continual help and support, we have no power to keep any of the commandments. Being able to experience this kind of "failure" is not a failure at all. Ironically and paradoxically, failures like these are actually signs of success, for through them we learn the essence of humility. Emanuel Swedenborg writes:

A person is not saved on account of temptations if he places anything of credit in them; for if he does this it is from the love of self, in that he congratulates himself and believes that he deserves heaven more than others. At the same time he thinks of his own pre-eminence and despises others in comparison with himself.

The temptations in which a person is truly victorious are attended with a belief that all others are more worthy than himself and that he is infernal rather than heavenly, for, while in temptation, such ideas are presented to him.

If after the temptation he comes into thoughts contrary to these, it is an indication that he has not been victorious. . . . He must then undergo similar temptations, or more grievous ones, until he has been reduced to such sanity that he believes he can take credit for nothing (Arcana Coelestia 2273).

The phrase "reduced to such sanity" might also read "reduced to such humility." There are times when we "hit rock bottom"—times when we know that we have no power from ourselves, but that all power is from God alone. It is at these times that it can be said that we are truly "sane." The idea that without God we are all essentially "powerless" is well known in the world of the twelve-step programs. For example, members of Alcoholics Anonymous say, "We admitted we were powerless over alcohol— that our lives had become unmanageable." They then add, "[We] came to believe that a Power greater than ourselves could restore us to sanity."[1]

Whether expressed in a twelve-step program or through the Sacred Scriptures, the lesson is the same. An early step in our spiritual development is to humbly admit that we have no power from ourselves. When Jesus delivered the Sermon on the Mount, the first lesson was about humility: "Blessed are the poor in spirit, for theirs is the Kingdom of Heaven" (Matthew 5:3). Similarly, followers of the Islamic religion learn to "enter the gate in a posture of humility" (*Qur'ān* 7:161) and to "prostrate themselves to Allah, acknowledging subjection . . . even as do their shadows, mornings and evenings" (*Qur'ān* 13:15). In the following journal entry a prisoner, following the teachings of his Islamic faith, humbly admits that from himself he has no power to overcome his addiction to nicotine. He writes:

> *Smoking. What is the key to quitting smoking for good? I have accepted the fact that I must quit, but I find it hard to stick to the commitment. Today I accept the fact that I cannot quit alone. I need help. My human will is not enough. I need the Divine intervention of Allah because I am far too weak to do anything without His help.*

This prisoner speaks of his powerlessness, the limitations of his human will, and his total reliance upon Allah. He is here practicing a fundamental tenet of the Islamic faith, for the Arabic word "Islam" means "submission"—specifically, total submission to the will of Allah. This kind of submission is the opposite of pride; it is the essence of humility.

The first temptation

One of the secrets of spirituality is that we are so created that life feels as though it is our own—that it originates within us—while the actual fact is that all life continually flows in as a gift from God. So, while it is fine to feel good about our loving feelings, wise thoughts, and generous behavior, we must always be quick to acknowledge that these are not "our own"—for God is the Creator and the Origin of everything that is good. Once again, this commandment teaches us, "Do not take what is not your own."

1. *Alcoholics Anonymous* (New York: Alcoholics Anonymous World Services, 1987), 59.

In the following example a prisoner catches himself taking credit for his God-given athletic ability. He writes:

Today someone commented that I played ball well. I usually enjoy this kind of praise and take all the credit. This time though, I gave God the credit. "It's a gift from God," I said. As soon as I said that, I knew I had said the right thing. I felt good. I felt right. I felt one with my world—not isolated. To acknowledge and appreciate God's gifts brings a new dimension to life. The air we breathe, the sun that warms, the million good things we experience every day are not possible without God's love and attention. Praise God.

"Taking what is not our own," has a long history. It goes all the way back to the Garden of Eden when Adam and Eve took what was not their own. God had just told Adam and Eve that they could freely eat of all the trees in that garden—all of the trees, that is, except the tree of the knowledge of good and evil. The serpent, however, urged Eve to take and eat the forbidden fruit, saying, "In the day you eat of it your eyes will be opened and you will be as God, knowing good and evil" (Genesis 3:5). When the serpent showed her that the tree was good for food, pleasing to the eye, and would make her wise, Eve succumbed to this first temptation. She took the forbidden fruit, ate it, and offered some to her husband who also chose to eat. This is the first theft recorded in the Bible. As a result of their disobedience, Adam and Eve were banished from Paradise.

This story may seem somewhat confusing. Doesn't God want us to know the difference between good and evil? Isn't this what all religion is about? Isn't this what all parents want for their children? Isn't this what we are all seeking, as we strive to become the best people we can be? So why would this knowledge be forbidden?

We can be certain that God *does* want us to have an accurate understanding of what good things are to be done, and what evil things are to be avoided. This is why we are given written revelation, or what is called "the Word of God." The Sacred Scriptures are given, in a variety of forms, not only to provide Divine guidance, but also as a protection, lest we decide to lead ourselves, believing the fickle and wavering fabrications of our own minds. Therefore knowing the difference between good and evil is not forbidden. What is forbidden is "man-made theology"—the attempt to rely on human reason rather than to trust in Divine revelation. Whenever we base our faith on "what seems good to us" (Eve "saw that the tree was pleasant to the eyes") rather than on the revealed Word of God, we are eating from the tree of the knowledge of good and evil. We have stolen from God what rightfully belongs to God alone—the power to discern between good and evil. The gift of human reason is given so that we may confirm the genuine truths of Divine revelation—especially the Ten Commandments—not to create "made-made theology" based on our limited perceptions and self-centered desires.

The serpent told Eve that if she ate of the fruit she would be like God, that it would make her wise, and that she would know good and evil. The simple truth is that we can never derive a knowledge of spiritual things, or attain "special enlightenment," through physical objects. No fruit, no leaf, no drug, no temple, no ritual, no sacred relic or holy oil, not even our own human reason or imagination, can give us a knowledge of good and evil. Only God can reveal this knowledge to us. And this comes to us through the Sacred Scriptures, according to our willingness to receive, our ability to understand, and our efforts to keep the commandments. To try to attain the knowledge of good and evil by some other way is to try to enter "like a thief in the night." As it is written in the New Testament, "Most assuredly, I say to you, he who does not enter the sheepfold by the door, but climbs up some other way, the same is a thief and a robber" (John 10:3).

In the following journal entry a middle-aged African shares a powerful experience from his high school years. It is a good example of "climbing up by some other way":

> When I was a student in high school I used to be very active in sports, especially soccer. There was only one weakness in my participation. I could not be an active participant without smoking Dagga. I was a sloppy player in the field without it. But when I smoked Dagga I was great.[2]
>
> In another area where I was active it was in class, especially in mathematics. My friend used to be respected for his knowledge of geometry whilst I was respected for my exceptional performance in Algebra. Although we were both Dagga smokers we did not smoke when going to class. It so happened that during our half-yearly examination, we first tested the idea of smoking Dagga before going for the first paper which was going to be mathematics. We knew that all eyes would be on us. We then decided to smoke a lot. We enjoyed our smoking so much so that we didn't even attend going to the chapel. To our surprise I finished the three-hour exam in fifteen minutes and my friend

2. Dagga is made from the dried tops of the plant whose botanical name is Cannabis Sativa. The active intoxicating agent is 9 Deltatetrahydrocannabinol (THC).

finished his exam in twenty minutes. The final results were twenty correct marks out of three hundred for me and thirty correct marks for my friend. That taught us both to stop smoking Dagga from that day.

These young men had come to believe that under the influence of "Dagga" they had extraordinary powers and that they would perform wonderfully on their mathematics exam. They were seriously mistaken!

We, too, seriously delude ourselves whenever we believe that "we know"—especially when it comes to spiritual things. Ultimately, we must come to the realization that only God has the power to discern between good and evil. And even though this knowledge is indeed revealed to us through the Sacred Scriptures of all religions, we can never have total perception, total clarity, or total understanding any more than we can stare directly at the sun. We may, of course, "enter in" to the Divine mysteries, and understand them more deeply to eternity. This is according to order. But to presume that we have anything more than a limited amount of understanding is to believe that a tiny candle, flickering in the darkness, is really the Sun of heaven. As Emanuel Swedenborg writes, "The wisest of the angels know that that they have nothing of wisdom from themselves, and that acknowledging this is being wise. They know also that what they know is as nothing compared to what they do not know" (*Heaven and Hell* 280).

As we enter more deeply into this commandment, we come to realize that the real "fall of man" occurs whenever we "fall victim" to the seductive illusion offered by the serpent—the illusion that "we think we know," and that, like God, we have a perfect knowledge of good and evil. As we fall victim to this illusion, we come into the delusive belief that the way we see things is the highest reality, and that we understand with the greatest clarity. In other words, we believe that we know what is right, and we know it better than others. We begin to believe the prophecy of the serpent: "Your eyes will be opened, and you will be like God, knowing good and evil." As we have seen in the journal entry about the young Africans who smoked Dagga, this delusive state brings with it an inflated sense of our own abilities and powers of perception. We begin to believe that the origin of goodness, wisdom, and even Life Itself, is within ourselves, or at least in the leaves of a plant. Having eaten of this forbidden fruit, we begin to believe that we are gods.

To walk humbly

The commandment against stealing is given to remind us that we must not take what is not our own. Whether we have taken a material object from a store without paying, or an idea that came from another person without acknowledging the source, we have stolen. We have taken what is not our own. Similarly, whenever we take credit for the benevolent impulses and noble thoughts that come to us, we commit spiritual theft. We have stolen what rightfully belongs to God.

Most deeply, this commandment asks us not to "climb up by some other way" (John 10:1), but to go to God humbly and prayerfully for inspiration and direction in our lives. As we read and meditate on the Sacred Scriptures of our respective religions, we come into ever greater light and perception. But even then, no matter how great the light, we still "see through a glass darkly" (1 Corinthians: 13:12). Because we are human and finite, we can only behold in part what we may some day perceive more fully. Therefore, in this commandment we are asked to trust in the Divine Word, to cultivate humility, and to give credit to God. As it is written in the Old Testament:

> *He has shown you, O man, what is good;*
> *And what does the Lord require of you,*
> *But to do justly,*
> *And to love mercy,*
> *And to walk humbly with your God?* (Micah 6:8).

The assignment: Be a credit giver

In this commandment we are told not to steal—"Do not take what is not your own." Do not take things that belong to others, whether objects or ideas. More deeply, we are to acknowledge that only God can give life, and that without God we can do nothing. We are to remember that we are not the origin of love and wisdom; rather that all the love and wisdom we have are free gifts from God. So be a credit giver. Give credit to God for those loving emotions you feel, those noble thoughts you think, and those useful deeds that you do. Keep this commandment. Do not steal.

Assignment

Give credit

Do not steal physically or spiritually.

In your journal, record your experience of keeping this commandment.

SUGGESTIONS FOR FURTHER REFLECTION AND APPLICATION

MEDITATION: "AND LEAD US NOT INTO TEMPTATION"

There is a continual temptation to fall into the pride of thinking that we know better than others. This is to steal from God, and to attribute God's wisdom to ourselves. As you practice keeping this commandment try using the words, "Lead us not into temptation" as a meditation to help you avoid the temptation to feel prideful and to invite the quality of humility into your life. Set aside a few minutes each day to stay your mind on the simple words, "Lead us not into temptation," remembering as you do so to be, not a credit taker, but a credit giver.

JOURNAL REFLECTION

Recall a time when you stole something—when you took something that was not your own. Describe the incident. What were your thoughts and feelings at the time? Do you feel differently about the incident today? If so, describe the difference.

ACTIVITY: "WHO STOLE THE COOKIE FROM THE COOKIE JAR?"

During the week notice any ways that you might be stealing physically, whether it be postage stamps from the office or cookies from the cookie jar at home. Also, be aware of the subtler forms of stealing; for example, when a cashier undercharges you and gives you back too much money. When you notice the desire to "take what is not your own," rise above it. Do not steal.

ACTIVITY: IDENTIFYING AND TAMING THE "KNOW-IT-ALL" WITHIN US

Recalling that humanity's first temptation was to steal the forbidden fruit and be "like God, knowing good and evil," notice tendencies in yourself to be a "know it all." In your conversations, be aware of how you come across to others. Do you speak with authority about things of which you have limited knowledge? Is there room for humility? Before offering your viewpoint, do you add phrases such as "This is only the way I see it," or "In my opinion," or "I may be wrong"? This week, pay attention to your conversations. Notice how dogmatically and how authoritatively you express yourself, even to the point of becoming "like God, knowing good and evil."

ACTIVITY: DON'T STEAL THE CONVERSATION

Avoid the tendency to "silently rehearse" what you want to say while others are still speaking. Give the gift of total attention. Learn to listen to others without interrupting, "stealing" the pauses, or giving in to the urge to add your comments to the conversation. Try leaving a pause of a few seconds after someone finishes speaking before you respond. Let someone else enjoy the chance to speak while you quietly give glory to God.

ACTIVITY: GIVE CREDIT TO OTHERS

Look for things that you can honestly admire in others, and give them credit for what they have done and are doing. Be a credit giver. Be generous in your praise of others, while you quietly give praise to God.

ACTIVITY: GIVE CREDIT TO GOD

Be aware of prideful thoughts and feelings as they arise in you, as well as prideful comments that you might make. Depending on your religious tradition, develop a habit of saying to yourself, "Praise the Lord," "Glory be to God," "Thank you, Jesus," or "Allah alone is holy." Remember that all glory belongs to God.

You shall not bear false witness against your neighbor.

OLD TESTAMENT—EXODUS 20:16

 For this cause I was born, and for this cause I have come into the world, that I should bear witness to the truth.

NEW TESTAMENT—JOHN 18:37

 Those who fear Allah, when a thought of evil from Satan assaults them, bring Allah to remembrance, and lo! they see aright!

QUR'ĀN 7:201

 To tell the truth is consistent with righteousness. There is nothing higher than the truth.

SANTIPARVA 109:4

 When a person abstains from false testimonies and turns away from them as sins, the love of truth and the love of justice flow in from the Lord through heaven. . . . As a consequence his utterances become utterances of truth, and his works become works of justice.

APOCALYPSE EXPLAINED 1020:2

CHAPTER EIGHT

Do Not Bear False Witness / Tell the Truth

O, while you live, tell the truth, and shame the devil.
—WILLIAM SHAKESPEARE

Defensive lying

TELLING THE TRUTH, rather than bearing false witness against our neighbor, has long been taught as a basic social ethic. As it is written in the Sacred Scriptures of India, "Abusing others, speaking untruth, detracting from the merits of all men, and talking idly, shall be the four kinds of evil verbal action" (*Laws of Manu* 12:6). The Buddha teaches, "Right speech is to abstain from lies and slander, from reviling, and from tattle" (*Majjhima-nikaya* 3:248-252). In the Old Testament we read, "Lying lips are an abomination to the Lord, but those who deal truthfully are His delight" (Proverbs 12:22). And as the New Testament draws to a conclusion, a stern warning is given: "The cowardly, abominable, murderers, sexually immoral, sorcerers, idolators, *and all liars* shall have their part in the lake which burns with fire and brimstone" (Revelation 21:8; emphasis added).

As we noted in the previous chapter, the first temptation recorded in the Old Testament occurred in the Garden of Eden when Adam and Eve were tempted to steal the "forbidden fruit." As the story continues, we note that this theft was followed immediately by a defensive cover-up: "Then the eyes of both of them were opened and they knew that they were naked; and they sewed fig leaves together and made themselves coverings" (Genesis 3:7). Rather than take personal responsibility for disobeying God's warning, they tried to cover up their wrong-doing by blaming others. Adam blamed both God and Eve: "The woman whom You gave to be with me, she gave me of the tree, and I ate" (3:12); and Eve placed the blame on the serpent. She said, "The serpent deceived me, and I ate" (3:13).

The defensive cover-up of Adam and Eve reminds us of the many ways that we, too, can cover up the truth with defensive lies. In the following journal entry a nine-year-old describes an incident in which he tells a self-protecting lie:

> *At school we had a tug-of-war. Right when we started I was pulling as hard as I could, but my team lost. I didn't want to feel embarrassed so I made up an excuse that I didn't hear him say "Go!" and that I wasn't ready because I was talking to somebody else. I really did hear it though. I just said I didn't. I told a lie.*

This young person made up an excuse because he "didn't want to feel embarrassed." His cover-up might seem harmless enough, but over time a pattern of making excuses to cover up our embarrassment, frustration, anger, fear or greed can be difficult to overcome. One of the first things for us to become aware of, therefore, is the automatic nature of our defensive lies. A colleague, noting the connection between defensiveness and lying, writes:

> *Often our lies are spur of the moment affairs. They take us by surprise. We find ourselves taking almost instinctive action to defend ourselves against the world. Here are some examples:*

> *During a break in aerobics class, the person next to you turns on you and suddenly bubbles, "Just saw Ghandi last night! Wasn't it a fantastic movie!" You are probably one of three people in the nation who found the movie excruciatingly boring. You spent the final hour wondering when you could get to a restroom. But you mumble something about "superior cinematography" and beat a hasty retreat.*

> *In the middle of a project at work you remember that you were supposed to call your wife over two hours ago. When she answers, you take a gamble that she's already used the phone during the day and blurt out, "Tried to call you earlier, Honey, but it was busy."*

These defense mechanisms flare up in our consciousness so briefly that we may find it hard even to call them "lies." Yet they set the stage for a life which increasingly closes us off from the world around us. A lie grows and multiplies. There is a good deal of nervous scrambling involved to cover things up, to rehearse stories making sure we've got them right, to remember which lie we have told, to whom and at what stage of it's growth.

While the time and energy wasted in lying is a nuisance, an even greater tragedy occurs when we have lost the God-given right to be honest. On even the simplest levels of our existence we cannot admit our preferences, our blind spots or our weaknesses, and receive forgiveness for them. We are unable to say, "I'm glad you liked the movie. I really didn't enjoy it myself" or "I was involved with things in the office here and I just forgot." [1]

The opportunities to defend ourselves with lies are manifold. Our lies may be as "harmless" as saying, "the check is in the mail" in order to gain a little time before actually mailing it. Or they may be more serious, as, for example, when a husband tells his wife that he has been working late when, in fact, he has been spending time with another woman. Whether our defensive lying is a relatively minor cover-up, or a darker, more deceitful one, it is a violation of the commandment, "You shall not bear false witness against your neighbor." How much simpler life could be if we would choose to rise above the tendency to defend ourselves with lies, and instead, tell the truth.

Lies we tell others

Earlier we defined religion as connecting to God and the neighbor by living according to the commandments. While honesty and openness can foster deep and meaningful connections, lying and deceit can have the opposite effect. According to Islamic tradition, Muhammad said, "The signs of a hypocrite are three: when he talks, he lies; when he makes a promise he breaks it; and when he is trusted he is disloyal" (*Hadith of Al-Bukhari*). The lies we tell others—whether they are motivated by embarrassment, fear, anger or greed—can have a disastrous effect on relationships. In the following journal entry a prisoner reflects on how lying has affected his life. He writes:

---

1. Kent Jungé, *Living Commandments* (unpublished manuscript, 1985), 58-59.

I was reminded of how I had lied earlier in the day. An inmate asked me for a "cadillac" [a cigarette], and I said to him I only had a few. I was telling a lie because I was sitting on a whole pack of them. I stood in my cell thinking about this lie I just told. It made me feel bad, and I thought about why I did it. I know it wasn't right, and I still feel bad about this, and I really want to get this burden off my chest. I am starting to realize how lying can really damage your relationships with others. I know this because it took me forever to get my parents to believe in me. I want people to believe in me, and I thank God for giving me a second chance to be honest in my relationships with others.

A church leader recounts the following experience:

As a part of our men's prayer breakfast we talked about honesty. One of the men is going through a very difficult time in his relationship to God. He prayed a beautiful prayer of humility as he confessed the difficult process that he was going through.

His honesty made me realize how men (including me) lie about how we are doing. How many times has someone asked me, "How are you?" and I lied by saying, "Great!" or "Pretty good!"

I saw how God used the honesty of this one man to open the hearts of the rest of us. I saw how each man began to confess similar struggles in his life. God honors honesty. I guess that's why He told us, "Do not lie!"

And a prisoner "catches himself" in a moment of dishonesty:

I was having a really bad day, and my counselor had come up and asked me what was wrong. I told him that nothing was wrong. He came at me again and asked me what was wrong, and I again told him the same thing. Later he asked one more time, and I finally told him there wasn't anything that he or myself could do about the problem so why bother talking about it. I guess I kind of failed on this week's assignment.

In each of these cases, "truth-telling" is seen as the key to healthy human relationships. Whether it is a prisoner lying about how many cigarettes he has, a church leader covering up his troubles, or a person saying that he is "just fine" when things are actually quite the opposite, our refusal to be authentic and honest robs us of the opportunity to connect with others and to experience the blessings of true friendship.

Sometimes people think that being "authentic" and "honest" means venting emotion without restraint. "I was just expressing how I really feel," some people say, or "I was just being honest." Medical researchers even report that suppressed emotion can cause bodily harm—ranging from headaches, digestive disorders and ulcers, to arthritis and cancer. But these researchers also point out that the unrestrained expression of negative emotion can be equally dangerous; it can produce high blood pressure and lead to heart attacks. Therefore, it is vitally important that we learn how to appropriately express our negative emotions—especially anger.

One of these ways is simply to "tell the truth" without defending ourselves or blaming others. This kind of honesty rises above the argument of whether it is better to "vent our emotions" or "suppress our anger." It begins, as do all of the commandments, with honest self-examination. It begins by being true to ourselves—that is, by being scrupulously honest about all things, and by refusing to live in self-deception. As Shakespeare has said:

> *This above all. To thine own self be true.*
> *And it must follow as the night the day,*
> *Thou canst not then be false to any man.*[2]

Being true to ourselves means that we express our position clearly—as we see it—without allowing our conversations to slip into arguments about who is right and who is wrong, or to totally disintegrate into war-like frays where we blast one another with our "justified" anger. Our conversations can be civil and polite. Taking a firm stand about something is not the same as making others wrong. Whether in the family, on the playing field, or in the workplace, we can take a firm stand for healthy communication. At the same time we can take a firm stand against our own tactless comments and angry outbursts that belittle others and tear away at their self-respect. Our communication may be clear, direct, and to the point—but it can still be tactful and kind. It may mean enforcing appropriate sanctions, but it can be done with compassion and with a hope for amendment. In the words of the Buddha, "Him I call a *Brahmin* who utters true speech, free from harshness, clearly understood, by which no one is offended" (*Dhammapada* 26:26).

---

2. William Shakespeare, *The Tragedy of Hamlet, Prince of Denmark*, Act 1, scene 3, lines 77-80.

What this commandment is calling us to do, then, is to be scrupulously honest in our dealings with others—speaking openly and kindly, neither shunning nor seeking confrontation, and thinking only in terms of how our words, or our silences, may serve. This commandment calls us to live with integrity by being true to our word, honoring our commitments, keeping our promises, and telling the truth. At those times when we may want to protect ourselves with a lie, or avoid a situation altogether, we are asked to stand for the truth. In the following journal entry, for example, a supervisor of a chemical plant refuses to protect himself by remaining silent about an $18,000 mistake. It should be noted that his writing shows no defensiveness, no blaming of others, no venting of emotion. He does realize, however, that saying nothing about the mistake would be a form of false witness and that he must be true to his beliefs. He decides to stand for what is right; and he does this by simply telling the truth:

Last week the crew I supervise at the chemical plant washed some test bottles in the wrong caustic concentration, and at the wrong temperature. This washing was the third segment of an $18,000 testing procedure. When we found out that this mistake had been made, one of my co-workers suggested that it would be easy to say nothing about it, because no one would ever know what had happened. I told him that the truth would have to be told, no matter what. So I informed both my superior and the customer. I have caught a lot of heat, been in several meetings, and have had to write several reports on the matter. But even after all this, I feel good. I know everything will work out because I stuck to the truth.

The peace this man attained through telling the truth surpassed anything he might have gained through defensive lying or a silent cover-up. Spiritually, emotionally, and physically it was the healthiest thing he could have done. Sometimes it seems easier to lie, to cover-up, or to conceal the truth; but it is always healthier to tell the truth. As it is written in the *Qur'ān,* "Cover not the truth with falsehood, nor conceal the truth when ye know what it is" (2:42). As the chemical plant supervisor said, "I caught a lot of heat . . . but even after all this, *I feel good.* I know everything will work out because I stuck to the truth."

Lying to ourselves

The incident involving the $18,000 mistake at the chemical plant is an instructive one. The supervisor could have rationalized the mistake by saying, "Well, not mentioning it is not really lying." This type of rationalizing is another form of "bearing false witness." It takes place through the many clever ways we manage to excuse, justify, and rationalize our behavior. In our apparent cleverness we may argue well, reason well, and debate brilliantly. As we pile up evidence to prove our point, we begin to think that we have every right to remain unforgiving, resentful and miserable. Though we may have won an argument and justified our behavior, we may have seriously damaged a relationship. Here are some examples of justifications and rationalizations identified by seminar participants:

My husband never listens to me; so why should I be nice to him?

Why should I go to practice? The coach won't put me in the game anyway—he plays favorites.

Why should I care about anybody? Nobody cares about me.

Sure I hurt the guy, but he had it coming.

I know it's not right to scream at the kids, but sometimes it's the only way to get them to do things.

So what if I go off my diet just this once? I've been under a lot of stress, and I'm entitled to a little fun in life.

I didn't write on the wall with my crayons. I wrote on the paint. [An actual statement from a four-year-old!]

I didn't steal my sister's money. I found it on the floor in her bedroom. It's not stealing if you find money on the floor.

Honoring parents can work for normal families. But my parents were cruel. I can't remember anything good about them.

In the following example a middle-aged African speaks of his long personal struggle to overcome alcoholism and the false witnesses (rationalizations and justifications) that kept him in bondage to his addiction:

> *I find this the most difficult assignment. It is hard to say I've never lied to myself. Often when I lie I have these "inner attorneys" that always help me justify my lies. In my old drinking times, I was serving the false god of drinking liquor. I was then drinking 365 days a year. Those were the worst times of my life. I would tell lies almost every day, not realizing that I was lying to myself. It was like an insult whenever anybody would try and talk to me about stopping my drinking. Every day I would deny that I was still drinking. Every day I would say that I had stopped. Although I was lying to myself I still believed in the Power of Prayer, and that is how I stopped.*

How can we recognize and overcome the false witnesses within—the rationalizations and justifications that keep us stuck in denial, self-pity and misery; the lies that prevent us from being all that we can be? One way is to set for ourselves a concrete goal, such as eliminating a certain food from our diet, fasting for a few days, exercising regularly, answering mail on a regular basis, contributing to a charitable cause, spending more time with our family, getting up earlier, etc. These simple tasks may not be "spiritual" in themselves; but having a simple goal in mind (e.g. "I will not eat sugar this week" or "I will exercise on Monday, Wednesday and Friday") will help us to observe how easy it is to lie to ourselves, to make excuses, to rationalize, and to justify our behavior.

"Lying to ourselves" means that we listen to and believe the clever arguments and rationalizations that come into our minds. They offer us "lower delights" such as laziness, self-indulgence, self-pity and unbridled anger. When we "buy into" the arguments and lies we deprive ourselves of a greater, fuller, and more joyful existence. Therefore, we need to examine these lower delights, contrast them with the higher delights that are available to us through keeping the commandments, and refuse to accept their false testimonies. When we exercise this kind of self-control and personal discipline we open the way for the Kingdom of Heaven to flow in. Emanuel Swedenborg writes, "When a person abstains from false testimonies and turns away from them as sins, the love of truth and the love of justice flow in from the Lord through heaven" (*Apocalypse Explained* 1020:2). And in the New Testament we read: "Come, you blessed of My Father; inherit the kingdom prepared for you from the foundation of the world" (Matthew 25:1).

The land of misunderstanding

For most of us it takes a lifetime of effort to recognize our patterns of thought and behavior, and to become aware of our true feelings and intentions. Even then, we cannot be absolutely sure of the deepest motives that drive us. If this is true for us as individuals, how then can we presume to know the thoughts, feelings, and deepest motivations of others? As it says in the Old Testament, "The Lord does not see as man sees; for man looks at the outward appearance, but the Lord looks at the heart" (1 Samuel 16:7). There is usually a world of difference between the deep and hidden reasons why people act as they do, and our interpretations of those actions. In fact, many (if not most) of our personal upsets can be attributed to our unhappy tendency to ascribe our own meanings to the words and actions of others. A seminar participant, who worked at a shelter for runaway teens, writes:

> *We once took care of a sixteen-year-old girl who told us that her foster mother had stabbed her. We were shocked. How could anyone do such a thing? It was bad enough that this young person had to be sent off to a foster home, but then to be stabbed by her foster mother—how awful! As time went by we had an opportunity to meet the foster mother and discuss the incident. She explained that her foster daughter was giving her a difficult time as she was trying to prepare the Thanksgiving dinner. Finally, feeling exasperated with her foster daughter, she asked her to leave the kitchen, and emphasized her point by poking her on the backside with the carving fork she was using to carve the turkey.*

When the image of being "poked" was transformed into the image of being "stabbed," a simple domestic scene was transformed into a picture of a bloody crime against an innocent girl. We may not know what *actually* happened in the kitchen on that day. To the young girl it felt like a "stabbing"; to the foster mother it was only a "poke." This story illustrates what can happen when our choice of language, whether deliberate or not, creates a distorted version of reality and misrepresents the true intentions of others.

Shading and twisting the truth, exaggerating details, deliberately changing a word or omitting aspects of a story in order to prove one's point, are all forms of lying. In some cases, such false witnessing can do serious damage to an individual's reputation and career. In this regard, consider the following journal entry from a seminar participant:

A certain person in my church was perceived by many people as being loud, aggressive, pushy, tenacious and unrelenting. I must admit that (like many others) I too had become a part of this choir of criticism. Whenever this individual spoke I saw him only as loud, pushy, obstinate and aggressive—just as others had described him.

But last week we spent a lot of time together, and I realized that he was wholly different than I had imagined. We drove together through 1,000 miles of rocky terrain, and through some very dangerous circumstances. And all the while I found him to be a man of tremendous courage, energy and perseverance. I also saw his kindness and his consideration of others.

As our friendship deepened I gained a whole new admiration for this man's wisdom, humor, insight and sensitivity. Truly, I had been unable to see this man's good qualities because of my imprisoning pre-conceptions.

Another seminar participant writes:

It was Mother's Day and my husband didn't bring me any flowers or even give me a card. I was hurt. It felt like he didn't really care and didn't really love me. Instead of going with these thoughts and feelings, I told him what it brought up for me. When he didn't buy me flowers or a card I made it mean that he doesn't love me. I asked him if there was any truth in that. He said absolutely not. He said that he just didn't want to buy into all the commercialism. It had nothing to do with his love for me. He really does love me and I don't have to make it mean something else. Wow!

When we misinterpret the motives of others and attach false meaning to their behavior, we are "bearing false witness against our neighbor." In the *Bhagavad Gita* this state of mind is called being "entangled in the meshes of delusion" (16:16). But there is hope. As long as we can honestly say, "I do not know what you meant by that," we can open up healthy communication. From there, we can go on to ask simple, non-accusatory questions such as, "What did it mean when you . . . ?"or "What were you thinking when you said . . . ?" or "What were you intending when you wrote . . . ?" We ask these questions to find out what is happening in another person's inner world, rather than think that we can read minds or judge motives. We ask these questions to discover the truth about another person's life rather than accept the false perceptions and distorted ideas that so often impose themselves on our consciousness. We ask these questions to find out what is true, rather than dwell in the land of misunderstanding.[3]

The power of truth

As we continue to observe ourselves in the light of this commandment, we may discover that sometimes several lies may be passing through our minds at the same time. "It's hopeless"; "It's no use"; "Nobody is any good"; "I have no self-discipline"; "I was born a slob, and I'll die a slob"; "I'm worthless"; and so on. A prisoner writes:

> *I'm always feeling that no one cares about me—mostly when I don't get mail from home, or if no one comes to see me. Of course I know that there are a lot of people out there in the free world that do care about me, but at times I feel that I am worthless—that I would be better off dead.*

This attitude of deep discouragement is echoed in the words of a young African school teacher. He writes:

> *When difficulties come by, when I see something not coming my way, or when I do something and fail, I tell myself that life is too difficult for me to be successful. Most of the time when I think of doing something, or starting a new venture, or when I have an idea of doing something, I think negatively about the result and even say to myself, "This will not work out."*

Sometimes deep discouragement can turn into profound despair. A woman, who has been incarcerated for murdering her child, writes:

> *How I wish that I could replace that which was taken. How I wish that I could venture beyond this life so I might actually find peace from the wrong I have*

---

3. Mental health professionals working in the field of "Cognitive Behavioral Therapy" refer to false perceptions of reality as "cognitive distortions," which they categorize and define as follows: "mental filtering" (dwelling on a single negative detail); "tunnel vision" (seeing only what fits our pre-conceived idea, while ignoring everything else); "selective abstraction" (arriving at a false conclusion by taking a detail or statement out of context); "arbitrary inference" (making an unfavorable judgment even when there is nothing to substantiate it); "over-generalization" (taking one negative incident as the overall pattern, as when we say, "You *never* come home on time," "You *always* put off doing your homework," or "No matter what I do, I fail."); "catastrophizing" (exaggerating the significance or severity of a particular event); "personalizing" (believing that the actions of others are directed at one's self [also called "taking things personally"]); "mind-reading" (believing that we know what other people are thinking); and others. For further information, see David D. Burns, *Feeling Good: The New Mood Therapy* (New York: Avon Books, 1980), 42-43, and Aaron T. Beck, *Love is Never Enough* (New York: Harper Perennial, 1989), 159-167.

done. No amount of earthly time nor good deeds could ever begin to erase the red-hot pain from my memory, or the sightless eyes from my every conscious moment. Yes, that's me, a wretch from hell bound someday back home.

This woman believed that her despair was a permanent condition and that nothing could ever relieve it, or take it away, except her own death. She did not realize that this was the time to turn to God, acknowledge her guilt, pray for forgiveness, and begin a new life. Although it was useful for this woman to experience deep remorse, this was not the end of the process. At some point she would need to turn to God for help. Otherwise, the "false witnesses" would continue to pound away at her guilty conscience, tormenting her, and driving her into deeper and deeper despair until they would succeed in their ultimate aim—ending not only her child's life, but her life as well. Such false witnesses persuade us that we are unredeemable. They tell us that there is no hope for us at all, not even in God.

False witnesses have been around for a long time. Three thousand years ago, in the Psalms, David wrote:

> *Lord, how they have increased who trouble me!*
> *Many are they who rise up against me.*
> *Many are they who say of me,*
> *"There is no help for him in God"* (Psalm 3:1-2).

This is a picture of human discouragement, even to the point of despair. Taken literally, it seems to speak about a man named David who has many enemies in the physical world. But on a deeper level, this Psalm is about each of us. It is not so much about our enemies in the natural world; rather, it is about our unseen spiritual enemies—the false witnesses that would destroy us in a moment if they could. One of their most devious ploys is to destroy our confidence in God—to totally discourage and dishearten us. "There is no hope," they say. "It's a losing battle." And even more diabolically, "God doesn't care about you at all."

Lies like these can lead to the false conclusion that God is powerless against evil, or even worse, that there is no God. This destruction of our faith in God is the ultimate aim of evil. The deeper our discouragement, the greater is the victory for the forces of evil. When we are in this state of mind—feeling that we are beyond redemption—we tend to lose sight of the opening words of the Ten Commandments. We forget that God is the Almighty Redeemer who has brought us forth out of the land of Egypt, out of the house of bondage. We forget that we have miraculously crossed the Red Sea, received the Ten Commandments, and are on the verge of entering the Promised Land. We forget that the battle for human freedom has already been won, that we can freely choose to serve God, and that we can live a life that leads to heaven.

During this state of forgetfulness the false witnesses can seem especially convincing. As we sink deeper and deeper into despair, it seems that all is lost. If we were ever hopeful about life, if we were ever convinced of God's power and goodness, if we were ever happy with our family, or excited about our jobs, we can't remember it now. We feel worthless, useless, good for nothing. It is as if we have "spiritual amnesia." We can't remember ever being happy. Life seems cruel and meaningless—filled with empty shadows and hollow gestures. It seems as though our few days upon the earth have been meaningless, and that we have been nothing more than actors "strutting and fretting upon a stage." As Shakespeare's Macbeth puts it, after hearing that his wife has died:

> *Tomorrow and tomorrow and tomorrow*
> *Creeps in this petty pace from day to day,*
> *To the last syllable of recorded time,*
> *And all our yesterdays have lighted fools*
> *The way to dusty death. Out, out brief candle!*
> *Life's but a walking shadow, a poor player*
> *Who struts and frets his hour upon the stage*
> *And then is heard no more. It is a tale*
> *Told by an idiot, full of sound and fury*
> *Signifying nothing.*[4]

That's how it feels in the depths of despair. Everything seems hopeless, lost. In the depths of his despair, David was tempted to think that there was no help for him in God. But he refused to believe this. Instead, he cried out to the Lord:

> *But You, O Lord, are a shield for me,*
> *My glory, and the One who lifts up my head.*
> *I cried to the Lord with my voice,*
> *And He heard me from His holy hill* (Psalm 3:3).

---

4. William Shakespeare, *The Tragedy Macbeth*, Act 5, scene 5, lines 24-28.

Notice how David's triumph is in exact proportion to his bearing witness to the truth—the truth that God is ever present, and that He has the power to save. And God *does* save, for in the next verse the miracle takes place:

> *I awoke, for the Lord sustained me.*
> *I will not be afraid of ten thousands of people*
> *Who have set themselves against me all around* (Psalm 3:5-6).

Spiritually speaking, David's "awakening" represents our own awakening to spiritual reality—the reality that no matter what our external circumstances might be, no matter how abandoned we might feel, God is always present, leading, guiding and comforting. In the following journal entry a prisoner feels a sense of depression coming over him as he anticipates another Christmas in prison, separated from family and friends. And yet, in the midst of what could be a desperate situation, he reaches inward to find spiritual solace and consolation. He writes:

> *As Christmas nears I feel a sense of depression coming on. This will be Christmas number three in prison, and before I get out (if I get out) I will have seen ten Christmases, possibly eleven, in prison. As I look over my circumstances, I come to realize that I am fortunate to be able to see this Christmas. Maybe God (Allah) is using this experience to teach me a lesson of thankfulness and to open my eyes. For truly I have spent many Christmases in prison—the prison of sin and ignorance. Now that my mind is on the way to freedom, I have no doubt that my body will soon follow! Tonight I not only accept my fate, but I thank Allah for this opportunity to expand my mind, soul and body for His glory.*
>
> *At times like these I reflect back over my life to see in what direction I am heading. I am very pleased with the direction I am going. I feel like a new person, a winner, a man in control of his fate. I am thankful tonight for life, love, troubles of life, and sadness, because it is times like these that make every heartache, pain, and struggle worthwhile. Even though there are injustices in the world, tonight I will be happy and accept my small, but significant triumph.*

Though he is separated from family and friends, this young man acknowledges the higher truth—the truth that God (Allah) is inmostly present, delivering him from evil and filling him with hope. His story is the living embodiment of the words that David spoke three thousand years ago: "In my distress I cried to the Lord and He heard me. Deliver my soul, Lord, from lying lips and from a deceitful tongue" (Psalm 120:1-2). This prisoner's deliverance, through acknowledging the truth of God's presence, is indeed a significant triumph.

"It is written . . ."

Emanuel Swedenborg writes:

> *When spirits begin to speak with a person, that person must be careful and not believe anything that they say, for they say almost anything; things are fabricated by them, and they lie. . . . If the person listens and believes, they press on and deceive, and seduce in divers ways. . . . They tell all things falsely. Therefore let people beware lest they believe them (Spiritual Diary 1622).*

Swedenborg is here referring to "false witnesses"—actual spiritual influences that strive to fill our minds with diabolical and deadly falsehoods. This is serious business for it involves spiritual life and spiritual death. It is for this reason that the Sacred Scriptures of all religions provide powerful teachings that can be used to refute the false witnesses that arise within us. As it is written in the *Qur'ān,* "We hurl the truth against falsehood, and it knocks out its brain, and behold, falsehood perishes" (21:18); also, "Those who fear Allah, when a thought of evil from Satan assails them, bring Allah to remembrance, and lo! they see aright!" (7:20). Through teachings such as these, we can say again and again, "Begone, you discouraging demons, you liars and false witnesses. **You shall not bear false witness against your neighbor!**" To the extent that we do this, standing steadfastly on the firm ground of truth, God works the miracle of deliverance. God hears our prayers and delivers us from what the *Qur'ān* calls "the slinking whisperer."[5]

One of the clearest examples of the use of truth to refute false witness is given in the story of Jesus' temptations in the wilderness. Each time the devil makes a tempting offer, Jesus refutes him with the power of truth. When the devil suggests that Jesus turn stones to bread, Jesus says, "*It is written,* 'Man shall not live by bread alone, but by every word that proceeds from the mouth of God.'" The devil tempts Jesus again from the pinnacle of the temple, saying, "Throw Yourself down," but Jesus replies, "*It is written,*

---

5. "I take refuge with the Lord of men, the King of men, the God of men, from the evil of the slinking whisperer who whispers in the breasts of men" (*Qur'ān* 114:1-5).

'You shall not tempt the Lord your God.'" The devil tries one last time, offering Jesus all the kingdoms of the world and their glory. There is, however, one important condition: Jesus must agree to bow down and worship him. But Jesus does not succumb. Again, He refutes the devil's false witness, and says, "*It is written,* 'You shall worship the Lord your God and Him only shall you serve'" (See Matthew 4:1-10; emphasis added).

In each case Jesus invokes the power of Sacred Scripture (*It is written . . .*) to refute the false witness of the devil. It is a powerful example of what each of us can do whenever we are similarly confronted and whenever false witnesses misrepresent reality in our lives. When discouragement and despair are knocking at the doors of our minds—eager to fill us with depressing thoughts about ourselves and about others, suggesting that there is no hope for us and no help from God—we can draw upon the inspiration of Sacred Scripture. We can see reality in the light of revelation. We can open a channel through which God can fill us with power and lift us on high. This is what it means to "Rise Above It."

The "deadly duo"

In the sequence of the Ten Commandments, the commandment against bearing false witness follows the commandment against stealing. These two commandments, taken together, help us deal with what may be considered the "deadly duo"—the trap of pride (believing that we are the origin of goodness, superior to others, and therefore "like God"), and the trap of despair (believing that we are evil and worthless, inferior to others, and abandoned by God). These two commandments, then, are given to protect us from identifying too strongly with states of elation (pride, conceit) and states of despair (guilt, worthlessness). The wisdom contained in these commandments is similar to that which is taught by the Buddha:

> *As a solid rock is not shaken by the wind, so wise men are not moved amidst praise and blame (Dhammapada 6:6).*

Prideful feelings arise when we mistakenly attribute goodness to ourselves, rather than acknowledge that all goodness flows in from God. Similarly, states of despair arise when we mistakenly attribute evil to ourselves, rather than acknowledge that all evil is a perversion and distortion of original goodness—also called "hell." In *Heaven and Hell,*

Emanuel Swedenborg reveals the secret of how these twin demons—pride and despair—can be overthrown. He writes:

> *If a person only believed, as is really true, that all good is from the Lord and all evil from hell, he would neither make the good in him a matter of merit, nor would evil be imputed to him; for he would then attribute to the Lord all the good he thinks and does, and all the evil that flows in he would cast down to hell, from which it comes. But because a person does not believe that anything flows into him from heaven or from hell, and therefore supposes that all things that he thinks and wills are in himself, and therefore from himself, he appropriates the evil to himself, and the good that flows in he defiles with merit* (302).

This commandment, then, calls us to awaken to that highest reality—that our God reigns. It calls us to ask God to deliver us from evil and defend us with truth. It calls us to focus on God's blessings, to remember God's promises, and to realize that each of us is of sacred importance. We are God's children, made in God's image and likeness, richly blessed and forever loved. Though we are not God (and never can be), we are created in such a way that we might forever receive the love and wisdom that continually flow in from God, in fuller and fuller measure, "pressed down, shaken together, overflowing our hearts" (cf. Luke 6:38). This is our Divine endowment, incorruptible and immortal, both in this world and the next. This is the truth that can sustain us when we are besieged by thousands of false witnesses. Our God, who leads us in wonderful ways, moment by moment, will never forsake us or leave us comfortless. This is the truth that can set us free.

The assignment: Tell the truth

For this commandment your assignment is to tell the truth: be true to yourself and to others; live in integrity and keep your word. Harness the power of truth to refute the false witnesses that enter your mind and occupy your thoughts. The truth is that God is all powerful, and that with God all things are possible.

Assignment

Tell the truth

**Be true to yourself and to others; keep promises;
clear up misunderstandings; refute false witnesses.**

In your journal, record your experience of keeping this commandment.

SUGGESTIONS FOR FURTHER REFLECTION AND APPLICATION

MEDITATION: "DELIVER US FROM EVIL"

The "deadly duo"—pride and despair—lead us into all temptation. Just as there is a temptation to fall into the pride of thinking that we know better than others, there is also a temptation to fall into the despair of feeling that we know nothing, that we are evil, that our lives are meaningless, and that there is no hope in God. The key to overcoming the deadly duo is to remain even-keeled, attributing neither goodness and wisdom, nor evil and falsity, to ourselves. In our previous meditation we used the words, "Lead us not into temptation" to overcome feelings of superiority; in this meditation we use the words "Deliver us from evil" to overcome feelings of inferiority and despair—especially the despair that sets in when we believe lies about others, about ourselves, and about God. Set aside a few minutes each day to stay your mind on the simple words, "Deliver us from evil," remembering as you do so that God is inmostly present through the truth of the Word, delivering us from all that is evil and leading us towards all that is good. Or you might prefer to meditate on the words of the Buddha: "As a solid rock is not shaken by the wind, so wise men are not moved amidst praise and blame" (*Dhammapada* 6:6).

JOURNAL REFLECTION
What "false messages" did you receive while growing up? These messages might have been about yourself, about your family, about life in general, or about God. For example, you may have been told that "you will never amount to anything," that "the world is a cruel place," that "God will punish you," or that "there is no God." Maybe it was something like, "You have to be a football hero to get along with a beautiful girl," or "Nice guys finish last." Whatever false messages you may have received, describe how one or more of them have affected you in terms of the choices that you made in your life.

JOURNAL REFLECTION
What "true messages" did you receive while growing up? How have these messages sustained you over the years? In what ways have you used these true messages to refute false witnesses?

JOURNAL REFLECTION
Recall a time when someone told a lie or spread a false report about you. How did it feel? What kind of damage did it do? Describe some of the ways it hurt you personally, socially, and/or professionally. Why do you think you still remember it?

JOURNAL REFLECTION
Think of a time in your life when you lied to someone or twisted the truth. What motivated you? What were you afraid of that caused you to cover up with a lie? What reasons did you use to justify your lie? What would have happened if you had told the truth?

ACTIVITY: BE TRUE TO YOURSELF
Give yourself a concrete assignment such as "This week I will not eat _____ ," or "This week I will exercise ____ times." Then, as the week progresses, notice the stream of lies, justifications and rationalizations that flow in to prevent you from doing what you know is best for you. Refute these false witnesses, and stick to your commitment. Be true to yourself.

ACTIVITY: BE TRUE TO OTHERS

While focusing on this commandment be aware of the commitments and promises you make. If you promise to do something, do it. If you are unable to honor your commitment, or keep your promise, deal with it honestly. Let this be an opportunity to "tell the truth" about what has happened. As you do so, practice stating the truth without blaming others or defending yourself. Finally, take responsibility; work out a mutually acceptable arrangement. For example, a father might say to his son, "I'm sorry. I know I promised to take you hiking this weekend, but my back has really been hurting me lately. What if we go to the ball game instead?"

ACTIVITY: BE TRUE TO GOD (REFUTE FALSE WITNESSES)

Take a large sheet of paper and draw a line down the middle. On the left side of the paper list some of the false messages (false witnesses) that come to you whenever you are upset or feeling low. These messages may come to you in the form of words, images or memories that flash into your mind. Try to capture the exact words/images/memories that come to you. For example, words like, "It's useless; the kids will always be selfish" may come to mind; an image of a teacher's stern face as she told you, "You'll never amount to anything" might flash into your consciousness; or a memory of not being picked for the team when you were a child might come into your awareness, along with the accompanying thought that you are worthless. All these can be added to your list of false messages/false witnesses.

When you finish the list, go over to the right-hand side of the paper, and in the space directly across from the first false message, refute it with a true message. The true message could be a statement of your own making, or it could be a verse of Sacred Scripture—some truth from the Word. For example, the false message, "You will never amount to anything," could be refuted by the statement, "God is with me in everything I do," or "With God, all things are possible." Follow this same procedure with each false message that you listed until you have refuted every false witness that you wrote down.

When you are finished writing out the refutations, tear or cut the paper down the middle. Then crumple up the false witness side and set it on something that is fireproof (like a sheet of aluminum foil). Then burn it! Watch those false witnesses go up in smoke. Finally, put the list of "true witnesses" in a safe place, or keep them in your pocket, wallet, or purse, so that you will be able to refer to them whenever the need arises.

False Messages	True Messages

You shall not covet your neighbor's house;
You shall not covet your neighbor's wife,
nor his manservant, nor his maidservant, nor his ox,
nor his donkey, nor anything that is your neighbor's.

OLD TESTAMENT—EXODUS 20:17

 Take heed and beware of covetousness, for one's life does not consist
in the abundance of the things he possesses.

NEW TESTAMENT—LUKE 12:15

 And let not those who covetously withheld of the gifts
which Allah hath given them of His Grace, think that it is good for them.
Nay it will be worse for them: soon shall the things which they covetously
withheld be tied to their necks like a twisted collar.

QUR'ĀN 104:1,2

 Free from self-will, aggressiveness, arrogance, and the lust to possess people
or things, he is at peace with himself and others.

BHAGAVAD GITA 18:53

 So far as anyone indulges in the lusts of the flesh,
he is a beast and a wild animal;
But so far as he takes delight in the desires of the spirit,
he is a human being and an angel.

TRUE CHRISTIAN RELIGION 328

CHAPTER NINE

Do Not Covet / Cleanse the Inside

Contentment is the greatest wealth.
—WORDS OF THE BUDDHA
THE DHAMMAPADA 15:8

Two aspects of coveting: "Amor Mundi" and "Amor Sui"

THROUGHOUT THE SACRED pages of the Old Testament, the words that are spoken on Mount Sinai are referred to as "The Ten Commandments." More accurately, they could be called "The Ten Words" because the original Hebrew phrase consists of two words: "*asor*" meaning "ten," and "*dabarim*" meaning "words." It is for this reason that the Ten Commandments are sometimes referred to as "The Decalogue," a term which comes to us from the Greek words "*deka*" meaning "ten" and *logos* meaning "word." Although religious leaders have sometimes disagreed about how the commandments should be numbered and divided, there has never been any dispute about the fact that there are ten of them. As it is written, "And He wrote on the tablets the words of the covenant, the *Ten* Commandments" (Exodus 34:28; see also Deuteronomy 4:13 and 10:4).[1]

According to the most ancient traditions, the commandment against coveting is divided into two parts and is treated as two separate commandments—the ninth and

---

1. In this regard it should be noted that the number "ten" in Sacred Scripture usually represents that which is complete, total, and perfect, even as the human body is perfected by the ten toes and ten fingers. The ten toes provide balance and support, and take us where we want to go; the ten fingers contain and give expression to the desires of the mind and heart. The Ten Commandments then—or the Ten Words of God—perfectly contain, perfectly support, and perfectly express the totality of wisdom concerning our civil, moral and spiritual life.

tenth commandments. *You shall not covet your neighbor's house* is regarded as the penultimate commandment, and *You shall not covet your neighbor's wife, manservant, maidservant, ox, donkey, or anything that is your neighbor's* is regarded as the final commandment in the series. According to Emanuel Swedenborg, there are deep, spiritual reasons for treating the commandment against coveting as two separate commandments. He writes:

> *There are two loves from which all lusts spring and flow forth perpetually like streams from their fountains. These loves are called the love of the world [amor mundi] and the love of self [amor sui]. . . .Now because the love of the world and the love of self are the foundations of all lusts, and all evil lusts are forbidden in these last two commandments, it follows that the ninth commandment forbids the lusts that flow from the love of the world, and the tenth commandment [forbids] the lusts that flow from the love of self* (Apocalypse Explained 1020:2).

Following Swedenborg's lead, we will deal with coveting in two parts. In the first part of the chapter, we will explore what Swedenborg calls "the love of the world" (*amor mundi*). We will look at some of the differences between a healthy love of the world where we dwell in contentment—seeing God in all things and in all circumstances—and an unhealthy love of the world, where we are never satisfied with what we have, and continually crave more.

Similarly, in the second part of the chapter we will explore what Swedenborg calls "the love of self" (*amor sui*). We will look at some of the differences between a healthy love of self where we appreciate our unique gifts while respecting the freedom and talents of others, and an unhealthy love of self where we either envy or despise others in comparison with ourselves, and desire to dominate, manipulate and control people. Ultimately, we will see that while *amor mundi* and *amor sui* are the root of all other evils, they are also the keys to self-examination. We will see that the holy words, "You shall not covet," offer a Divine invitation to cleanse not only our outward actions but also our hidden desires. As Jesus says, "First cleanse the inside of the cup" (Matthew 23:26).

The literal level of the commandments against coveting tells us more than what *to do* and what *not to do* on the external plane of our lives. These commandments are not only about our *external* actions; they are about our *internal* desires. They direct us to do more than keep the literal level of the previous commandments as a general code of moral conduct, or as a means of keeping society in order. While the literal level of each commandment must be observed, the literal level of the commandments against coveting bids us to go further. These commandments ask us to re-examine not just the actions of our bodies, but also the thoughts of our minds and the desires of our hearts. They help ensure that we will not merely refrain from murdering, committing adultery, stealing, and bearing false witness on the physical level, but on the spiritual level as well. They ask us to *cleanse the inside*. While the literal observance of the commandments prepares us for temporal citizenship in this world, the spiritual observance of the commandments prepares us for eternal citizenship in the Kingdom of God.

PART ONE: "YOU SHALL NOT COVET YOUR NEIGHBOR'S HOUSE."

Amor Mundi: the love of the world

"Coveting" comes from the Latin word "*cupere*" meaning "to desire." It is often associated with passionate, insatiable longings, secret cravings, and the lust to possess what belongs to others. Covetous desires are deep and driving; they torment us and rule us. We feel as though we can never be happy unless these desires are satisfied. The strange irony is, however, that such desires can never be satisfied. Their very nature is to want more and more, and to continue wanting. As it is written in the Hindu Scriptures, "Desire never rests in the enjoyment of lusts, as fire surely increases the more oil it is offered" (*Laws of Manu* 2:94).

The commandment, "You shall not covet your neighbor's house" speaks to us of our inordinate longings to possess the things of the world. We can't just enjoy the fact that the world is filled with beautiful objects and wonderful things—we want to possess those things for ourselves. If our friend gets a new car or a promotion at work, instead of being happy for our friend, we feel envious of our friend's good fortune. We wonder, "Why can't I get a new car or a better paying job?" If we hear that our friends enjoyed a wonderful vacation, or put a new addition on their home, we do not feel happy for them. Instead, our covetous desires get in the way. We want what they have for ourselves.

This is what Swedenborg refers to as the unhealthy aspect of *amor mundi*—the selfish desire to possess what others have. Consider the following journal entry:

This past weekend, my sister and brother-in-law came over to see us. We all hugged and were so glad to see each other.

When I walked into the kitchen I looked out the window and saw a brand new Honda Accord parked outside. I had been wanting a new car for a while now.

"Is that your car?" I asked my sister. "Yes!" She replied enthusiastically. A feeling of jealousy flooded me immediately.

We went out to have a closer look at the car. I sat in the driver's seat and took in all the options it had: sun/moon roof, electric everything; CD player. Instead of being glad for my sister, who has not had a new car in years, I was envious.

I worked hard at a job five days a week, forty-plus hours a week. My husband also worked extremely hard at his job. My sister, on the other hand, has not worked for years. How could she afford a new car when I couldn't? I felt as though I must have a new car, too. I was not going to be outdone!

As we stood there looking at the car, my sister put her arm around me. She explained how long and hard both she and her husband had worked to save the money to buy this car, and what sacrifices they had to make. She explained that the car was really an expression of her husband's love for her and meant so much to her.

Well, I just melted. How could I have coveted so? God tells us we should keep free from the love of money and be content with what we have. I realized that I was serving the false god of envy and breaking the commandment, "Thou shalt not covet." I hugged my sister, and with real feeling I told her how happy I was for her, and how proud I was of her new car. Then we all went for a ride with the windows down and the sun roof open. God's love was pouring in!

This seminar participant identified her feeling, named it as "envy" and was able to rise above it to a place where she could be genuinely open to her sister's joy. She writes, "With real feeling I told her how happy I was for her." As Emanuel Swedenborg says, "To feel the joy of another as joy in one's self, this is loving" (*Divine Love and Wisdom* 47).

Stingy and Greedy

In India, when hunters want to catch a monkey, they set out a heavy wooden box with a small hole on top. The hole is just large enough for a monkey to squeeze a paw through. Inside the box there is a banana. It's the monkey's bait. The hunters hide and wait for the monkey to show up, smell the banana, and reach inside to grab it. As soon as the monkey grabs hold of the banana the hunters close in to capture him. The monkey tugs and pulls but to no avail. He just can't pull the banana through the hole. It never occurs to the monkey that he could just drop the banana and run away. Instead he refuses to let go—even though it may cost him his life!

In the *Dhammapada* we read, "The craving of a thoughtless man grows like a creeper. Like a monkey wishing for fruit in the forest he bounds hither and thither" (24:1). The monkey bounding "hither and thither" seeking for fruit in the forest is sometimes seen as a symbol of the restless person who cannot find peace within, but who is constantly searching for some sensuous pleasure. The monkey also symbolizes an unhealthy "love of the world," an insatiable desire to acquire more and more, as well as the refusal to let go of what we have.

As long as we live in this material world, we will have the opportunity to resist covetousness in its many forms. Let's take a look at two of those forms: we call them "greedy" and "stingy." A greedy person is never satisfied and continually yearns to have more; a stingy person clings to possessions and is reluctant to give anything away. While greediness is an inordinate desire for acquiring things, stinginess is an inordinate desire for holding on to our possessions once we have acquired them. Wanting more, and not being able to let go of what we have, are two sides of the same coin. When these negative traits hold us captive we find that our lives are surrounded with clutter, both internally and externally. While "Greedy" yearns to acquire more and more things, "Stingy" can't let go of anything. In the end we find ourselves drowning in seas of physical, mental and emotional clutter.

In the following example, an individual finds himself surrounded by CD's (compact disks)—more than he will ever have time to listen to. He writes:

I have always loved music. You might say that I have a passion for music. So when CD's first came out I was ecstatic. The sound quality was so terrific. It was like being in the front row of a great concert! When I started to buy my first CD's it was so much fun. Every Friday when I got my paycheck I would head straight for the music store and buy two or three CD's. As my collection of CD's grew I wanted more and more. I actually craved increasing my collection. It became an all-consuming addiction. I was spending money on CD's that I should have been spending on other things. I was truly caught in the trap of craving, coveting and stockpiling possessions.

This person's obsession with collecting CD's is an example of a tendency that many of us may have. Although it may begin as an innocent hobby— collecting CD's, books, dolls, coins, baseball cards or antiques—our inclination to covet can easily escalate into a full-blown, all-consuming addiction. We find ourselves surrounded by the objects of our desires, yet still unsatisfied, wanting more, and unable to let go of our many possessions. According to Lao-tzu, "There is no greater sin than the desire for possession" (*Tao Te Ching* 1:46).

We tend to think that possessiveness is a problem only for those who live in affluent countries. But the reality is that it can be a a problem for anyone, in any culture, whether rich or poor. In the following journal entry a man of modest means from a small African village writes about his unwillingness to share his possessions:

In the Zulu language my name means "wanting his own" and I believe that it fits me well. I have been extra-possessive, and have coveted many things. This state is my strongest god. I have made a strong idol and a beautiful image decorated with ornaments of "this is my own," and no other person is to interfere with my property. God has prospered me so that I can give material things to other people, but I always feel that "this is my own," and I do not want to share with others. I now pray that I may share without labeling what is "mine" and "mine alone."

Regardless of our economic status, age, religion, nationality, or even the time period in which we live, the commandment against coveting applies to each of us. In the sixth century B.C., the Chinese philosopher Lao-tzu taught, "The sage does not accumulate possessions; he lives for other people, and grows richer himself" (*Tao Te Ching* 6:61). Piling up wealth without any thought of service in mind, but merely to hoard it for one's self, is warned against in the Sacred Scriptures of all religions. In the Islamic Scriptures we read:

Let not those who covetously withhold of the gifts which Allah hath given them of His Grace, think that it is good for them: Nay, it will be the worse for them; soon shall the things which they covetously withheld be tied to their necks like a twisted collar, on the Day of Judgment (Qur'ān 3:180).

In the New Testament, Jesus tells the story of a certain rich man who had plentiful crops, and who decided that he would build even bigger barns to store his surplus. In the story, the rich man is warned not to place his trust and security in worldly possessions, because *eternal* life does not consist in the abundance of *things*. We read:

And He said to them, "Take heed and beware of covetousness, for one's life does not consist in the abundance of the things he possesses." Then He spoke a parable to them, saying: "The ground of a certain rich man yielded plentifully. And he thought within himself, saying, 'What shall I do since I have no room to store my crops?' So he said, 'I will do this: I will pull down my barns and build greater, and there I will store all my crops and my goods. And I will say to my soul, "Soul, you have many goods laid up for many years; take your ease; eat, drink, and be merry."' But God said to him, 'You fool! This night your soul will be required of you; then whose will those things be which you have provided?' So is he who lays up treasure for himself, and is not rich toward God" (Luke 12:16-21).

This story is the Christian counterpart to the wisdom of the Islamic Scriptures: "Woe to him who pileth up wealth and layeth it by, thinking that his wealth would make him last forever" (*Qur'ān* 104:2-3).

It is important to remember that this commandment specifically forbids *coveting*. It doesn't prohibit us from having desires, dreams, and longings that are based on our love to God and our love for the neighbor. In other words, we may still dream dreams and have visions for our future. We may still desire to own a decent home or have a reliable car. We may still yearn for a loving relationship with our spouse. We may still hope that we can have sufficient food for our families. We may legitimately desire to live in a neighborhood where it is safe to raise our children. These are normal desires and are not in themselves "stingy" or "greedy."

But a problem arises when normal desires become insatiable lusts. This is the point at which perfectly legitimate desires become anxious, desperate longings. We are unable to let go of these longings until they are fulfilled. Ancient wisdom teaches that we do not have to surrender all desires—just our craving to obtain them. In the Sermon on the Mount, Jesus says, "Do not worry about your life, what you will eat or what you will drink; nor about your body, what you will put on . . . . for your heavenly Father knows that you need all these things . . . . Therefore do not worry about tomorrow" (Matthew 6:25, 32). In opening up the spiritual meaning of this passage, Emanuel Swedenborg writes:

> *This passage does not mean that a person should not procure food and clothing and even resources for the time to come; for it is not contrary to order for a person to provide for himself and his own. But those who care for tomorrow are those who are not content with their lot; who do not trust in the Divine, but in themselves; and who have regard for only worldly and earthly things. With such there universally reigns care about tomorrow, and a desire to possess all things and to dominate over all people. They grieve if they do not obtain the objects of their desire, and feel anguish at the loss of them . . . .*
>
> *The case is very different with those who trust in the Divine. These also care about tomorrow, and yet they do not care, because they do not think about tomorrow with concern, still less with anxiety. Their spirit remains in equanimity whether they obtain the objects of their desire or not; and they do not grieve over the loss of them, being content with their lot. If they become rich they do not set their heart on riches; if they are raised to honors they do not regard themselves as more worthy than others; if they become poor, they are not made sad; if their circumstances are wretched they are not dejected. They know that for those who trust in the Divine all things advance towards a happy state to eternity, and that whatever befalls them in time is a means to that end (Arcana Coelestia 8478:2, 3).*

The key phrase here is "their spirit remains in equanimity whether they obtain the objects of their desire or not . . . [for they] trust in the Divine." It is not that they are devoid of all desire, but rather they do not have *anxious* desires which rob them of the blessings within the present moment. They care, but they do not worry. They plan for tomorrow, but they do not despair if their plans do not work out. They have dreams, but they hold them lightly, knowing that God is ruling the universe. Whatever their circumstance, they know that "all things advance towards a happy state to eternity, and that whatever befalls them in time is a means to that end."

Spiritual possessions

In sacred symbolism, "possessions" and "riches" often refer to spiritual truths. Just as we may be stingy and greedy about worldly possessions, we can also be stingy and greedy about spiritual possessions. If we have been busy studying the great spiritual teachings, we have undoubtedly discovered many beautiful treasures along the way. We have learned much about spiritual life, and collected insights like sparkling gems. These acquisitions are indeed "great possessions."

But a knowledge of spiritual life is not spiritual life itself, just as a lecture about heaven is not heaven. The great spiritual teachings of all time are merely empty facts, unless they are converted into sustenance for our desert states, and energy for useful service. The statement, "It is easier for a camel to go through the eye of a needle than for a rich man to enter the kingdom of God" (Matthew 19:24) refers to our tendency to set our heart on acquiring great knowledge, thinking that in so doing we will be allowed to enter the Kingdom of God. In this regard, Emanuel Swedenborg writes:

> In the natural sense the rich are those that have an abundance of riches and set their heart upon them; but in the spiritual sense they are those who have an abundance of knowledge and learning, which are spiritual riches, and who desire by means of these riches to introduce themselves into the things of heaven and the church by means of their own intelligence. And because this is contrary to Divine order it is said to be "easier for a camel to go through a needle's eye" (Heaven and Hell 365:3).

A camel in sacred symbolism—especially because of its ability to conserve water in its cells and store up fat in its hump (to be used during the long desert journey)—represents the accumulation of knowledge. As the camel conserves water and stores up fat, we can learn and store up spiritual knowledge which can be miraculously converted into life giving sustenance during our "desert" states. This is a legitimate use of stored up knowledge. But piling up knowledge, or priding ourselves on our learning, will do us no good. In order to pass through "the eye of the needle," we must become "poor in spirit." We must draw upon our spiritual riches, no matter how limited. We must humbly ask God to convert them into spiritual nutrition for our journey, and loving energy for useful service.

This is the lesson that Jesus teaches the rich young ruler who asked, "What good thing shall I do that I might inherit eternal life?" Jesus said to him, "If you want to enter into life, keep the commandments." The rich young ruler said, "All these things I have kept from my youth. What do I still lack?" It was at this point that Jesus said to him, "If you want to be perfect, *go, sell what you have and give to the poor, and you will have treasure in heaven . . .*" (Matthew 19:16-21; emphasis added).

For those of us who have become overly attached to our possessions, selling them may be the best thing to do. But there is a deeper lesson in this teaching. When we "sell" something we give up ownership. It no longer belongs to us. Similarly, we must give up the idea that our "good works" are from ourselves, and that we "own" them in any way. As we said in the commandment against stealing, we must acknowledge that any good thing that we do is from God alone, who acts into and through us to the extent that we keep the commandments. It is only then that we can "give to the poor." In other words, from a humble spirit, emptied of selfish desire and cleansed of self-interest, we can give to others the riches that God has given to us. But the rich young ruler was not yet able to do this. His unwillingness to part with his possessions is a picture of each of us at those times when we are unable to humbly acknowledge that the riches we have—whether material or spiritual—belong to God. Instead we covetously hold on to them, thinking that these possessions are the key to happiness. But they are not. We read therefore that, "He went away sorrowful, for he had great possessions" (Matthew 19:22).

Treasures in heaven

In recognizing and overcoming covetousness we gradually learn to let go of every selfish desire and every attachment that binds us to this material plane. As Jesus said,

> Do not lay up for yourselves treasures on earth, where moth and rust destroy and where thieves break in and steal. But lay up for yourselves treasures in heaven, where neither moth nor rust destroy and where thieves do not break in and steal. For where your treasure is, there your heart will be also (Matthew 6:19-21).

Jesus spoke of "the hidden treasure"— the treasure which we cannot see with the eye, nor hear with the ear, nor feel with the touch, but which is richer by far than anything the world can offer. He referred to it as "treasure hidden in a field, which a man found and hid; and for joy over it he goes and sells all that he has and buys that field" (Matthew 13:44).

This "hidden treasure" is available whenever we shift our focus from what is missing in our lives to what is present in our lives. A participant writes:

> *When I drove into the parking lot this morning I noticed the "nice" cars (BMW's, Lexus, Mercedes, etc.) that seemed to line the parking lot. As I drove up each level of the parking deck, it seemed like cars were jumping out at me and saying, "Look at me! Look how nice I am!" I don't usually notice things like that, but I have to admit that I got to thinking about how much some of those cars cost and wondered who they belonged to.*
>
> *As I allowed my mind to focus on these material things, I realized that I was "coveting" my neighbor's property. I know that I was allowing a desire to build up in me that focused more on the things that this world has to offer, than the things that God has to offer. I know that I should have just ignored those cars and not even have given them a second thought. I started to say to myself, "Seek ye first the kingdom of God."*
>
> *As I rounded the third level of the parking deck, I saw a young man who was severely handicapped. I saw him struggling mightily with two crutches and literally dragging himself into the building. I knew then that God had provided an instant response to my situation. I realized that I was lacking NOTHING in comparison to many others. God quickly changed my focus from what was "missing" in my life, to what was "present" in my life. Praise God from whom all blessings flow!*

As this seminar participant discovered, the treasures of heaven are there for each of us—but in order to obtain them we must practice the spiritual discipline of this final commandment. We must not covet; we must surrender ourselves to the will of God, who removes our lusts and replaces them with "the treasures of the unseen, the treasures that none knoweth but Allah" (*Qur'ān* 6:59).

Sometimes "heavenly treasures" are hidden away in the simplest things of life, but we do not see them or appreciate them because of the frantic pace of our lives. Overwhelmed by numerous commitments, activities, meetings and appointments, we often do not have time to catch our breath. We race furiously from our son's soccer game, to our dentist appointment, to the department store to buy new shoes, to the grocery store to restock the refrigerator, and then to the bank to cash a check before they lock the doors. Our lives are filled to the brim with things *to do*, and little time *to be*—things to achieve, and little time to appreciate. Greedy to accomplish more, we pack our daily schedules with things to do and places to go, believing that achieving our goals is more important than being still, quieting the mind, and appreciating the many treasures and simple joys stored up for us within the present moment. In this regard, consider the wisdom of this nine-year-old girl:

> *Grandmothers don't have to do anything except to be there. If they take us for walks, they slow down past things like pretty leaves and caterpillars. They never say, "Hurry up." When they read to us, they don't skip or mind it if it is the same story over again. Everybody should try to have a grandmother, especially if you don't have television, because they are the only grown-ups who have time.*[2]

In the midst of our rush to attain our goals, we often overlook the heavenly treasures along the way. As Mahatma Ghandi once observed, "There is more to life than increasing its speed." When our mind is concentrating on the next thing that we need to do, we are unaware of the possible treasures that exist within the moment. While driving a child to an athletic practice, we can choose to think about the plumber who is coming tomorrow, or we can choose to have a conversation with our child and strengthen our relationship right now. Contained within the present moment are simple gifts and heavenly treasures waiting to be discovered. They are available to each of us to the extent that we are able to let go of covetousness and be content in God.

Throughout the study of this part of the commandment we have seen that covetousness is an unwillingness to let go of our desire to possess the things of the world. In essence it is a *trust in things*, rather than a *trust in God*. As it is written in the Old Testament, "Some trust in chariots, and some in horses, but we will remember the name of the Lord our God" (Psalm 20:7). In the Sacred Scriptures of the Islamic faith, we read, "Do not strain thine eyes in longing for the things of this world . . . for the provision of thy Lord is better and more enduring (*Qur'ān* 20:131). Truly, being content in God, trusting in God's leading, and doing God's will is the greatest wealth. As Emanuel Swedenborg writes, "Peace has in it trust in the Lord, that He governs all things, provides all things, and leads to a good end" (*Arcana Coelestia* 8455).

2. "What is a Grandmother?" Originally published in the *Bulletin of the Children's Hospital of Los Angeles*. Reprinted in *The Park News* (Glenview, Illinois: Immanuel Church of the New Jerusalem, August 22, 1986): 1.

Learning to distinguish between the transitory pleasures of earth and the eternal treasures of heaven is a gradual process, and, for most of us, it takes a lifetime. As Confucius says, there are three things that each of us must guard against: in our youth we must guard against physical lust; in our middle years we must guard against quarrelsomeness; and when we are old we must guard against covetousness (*Analects* 16:21). This is perhaps why the commandment against coveting is the last of the Ten Commandments, and why the Sacred Scriptures of India teach that overcoming attachment to the things of this world is the great and final battle in our lives: "He who is without craving . . . is called the great sage, the great person. This is the last body" (*Dhammapada* 24:19). "With the destruction of craving I am freed" (*Dhammapada* 24:20).

The things of the world are provided for our enjoyment and are necessary for sustaining our physical lives. While we can appreciate these gifts, we need not make them the center of our lives, or believe that our happiness, security or self-worth is determined by how much we own. Examining the desires of our heart and letting go of our covetous desire to acquire things opens us to the presence of spiritual riches and the treasures of heaven.

PART TWO: "YOU SHALL NOT COVET YOUR NEIGHBOR'S WIFE, NOR HIS MANSERVANT, NOR HIS MAIDSERVANT, NOR HIS OX, NOR HIS DONKEY, NOR ANYTHING THAT IS YOUR NEIGHBOR'S."

Amor Sui: the love of self

The commandment against coveting begins with the words, "You shall not covet your neighbor's house." We have discussed how a physical "house" can represent our love for possessing and accumulating the things of the world. The second part of the commandment against coveting continues with the words, "You shall not covet your neighbor's wife, nor his manservant, nor his maidservant, nor his ox, nor his donkey, nor anything that is your neighbor's" (Exodus 20:17).

While it is true that we should not covet anything of our neighbor's material possessions, the second part of this commandment takes us inside the neighbor's house to more interior things. In this part of the commandment a "house" represents the human mind. Just as people enter and leave a house, thoughts and feelings enter and leave the mind. Also, just as we dwell in a house, we dwell on ideas; and just as we establish our place of residence, we establish certain mental habits. These mental habits—our customary ways of thinking and feeling—become our mental habitations and spiritual dwelling places. In the Psalms of David we read, "I shall dwell in the house of the Lord forever" (Psalm 23:6; King James Version).

This commandment speaks to each of us whether we are married or unmarried, have servants, own livestock or have any other possessions. It speaks to us of the important and living aspects of a person's mind and life. In sacred symbolism the "wife" often refers to our deepest love, highest aspirations, and most cherished values. The "manservant" represents our rational thoughts and belief systems; the "maidservant" signifies the feelings associated with those thoughts and beliefs. The "ox" and the "donkey" symbolize the most external level of our lives—what we say and what we do.

Because this is an interior commandment, it relates to coveting interior things. The Lord's warning—that we should not covet these things in our neighbor—means that we should not exert selfish domination or control over the feelings, thoughts, or actions of others. According to Emanuel Swedenborg, this commandment teaches that coveting what is inside the neighbor's house (mind) is "to eagerly desire to subject another to one's own authority, or bidding . . . . This commandment has reference to the love of self (*amor sui*), especially to the love of ruling over others."[3]

Controlling those we love

The commandment against coveting reminds us to accept and respect the feelings, thoughts and lives of other people. It reminds us that while we are free to offer our viewpoints, we must not compel people to love the things we love, believe the things we believe, or do the things we want them to do. Letting go of control is especially difficult at home with members of our family. In the following journal entry, a father deals with his own control issues as he struggles to accept a vocational decision that his daughter has made. He writes:

---

3. Swedenborg's Latin phrase is "*amorem imperandi*" which suggests the love of commanding, or of exercising imperialistic rule. It is translated here as "the love of ruling over others" (See *Apocalypse Explained* 1022:2).

My daughter announced that she wanted to study to become a nurse. My first reaction was that she had lost her mind. This is the middle of the AIDS scare in America. I rebelled to the extent that I almost became ill. There were many sleepless nights. She is young. She is my beautiful daughter. I don't want her to die of a disease she does not deserve. What kind of a father would I be if I were to allow her to throw away her life this way? I have loved her and know what is best for her.

While trying to get her to reconsider, she said something that stopped me in my tracks. "Dad," she said, "What if it is God's will for me to become a nurse?" Suddenly I realized that I had been coveting my daughter's life, trying to control her in a way that was not right. After all, it really is possible that her desire to be a nurse is a direct response to God's call. My protest ceased and I no longer tried to get her to reconsider. The case was closed.

The theme of not controlling the lives of our children occurs again in the following excerpt from another participant's journal. The scenario is a familiar one—trying to get a child to keep his room clean:

Memorial Day started out to be a nice relaxing day. The family decided that we would straighten up the house and then take the rest of the day and just do whatever. Well, as I passed my son's room I couldn't believe what I saw. He had just cleaned his room two days ago and now it looked as though a tornado had passed through it. "Control" is a continual problem with me, and I was determined to put an end to this pig-style of living. I was especially upset because I had just spent the last month painting and papering the inside of the house. I was determined that I was not going to let all my efforts to make the house look better go to waste.

What I wanted was for him to immediately go in there and clean that room. I was so upset that I intended to get my point across once and for all. As I went into the family room, where he was doing some trivial thing, I started to yell, but stopped myself before any words came out. I remembered the assignment about not controlling. I thought about our discussion in class and about keeping the commandments. I knew that in that moment I was violating several of them! Mostly, I knew that I was not in control of myself, but I was willing to control my son.

I went outside and started to work on the car, and thought about what had just happened. As I talked with God and let the frustrations pass I was able to see things more clearly. I thought back to when I was growing up and how it was to be a kid. My attention was not on cleaning but on everything that brought joy and pleasure to me. Because of these insights I was able to go back and talk to my son kindly. This resulted in the room being cleaned without any hurt feelings. I was also able to keep the commandments.

We find that our desire to want others to see things our way, to accept our priorities as their priorities, to believe what we believe, and to do what we want them to do, creates an illusionary reality where our thoughts and feelings are the only ones that really matter. We feel as though we are the center of the universe; and everything else—as well as everyone else—is created to serve our needs. This tendency to regard ourselves as more important than others must be carefully examined and honestly evaluated. It is important, therefore, to be able to identify its chief features. A primary feature is the delusive persuasion that our thoughts are more valid than the thoughts of others, our opinions are more important, and our feelings are deeper. In fact, at its extreme, this feature regards one's self as all-important, and others as having little or no value except for how they might be able to serve one's own self-interest. No one else really exists except as bit-players in the drama of our lives where we and we alone hold center stage, commanding the attention, the service, and the favors of all.

To the self-absorbed individual, other people are little more than shadows and images without feelings, thoughts, or life. Whether it is a husband who regards his wife's opinions as worthless, a business owner who looks upon her workers as existing for the sole purpose of increasing her profit, or a doctor who disregards the feelings of his patients, the situation is similar. Other people are seen as relative "nothings." In commenting on the tendency to be dismissive of others and to discount their feelings, Emanuel Swedenborg says that people who are absorbed in self-love "imagine that they alone live; they look upon others as images" (*Divine Love and Wisdom* 144).

In the following example a father is introduced to the reality that his son is more than a mere reflection of himself, but rather a young man with his own thoughts and feelings. He writes:

I had given my sixteen-year-old son permission to fix up a place for himself in the old garden shed. It hadn't been used for years, but still had electricity. He put a lot of energy into cleaning it up, and within a few weeks had it looking quite nice.

But last night I found him out in the shed, late at night, watching TV. We have very strict rules in our house about the amount of TV we watch and the content of what we watch, and we have never allowed our kids to have their own TV sets. So it was a big surprise to find out that he had "smuggled" a TV set into the garden shed. When I saw him in there watching TV my heart sank. I thought, "He is disobeying me. He just does whatever he wants. He has abused this privilege." I was really upset. I opened the door of the shed, walked inside and said, "All right, turn the thing off, and close the place down." He shut off the TV, turned off the lights, and we went outside together.

We went at it. I was insisting that he was disobedient and selfish and only did what he wanted to do. He was insisting that I wanted him to be "perfect," that I wanted him to fit into my mold, and that I was trying to control him. "You want me to think just like you," he said. "But I am not you, and I don't think like you. I need to find things out for myself."

He was probably making a good point, but I was so upset that I couldn't hear it. It was a meaningless battle with no winners and two losers. Realizing that this was going nowhere, I said, "Let's talk about this tomorrow. Meanwhile you are not allowed to use the shed until further notice."

That evening and the next day I was able to give it a lot of thought. I began to realize that as a father I do have a responsibility to establish and enforce reasonable rules for our family life. We have other children who must abide by the rules we have established, and it would be unfair to make an exception for our son. However, I also realized that he is growing older, needs greater freedom, and could perhaps watch TV in the shed occasionally for a special event. When we met to discuss the issue my son had obviously done a good deal of thinking too. He said, "Dad, I've thought about it. I had that TV out there for two days, and it was all junk. I really don't need it."

I was surprised and almost took him up on his offer, but decided that I still needed to make a stretch toward relinquishing control. "I'm glad to hear that," I said, "but I think you still might want to use the TV on special occasions." He *beamed, and the matter was settled. He spent the rest of the day voluntarily mowing the lawn, trimming brush, and pulling weeds. For me, working on "not coveting"—especially not trying to control my son's affections, thoughts and actions—really paid off. In fact, it saved our relationship. I realized that I must not play God, and that my son and I can still have a great relationship, even when he doesn't choose to obey **MY** commandments!*

This father learned that there was a world of difference between his desire to enforce the "rules of the house" and his own need to obey the commandments of God. In the process he realized that his son was much more than an image of himself: he was a unique and precious human being, made in the image and likeness of God.

In the next example, a father graciously invites us into his inner world as he describes his struggle to overcome the desire to control his handicapped daughter:

I have a daughter who is mentally challenged. She does not have the normal power to reason. She has a strong compulsion to talk. She breaks into conversations and talks about subjects which have no relationship to whatever is being said.

When she does this, I can feel that old demon anger climbing up my spine. Even before it happens I know how I am going to react and that I am going to say something that will wound her. I wonder why I just can't keep my mouth shut. I realize that I could just let my daughter say whatever is on her mind and there would be no real damage done. So why do I feel that I always have to "control" the situation?

I think about the many times she has done this in her twenty-four years, and I know in my heart that she does not mean any harm. All she wants is to feel accepted. She just wants to be a part of the group. There is nothing wrong with that.

This evening, while visiting with some friends, my daughter broke into the conversation and blurted out something completely unrelated to the topic. This time I responded differently. I just sat there and refused to control the situation. I let her finish her story. Instead of trying to control her, I controlled my tongue. It worked. I pray that God will help me accept my child and not try to control what she says.

This father decided that it was wiser to "control his tongue" rather than to control his daughter. In the Hindu Scriptures it is written, "If a man were to conquer in battle a thousand times a thousand men, and another only conquered one—himself—he who conquered himself would be the greatest of conquerors" (*Dhammapada* 8:4). Similarly, it is written in the Old Testament, "He who is slow to anger is better than the mighty, and he who rules his spirit [is mightier] than he who takes a city" (Proverbs 16:32).

In the previous journal entries we were invited to explore the inner world of individuals who were struggling to keep the commandments in relation to their children, and who wanted to love them without controlling them unnecessarily. In the following example, a husband struggles over the fact that his wife has taken on a job that limits the amount of time she can spend at home. He writes:

> *I don't need new cars, a big house, designer clothes, or a car phone. I do, however, desire to have a strong family unit. I see myself as the breadwinner and look to my wife to be the homemaker. I know that sounds old-fashioned, but that is how I feel.*
>
> *This year my wife was asked to be the director of the Vacation Bible School. She stays up late working on plans and organizing the upcoming week. She has attended an association clinic, and conducted a clinic at the church. She is trying to get everything organized to facilitate a successful Bible School.*
>
> *While I am proud of Pat's efforts, I am also jealous and covet her time for me. I miss her being available for me when I want to talk about my day or discuss her day or whatever. I miss the dinners she hasn't had time to prepare. It has been a struggle, but I have decided that what she is doing is an important cause for the Kingdom of God. Her dedication and diligence make me feel ashamed of myself for even noticing her absence in taking care of my every need. My needs pale in comparison to the greater need she is filling.[4]*

Of sacred significance

The commandment against coveting, then, when understood more deeply, calls us to see all people as having sacred importance, for we are all children of God. In serving

---

4. It should be noted that "missing someone" is not necessarily "coveting"—although it could be. Sometimes this kind of basic human desire (simply wanting to be with one's spouse) is good to communicate, and need not be suppressed, denied, or dismissed as merely "coveting."

one another we serve God. Those who hold the highest offices in a country are often called "public servants," and their specific task is to govern in such a way that individual freedom and human diversity is protected and honored. "The highest duty of a ruler is to protect his subjects" (*Laws of Manu* 7:144). In brief, public officials—no matter how prestigious their office—must not "lord it" over others. They must serve. As Jesus said to the disciples:

> *You know that those who are considered rulers over the Gentiles lord it over them, and their great ones exercise authority over them, yet it shall not be so among you; but whoever desires to be great among you shall be your servant* (Mark 10:42-43).

Each of us is born to make a special and distinct contribution to our family, to our community, and to the world. It is therefore meaningless and fruitless to enter into comparisons between people. Even though subordination can be useful, the truth remains: no one is above us, and no one is below us. There is a special place and a special calling for each of us. That is why, in the eyes of God, each of us is a "special treasure"(Psalm 135:4). Even though it may appear that some people have superior talents or more important positions in society, the reality is that we all have a significant role to play in the universal human family. Just as the body is one, even though it has many parts, the world community is one, even though it is made up of many people. As it is written:

> *Now there are diversities of gifts, but the same Spirit. There are differences of ministries, but the same Lord. And there are diversities of activities, but it is the same God who works all in all . . . .*
>
> *The eye cannot say to the hand, "I have no need of you"; nor again the head to the feet, "I have no need of you." No, much rather, those members of the body which seem to be weaker are necessary. And those members of the body which we think to be less honorable, on these we bestow greater honor . . . . If one member suffers, all the members suffer with it; or if one member is honored, all the members rejoice with it"* (1 Corinthians 12:4-6, 21-23, 26).

When our communities, schools, religious institutions, businesses and families are organized according to spiritual principles, there is no envy, no jealousy and no competition. There is a place for all—and all know their place. Each person is, so to speak, a center for everyone else, and each person's contribution is valued, esteemed and honored. People know and understand that they have come together, not to be served, but rather to serve a higher purpose. In such a setting every job is important, whether it is the janitor sweeping the school, the receptionist at the front desk, the President of the Corporation, or the waterboy on the athletic field. When the garbage collectors go on strike, and the trash piles up, disease begins to spread rapidly. People begin to understand that the labor of the garbage collector is as important to society as the research of the scientist who discovers a vaccine, or the work of the physician who administers it.

The sacred significance of every human being is based on the spiritual law that all people are born to serve a Divine purpose in both this world and the world to come. That Divine purpose is served as God is allowed to act freely through each and every individual. This is how Divinity is manifested and becomes present in the world. As it is written in the Hindu Scriptures, "He who sees the Supreme Lord abiding equally in all beings, never perishing when they perish—he verily sees" (*Bhagavad Gita* 13:27). The same wisdom is expressed in the Upanishads: "As the same fire assumes different shapes when consuming objects of differing shapes, so too does the Supreme Lord, though One, take on the shape of every creature in which He is present" (*Katha Upanishad* 2:2). And in the Christian Scriptures we read, "I was hungry and you gave Me food; I was thirsty and you gave Me drink; I was a stranger and you took Me in . . . . Inasmuch as you did it to one of the least of these My brethren, you did it to Me" (Matthew 25:35, 40).

The power of love

The commandment against coveting, as we have seen, is not just about giving up possessiveness; it is also about giving up control. This can be a difficult task, especially when we are convinced that *our* way is the "right" way. Therefore, developing a sense of humility is essential. It is essential to acknowledge that we do not have all the answers. It is essential to remember that what we know is relatively nothing compared to what we do not know. It is essential to realize that there are other ways of viewing the world, and that people have different needs, different tastes, different preferences, and different ways of thinking.

In this context, the words, "You shall not covet," mean that we should be willing to part not only with our possessiveness (*amor mundi*), but also with our belief that *our* view is the only view, and that *our* way is the only way (*amor sui*). In brief, this commandment asks us to make room for other viewpoints, to consider other opinions, and to allow for other alternatives. In the first century A.D., in an address to the Roman Senate, Lucius Seneca said, "He who decides a case without hearing the other side . . . even though he decide justly, cannot be considered just." Most importantly, this commandment calls us to hear God's side, and to recognize the hidden ways that God accomplishes all things. We read in the Old Testament, "As the heavens are higher than the earth, so are My ways higher than your ways" (Isaiah 55:8).

As we have pointed out, this commandment asks us to examine not just the outward actions of our lives, but our inner thoughts and desires as well. In the New Testament, Jesus speaks words of greatest comfort to all who have gone astray in their outer lives; but when speaking to the scribes and Pharisees—those who have observed the literal teachings of the commandments—Jesus' words are far from comforting. "Woe to you, scribes and Pharisees, hypocrites! For you cleanse the outside of the cup and dish, but inside they are full of extortion and self-indulgence" (Matthew 23:25-26). Jesus is here referring to the self-righteousness of the Pharisees, who believed that their salvation was secure because they rigorously adhered to the external teachings of the commandments. Jesus continues, "Woe to you, scribes and Pharisees, hypocrites! For you are like whitewashed tombs which indeed appear beautiful outwardly, but inside are full of dead men's bones and all uncleanness" (Matthew 23:27). His appeal to them, as it is to each of us, is summarized in those simple words, "Blind Pharisee, first cleanse the inside of the cup and dish, that the outside of them may be clean also" (Matthew 23:26).

To "cleanse the inside" of the cup and dish is to identify and flee from every emotion, every desire, every impulse and every thought that is contrary to the commandments. It is to rise above every selfish desire, every longing to control others, every craving for approval, and all urgency to have things go our way. We may not like the situation that we are confronted with at the moment—whether it be a letter informing us that we have lost our job, a medical diagnosis in which we discover that a family member has a terminal illness, or some other undesirable circumstance. However, regardless of the circumstance or situation we find ourselves in, we can rest in the blessed assurance that a loving and wise God is controlling the universe. As Emanuel Swedenborg writes, "Nothing whatever, not even the least thing, shall arise, except that good may come from it" (*Arcana Coelestia* 6574). And in the *Bhagavad Gita* we find this beautiful promise: "United with Me, you shall overcome all difficulties through My grace" (18:58).

The commandment against coveting, then, is about cleaning the inside of our lives. It is about identifying those lusts and desires that drive us and rule over us; it is about asking God to remove them from our hearts. Indeed, it is asking God to give us a new heart, and a new spirit filled with holy desires and noble thoughts. This is not too much to ask for. In fact, it is a Divine promise, for it is written, "I will put My law in their minds, and write it on their hearts" (Jeremiah 31:33); "I will give you a new heart and put a new spirit within you" (Ezekiel 36:26); "I will put My Spirit within you and cause you to walk in My statutes . . . . I will deliver you from all your uncleanness" (Ezekiel 36:27, 29). "I will pour out My Spirit on all flesh; your sons and your daughters shall prophesy, your young men shall see visions, your old men shall dream dreams" (Acts 2:17; see also Joel 2:28-32). Truly, as we call upon God to help us remove unholy desires and ignoble thoughts, God flows in with new desires and new thoughts. As it is written, "Trust in the Lord and do good . . . and He shall give you the desires of your heart" (Psalm 37:3, 4). And Emanuel Swedenborg writes, "So far as anyone indulges in the lusts of the flesh, he is a beast and a wild animal; but so far as he takes delight in the desires of the spirit, he is a human being and an angel" (*True Christian Religion* 328).

The lusts of the flesh include the angry, vengeful feelings that we harbor towards others—those emotions that would separate and divide us. But when we *cleanse the inside*, God gives us the desires of the spirit: the desire to be reconcilers rather than dividers, live givers rather than murderers. The lusts of the flesh would drive us into adulterous liaisons, where we would dishonor marriage and break our covenant with God. But when we *cleanse the inside*, God gives us the desires of the spirit: the desire to honor marriage, to be tender-hearted and forgiving, and to work through difficulties with patience and compassion. The lusts of the flesh would compel us to take inordinate pride in our achievements, to feel that we are better than others, and ultimately to take credit for what rightfully belongs to God. But when we *cleanse the inside*, God gives us the desires of the spirit: the desire to humbly acknowledge that all praise and honor belong to God alone. The lusts of the flesh would have us bear false witness against our neighbor, against ourselves, and even against God. But when we *cleanse the inside*, God gives us the desire to speak the truth boldly, and to refute false witnesses with the power of the truth that comes to us through the Sacred Scriptures.

To the extent that we are willing to keep the Ten Commandments, the world will be seen as God's kingdom, governed by God's law, ruled by God's power, and filled with God's glory. When Jesus faced the final temptation in the wilderness, the devil offered Him "all the kingdoms of the world and their glory." It was the ultimate temptation: the "kingdoms of the world" represent every material blessing that the world can offer (*amor mundi*); and "their glory" represents all the power and honor that could ever be attained (*amor sui*). "All these things I will give You," said the devil, "if you will fall down and worship me." Jesus' response still rings out across the centuries: "Away with you, Satan! For it is written, 'You shall worship the Lord your God, and Him only shall you serve'" (Matthew 4:9-11). It is for this reason that the Lord's Prayer ends with the words, "For Thine is the kingdom, and the power, and the glory, forever. Amen."

In this final commandment we are invited to experience the life that leads to heaven. In striving to overcome the love of the world, we discover a world of love; in striving to overcome the love of power, we discover the power of love. We come to know—ultimately and deeply—that the God who rules the universe is a God of love and wisdom; a God who cares deeply for each of us, now and forever. This is the great God of all creation, the Redeemer and Savior, the One True God of all people, in all faiths and in all lands.

Assignment: "I will not do this."

This brings us full circle, right back to the first great spiritual principle: *There is only One True God.* We have identified the most tyrannical false god of all—our self! What a relief to discover that we do not have to run the universe, or control the way people feel, think, or act. At last, we can get off the throne, get out of the way, and let God be God. Our task, then, is to get our own house in order by cleansing the inside of the cup and dish—that is, by identifying and fleeing from any and all desires that are contrary to the Ten Commandments. Whenever something presents itself to our minds, whether it arises from an inordinate love of the world (*amor mundi*) or an inordinate love of self (*amor sui*), we need only think, "I will not do this because it is opposed to the commandments of God." Then notice how God flows in with noble thoughts and loving emotions. *This* is the Kingdom of Heaven.

Assignment

Cleanse the Inside

**Accept all circumstances as opportunities
to keep the Ten Commandments.**

In your journal, record your experience of keeping this commandment.

SUGGESTIONS FOR FURTHER REFLECTION AND APPLICATION

MEDITATION: "FOR THINE IS THE KINGDOM, AND THE POWER,
AND THE GLORY, FOREVER."
This concluding meditation focuses our attention on God's omniscience, omnipotence and omnipresence. It acknowledges that God knows all things, has all power, and is perpetually present with each of us. As you stay your mind on the words, "For thine is the kingdom," acknowledge that every material thing belongs to God. As you do so, let go of anxious desires to possess things. Next, stay your mind on the words, "and the power and the glory," acknowledging that all power and glory belong to God. As you do so, let go of anxious desires to control what other people love, believe, and do. Set aside a few minutes each day to stay your mind on the simple words, "For thine is the kingdom, and the power, and the glory, forever," remembering as you do so, that we can give up all anxious desires and trust in God—forever.

JOURNAL REFLECTION
Write about a time in your life when you wanted something desperately. In what way would you now describe this as "coveting"? What did you do to get it? Did it work?

REFLECTION: "THE CLOUDS OF HEAVEN"

Seek God's presence and direction through the Sacred Scriptures. Inquire of God, seeking Divine direction with all your heart, and desiring nothing else. As it is written in the Old Testament, "One thing have I desired of the Lord, that will I seek: that I may dwell in the house of the Lord all the days of my life, to behold the beauty of the Lord and to inquire in His holy temple" (Psalm 27:4). This is what it means to see "the Son of Man" (the Divine truth) coming in "the clouds of heaven" (the Sacred Scriptures) "with power and great glory" (Matthew 24:30).

ACTIVITY: CLEARING OUT THE CLUTTER

Examine your life in terms of "clutter." Is there an attic, a closet, a garage, or a room in your home that has gotten filled up with unnecessary clutter? Have you been unwilling to "let go" of things, and allowed them to pile up in your life? Have you tried to get "better organized" as a means of controlling and managing the clutter—building "bigger barns"—rather than parting with your possessions? In terms of the commandment against coveting, take a careful look at your home and your life. Think in terms of what possessions you really need, and what you could sell, give away or get rid of. Then do it! Have a yard sale, give to a charitable organization, recycle, or put things in the trash. Clear out the clutter.

ACTIVITY: "TALK-ABOUT" (FOR GROUPS)

- Pair up with a partner. Take one minute each to talk about a time when you felt controlled or manipulated by someone else. (You needn't name any names—just talk about your experience.)

- Change partners. Take one minute each to talk about someone who has cared a great deal about you, but who did not control or manipulate you.

- Change partners again. Take one minute each to talk about one method that you use to control or manipulate others. For example, the "silent treatment," raising your voice, sulking, etc.

- Change partners one last time. Take one minute each to talk about what your behavior would look like if you were not trying to control or manipulate others.

ACTIVITY: LEARNING TO "LET GO" OF CONTROL, ANXIETY AND WORRY

Much of our time is spent trying to control other people and worrying about outcomes in our lives. This commandment gives us Divine sanction to "loosen up" and "let go." In keeping this commandment, then, practice the spiritual disciplines of trust and acceptance. Let go of anxiety and worry. Live in integrity, making each move in the game of life from God-consciousness, while letting go of anxiety and worry about the moves that others make. Give up anxious control.

REFLECTION: AMOR MUNDI AND AMOR SUI

The distinctions made between *amor mundi* (the inordinate "love of the world") and *amor sui* (the inordinate "love of self") provide useful concepts for self-examination. While we like to believe that most of our decisions are made out of genuinely altruistic and unselfish motives, they can be tainted with either an inordinate love of the world (the desire for materialistic gain), or an inordinate love of self (the desire to enhance our reputation, prestige and power.) For example, we may study for a Ph.D. in order to gain as much knowledge as possible in our field so that we may do the best possible job. But we may also pursue a Ph.D. primarily to obtain a well-paying job (*amor mundi*) or to enhance our reputation and power (*amor sui*). The same distinction can be made in whether or not we decide to complain about a speeding ticket. It might be that we are upset about paying such a large fine (*amor mundi*). Or it might be that we do not want people to know that we have broken the law, because it may harm our reputation (*amor sui*). As we practice using these terms as a method for making spiritual discernments, we will find that the lower motivations—the love of honor, reputation and gain—will subside, and higher motivations will take their place—motivations such as the desire to be of service to others, and this without thought of personal reward or gain.

ACTIVITY: A SPIRITUAL TREASURE HUNT

Try letting go of worries and concerns long enough to appreciate the present moment. While driving with a friend or family member to school, to work, to an athletic event, or to the mall, place your awareness on the person you are with. Whether you are the person doing the driving or the passenger who is riding in the car, use this opportunity to strengthen your relationship. This can also take place in a waiting room, or even while standing in line. Discover the treasures of your relationship, enjoying conversation, telling jokes, singing or reminiscing. Happy treasure hunting!

REFLECTION: A POEM

The following poem was written and submitted by a prisoner. It is a profound analysis of the kind of rationalizations and justifications that keep us "holding on" to our possessions. As you read through the poem, think about the destructive effects of coveting. Can you identify with any of these people?

The Cold Within

Six men trapped by happenstance
In the dark and bitter cold.
Each one had a stick of wood,
Or so the story's told.

Their dying fire needed logs;
The first man held his back.
For of the faces 'round the fire
He saw that one was black.

The next man looking across the way
Saw one not of his church;
And he wouldn't bring himself to give
The fire his stick of birch.

A third man sat in tattered clothes;
He gave his coat a hitch.
Why should he use his stick of wood
To warm the idle rich?

The rich man just sat back and thought
Of the wealth he had in store,
And how to keep what he had earned
From the lazy, shiftless poor.

The black man's face bespoke revenge,
As the fire passed from sight.
For all he saw in his stick of wood
Was a chance to spite the white.

The last man of that forlorn group
Did nothing except for gain.
Giving only to those who gave
Was how he played that game.

So, their sticks held tight in death's firm grasp
Was proof of human sin.
They did not die from the cold without;
They died from the cold within.[5]

The destructive effects of coveting cannot be underestimated. It is for this reason that Jesus said, "What is a man profited if he gains the whole world and loses his own soul?" (Matthew 16:26).

---

5. Unpublished poem written by Matt O'Donnell. Used with permission.

Be exalted, O God, above the heavens;
Let Your glory be above all the earth.

—PSALM 57:11

Above the Clouds, the Sun is Always Shining

And still I rise.
— MAYA ANGELOU

Glimpses of heaven

THE FINAL COMMANDMENT calls us to surrender our selfish desires so that we may be led into a new way of living, into a mode of existence on a higher plane, a realm that is above our normal consciousness. We are called to give up our inordinate love for possessing the things of the world (*for Thine is the kingdom*) as well as our inordinate love of self, our pride, our attempts to control others, and our "power trips" (*for Thine is the power*). It is a new level of consciousness where, no matter what the appearance, God is always present.

The reality, consistently taught in the Sacred Scriptures of all the world's great religions, is that we are all being led perfectly at every moment, and that when we give up our selfish desires, God immediately flows in with love, wisdom and power. God wills to give us everything, to fill us with overflowing joy and happiness. The only obstacles are those that we do not remove, either willfully or through ignorance. Every seemingly chance occurrence, however we perceive it, is under the watchful eye of an all-knowing God. Even God's permissions—not what God wills, but what God *allows* to happen to us—are under the watchful and loving eye of the Divine Providence. "For Allah has full knowledge of all things" (*Qur'ān* 29:62).

Life in the physical world sometimes seems hard and unfair, and things happen that are often difficult to deal with. But God opens our eyes to spiritual reality—the eternal world that exists forever, within and beyond the world of time and space. When our minds are opened, and when we are given a glimpse of that higher dimension, we know that there is One True God, infinitely loving and wise. We know that God cares for us in every moment in ways that we may never fully comprehend, and that God is leading us even now into the glory of the heavenly kingdom, and into all the joy that we are willing to receive.

Rising above it

Words fail at this point. The only thing that comes to mind is a rainy, winter day in Pittsburgh, Pennsylvania. It had been raining for weeks, and the clouds were dark and gloomy. We had boarded a plane, and were watching the airfield pass by as our plane taxied down the runway gathering speed for the take-off. When the lift-off came, it was strong, smooth and powerful. That huge iron bird, weighing thousands of pounds, was soaring through the air, piercing through the dense clouds that rushed past our window. A few moments later, we were on the other side of the clouds. And there, silent and serene, shone the sun in all its glory. Though we were far above sea level, a line from the "Ancient Mariner" came to mind: "*We were the first that ever burst / Into that silent sea.*"[1]

In that moment it was abundantly clear that above the clouds the sun is always shining. The sun shining above the clouds was a perfect symbol of God's love—constant and unceasing—shining upon the entire world, the good and the evil, the just and the unjust, now and forever. In that moment, we could see clearly that above the gloom, and above the sorrow, there is a higher, more glorious level of consciousness, a level of consciousness that is always available to us—as we strive to keep the commandments.

---

1. Samuel Taylor Coleridge, "The Rime of the Ancient Mariner," Part II, lines 103-104.

Where two or three are gathered together in My name,
there I am in the midst of them.

—MATTHEW 18:20

Conscious Reporting: the "4 by 4"

To live more truly

IS SPIRITUAL GROWTH a private matter—something that takes place solely between an individual and God? Or is it something to be shared with others? In the New Testament we read, "When you pray, go into your room, and when you have shut your door, pray to your Father who is in the secret place, and your Father who sees in secret will reward you openly" (Matthew 6:6). Jesus told the disciples to bear their problems bravely and not go around with sad faces. "When you fast," He said, "anoint your head and wash your face so that you do not appear to men to be fasting . . . and your Father who sees in secret will reward you openly" (Matthew 6:16-18). Some have taken these passages to mean that truly spiritual people must bear their burdens alone, and not discuss their problems with others. Instead they should go directly to God for support and guidance. For them, spiritual development is intensely personal and private; it is holy ground—something that takes place in the quiet chambers of the human heart, the secret meeting place of God and man.

This approach to spirituality—seeing it as a private, highly individual and intensely personal experience—is true. No one else can do the work of regeneration for us; we must do the individual, personal work ourselves. Yet, there is another aspect to spiritual development. Throughout the Gospels, Jesus exhorts the disciples to serve one another, to comfort one another, and to love one another. In response to Jesus' words, the early Christians established supportive communities based on mutual service. And the early apostles confirmed the words of Christ by teaching such things as "Bear one another's burdens" (Galatians 6:2), "Confess your trespasses to one another," and "Pray for one another that you may be healed" (James 5:16).

Spiritual development is a highly individual, yet deeply communal process. On the one hand, it is about our relationship to God—a relationship that goes on secretly, and in private. On the other hand, sharing our journey with others is a necessary and useful part of our spiritual life. As Jesus said, "Where two or three are gathered together in My name, there I am in the midst of them" (Matthew 18:20).

The idea of "two or three" gathered together in spiritual community is a familiar one in all religions, whether the gathering together takes place in a church, ashram, wigwam, synagogue, temple or mosque. The Indian sage, Eknath Easwaran, writes:

> *An essential part of the spiritual life is joining together with those who are spiritually-minded, those who want to promote our growth, and who want us to promote theirs. This should not be considered a luxury or an indulgence. The Buddha would say that most people throw themselves into the river of life and float downstream, moved here and there by the current. But the spiritual aspirant must swim upstream, against the current of habit, familiarity, and ease. It is an apt image. We know how the salmon fights its way along, returning at last to its original home. Those who set out to change themselves are salmon swimming against the relentless flow of the selfish life. Truly, we need every bit of support we can get; we need friends, loyal companions on the journey. We have to do the swimming, of course; nobody else can do it for us. But there will be an easier and swifter passage if we can swim with those who encourage us, who set a strong pace and will not stop until they reach their destination. The burdens are shared, easing them; the joys are shared too, multiplying them.*
>
> *In Sanskrit, this sharing is called satsang. The word derives from two smaller words: sat, meaning "the good" or "truth" or "reality," and sanga, meaning "group" or "association." Thus it signifies the seekers of the highest, banded together.*

Every day devout Buddhists chant three phrases, one of which touches upon this fellowship of seekers. "I take refuge in the Buddha"—he who shows the way, the perfect reminder that nirvana, or liberation, is indeed possible here on this earth in this lifetime. "I take refuge in the dharma"—in the deepest law of our being, that all of us are one. "I take refuge in the sanga"—in the company of those who have come together for the supreme purpose of attaining liberation.[1]

This Buddhist approach to spirituality recognizes the essential unity of all people, and our need for the encouragement and inspiration of fellow seekers along the way. The Sufi mystic and poet, Kahlil Gibran, also shares this point of view. He points out that spiritual companionship is essential to our spiritual growth, for it is the means whereby we learn different aspects of the truth from one another—aspects of the truth that we cannot see by ourselves. These various aspects of the truth, which we learn through other spiritual aspirants, eventually "blend together" to make a beautiful flower garden. Gibran writes:

Thou art my brother because you are a human, and we both are sons of the Holy Spirit; we are equal and made of the same earth. You are here as my companion along the path of life, and my aid in understanding the meaning of hidden Truth . . . .

You and I are all children of one religion, for the varied paths of religion are but the fingers of the loving hand of the Supreme Being, extended to all, offering completeness of spirit to all, anxious to receive all . . . .

Your Truth shall meet my Truth in the coming world and blend together like the fragrance of flowers and become one whole and eternal Truth perpetuating and living in the eternity of Love and Beauty.[2]

As Gibran points out, we are here to learn from one another "as companions along the path of life" even though our religious traditions may vary. Those variations are

---

1. Eknath Easwaran, *Meditation: A Simple Eight-Point Program for Translating Spiritual Ideals into Daily Life* (Petaluma, California: Nilgiri Press, 1991), 190-191. Eknath Easwaran is founder and director of the Blue Mountain Center of Meditation, Tomales, California. Reprinted by permission of Nilgiri Press.
2. Kahlil Gibran, *Tears and Laughter* (New York: Philosophical Library, 1949), 83-84. Reprinted by permission of Philosophical Library.

merely the different "fingers of the loving hand of the Supreme Being," reaching out to all people, everywhere and at all times, eager to gather them together "as a hen gathers her chicks under her wings."[3]

In the end, the question of whether spiritual growth should be done privately or shared with others is no longer an issue. Those who choose to do spiritual work know that spiritual growth is intensely personal. At the same time, they understand that they also need the support of others who can inspire them along the way, help them when they falter, and rejoice with them when they succeed. As Helen Keller says: "I long to communicate with fellow believers who can inspire me to live more truly as I believe."[4]

The "4 by 4"

When appropriate guidelines are in place, a "satsang" or "sharing group" can greatly benefit those who participate. Therefore, in this section we offer a general explanation of how we run the *Rise Above It* seminars, with a specific focus on guidelines for reporting spiritual experiences in small group settings.

The *Rise Above It* seminar can be given to any number of people. We have offered it to groups as small as eight and as large as eighty. It could probably be offered to groups as small as four and as large as four hundred. Normally we meet once a week for two hours over a ten-week period. Each class involves an introductory or "warm-up" activity, a review of the commandment we have been working on, small-group sharing in what we call a "4 by 4," a short break, an introduction to the next commandment, an assignment, and a closing activity.

While the seminar itself is fairly simple and follows standard rules of pedagogy, the 4 by 4 is somewhat unique and therefore requires some additional explanation. Regardless of the size of the larger group, we always provide time during the class for people to meet in groups of four. We call these four-person groups 4 by 4's because each person in the group gets four minutes to share his or her experience of keeping the commandments during the previous week. If there is an uneven number of persons in the larger group, some of the 4 by 4's may wind up having three or five people in them.

---

3. "O Jerusalem, Jerusalem, the one who kills the prophets, and stones those who are sent to her! How often I wanted to gather your children together, as a hen gathers her chicks under her wings, but you were not willing" (Matthew 23:37).
4. *Light in My Darkness,* 158.

For example, if twenty-five people enroll in the seminar, they will divide into five four-person groups and one five-person group. If there is sufficient space in the facility being used, it is helpful for the groups to meet in different locations. The membership of each group is selected at random and changes each week. Over the course of ten weeks, the 4 by 4's help participants to connect with other seminar participants in ways that are deep and meaningful. For some, this has been one of the most significant aspects of the course.

In order to ensure that each person in the 4 by 4 gets four minutes of sharing time, one person in the group is given a timer that can be set to beep in exactly four minutes. When the beeper sounds, the person who is speaking brings his or her sharing to a close. The person who is timing then asks, "Who would like to go next?" And so it goes until everyone in the group has had a chance to speak. In a two-hour seminar, we usually take a 10-15 minute break so that after the 4 by 4's people can have refreshments, use the restroom, continue their discussions, or have some quiet time. At the end of the break, we reconvene the group and introduce the next commandment.

For those who share in a 4 by 4 the following etiquette is recommended:

1. Make a commitment to do your assignment each week.

2. Come to the seminar each week ready to share during 4 by 4's. You may either read from your journal or speak directly to the other members of your group.

3. Use discretion. In the course of a week, you will have many opportunities to "keep the commandments." You do not need to report on those experiences that might be damaging to your reputation or to the reputation of others.

4. Do not complain or blame. However, you may speak about those times during the week when opportunities to complain or blame came up for you, and how you responded at those times.

5. Keep the focus on *your experience* of keeping the commandment for the week. Your sharing in the 4 by 4 is about *you* and your response to the commandment—not about your theories, or about other people.

6. Be sure that your sharing addresses questions such as:

—*What came up for you as a result of keeping this commandment?*

—*What opened up for you as a result of keeping this commandment?*

—*How did you manage to remember to keep this commandment?*

—*What shifted for you when you remembered to keep this commandment?*

—*What was it like for you when you remembered this commandment but didn't want to keep it?*

—*What changes came about in your relationships to others in the process of/as a result of striving to keep this commandment?*

—*What did you learn about yourself by keeping this commandment?*

—*In what ways did you feel God's presence by keeping this commandment?*

7. If you didn't work on the assignment, use your time to talk about why. Be honest with yourself and with others. Examine your sense of commitment.

For those who listen in a 4 by 4 the following etiquette is recommended:

1. *Do not interrupt.* Give your total attention to the person who is speaking .

2. *Do not "rehearse."* While someone else is sharing, do not be thinking about what you will say when it is your turn to speak. Instead, give your total attention to the person who is speaking .

3. *Acknowledge those who share.* Words like, "Thank you," "I appreciate what you said," "Thanks for sharing that with us," or even a compassionate smile can be a comfort to a person who has just shared. Conversely, the absence of any feedback can be awkward, and it can send a negative message to the person who has shared. When we taught this seminar among the Zulus, the participants in the 4 by 4's all said spontaneously, *Siyabonga* ("We are grateful"). Ghanian participants said, *Meda wo ase pa* ("Thank you so much").

4. *No advice-giving.* The 4 by 4 is not about solving problems; it is about sharing our experience of keeping a particular commandment and allowing ourselves to be inspired by the efforts of others who are also striving to keep the commandments.

5. *Honor confidentiality.* What is said within the 4 by 4 should remain within the 4 by 4. It should not be discussed with others outside of the group experience.

CONCLUSION: AN ANCIENT TRADITION

As we meet in small groups and share our spiritual growth experiences, we are not scientists looking for answers or psychologists solving problems; rather, we are pioneers on a journey of self-examination, striking out into new territory, encountering hazards, fighting inner dragons, and discovering miracles. Each week, as we gather together around the fire of God's love, we have an opportunity to share in an ancient tradition—the telling of wonderful stories of our high adventures in the inner world of the human spirit. This is not a time to give advice, to do psychological analysis, or to become self-righteous. Rather, it is a time for child-like wonder and awe as we listen to and share real stories and great adventures that could only have been written by the Hand of God.

Two thousand years ago a young man, infested by demons, was restored to his right mind by Jesus Christ. When the multitude of demons was driven out of the young man, he immediately wanted to get into the boat with Jesus. But Jesus said to him, "*Go home to your friends and tell them what great things the Lord has done for you, and how He has had compassion on you*" (Mark: 5:19; emphasis added).

The 4 by 4 is an attempt to continue this tradition. It provides an opportunity to bear witness to the extraordinary things that go on in our everyday lives when we strive to live consciously in the light of the commandments. Each person in the 4 by 4 becomes a living, joyful witness to the great things God has done—and is doing—in each of our lives. As we persevere in keeping the commandments personally, and sharing our struggles collectively, we come to realize the many ways in which God has had compassion on us all.

About the Cover

A WINDY MORNING IN BOSTON HARBOR

The cover photograph pictures the early dawn of a new day. Although some stars still twinkle in the night sky, the sun is already dispersing the clouds and filling the world with warmth and light. Meanwhile, an unidentifiable individual stands on the beach, enjoying the early morning breeze, and holding a long pole with streamers attached to it. The streamers, dancing in the wind, may symbolize the human spirit in each of us meeting difficulties with grace, and even allowing those difficulties to lift us higher.

In the background are the following religious symbols:

The Jewish Menorah (Judaism)

The seven-branched candelabrum ("the Menorah") is one of the oldest symbols of the Jewish faith. The Hebrew word "Menorah" means "lampstand." As a symbol of Judaism it dates back to the instructions that were given by God for constructing the Tabernacle — the place where the Ten Commandments were to be housed. "Make a lampstand of pure, beaten gold . . . . Then make seven lamps for the lampstand" (Exodus 25:31, 37). The seven lamps represent the holiness of Divine Wisdom which shines like light; the lamps are to be fed with olive oil, representative of Divine Love. This flame must never go out, or be extinguished, for it symbolizes Eternal Love and Wisdom burning brightly and continuously. Like the sun, it is a perpetual symbol of the Divine Presence among us.

The Christian Cross (Christianity)

The cross, or "crucifix," has become the central symbol of the Christian faith. To many people the cross represents the suffering that Jesus Christ endured on behalf of the human race, and through which humanity's sins were forgiven. Others focus on the resurrection—the miraculous rising of Jesus Christ above death and suffering. They regard the empty cross as a symbol of the eternal life that awaits all who believe in Jesus Christ and who keep His commandments.

Esoteric Christians see the cross as a symbol of the crucifixion (death) of the "lower self," and resurrection ("re-birth" or "transformation") into a "higher self." This spiritual rebirth is referred to as the birth of "the Christ," or simply, "Christ Consciousness."

The Crescent Moon (Islam)

The origin of the Crescent Moon and Star—which have become associated with the Islamic faith—is unclear. It is said that in 339 B.C. a brilliant waxing moon saved Byzantium (now Istanbul) from an enemy attack. In order to express their gratitude, the citizens of Byzantium adopted the Crescent Moon of the goddess Diana as the city's emblem. Many years later the Sultan of the Ottoman Empire had a dream in which he saw the Crescent Moon stretching out and encompassing the entire world. Taking this as a prophetic sign, the Sultan adopted the Crescent Moon as a symbol for his nation.

Others say that on the night that Muhammad received his initial revelation from Allah there was a conjunction of the moon and Venus in the early morning sky. Traditionally, the moon and stars represent faith in God, for they give light to all, even in times of darkness. Similarly, the Word of God gives light to all, and transforms the darkness of night into the light of day.

The Sacred Syllable (Hinduism)

The sacred syllable "Om," or more properly "AUM," has become a symbol for Hinduism. This sound is the essence of all mantras, and is said or sung before and after all prayers. In Sanskrit, the ancient language of the Hindus, this three-letter sound begins and ends with a fourth sound which is beyond the range of human hearing. It is called the "sound of silence." Although inaudible, this "sound of silence" is sometimes referred to as the "the sound of the universe." The repetition of the Sacred Syllable, "AUM," takes the practitioner beyond thought, into the stillness, into the silence, into the depths of pure consciousness, and finally, into the heart of God. In the *Bhagavad Gita*, Krishna (the Blessed Lord) says to Arjuna, "Among the sages, I am Wisdom. Among the words, I am the Sacred Syllable, 'AUM'" (10:25).

The Wheel of Law (Buddhism)

The wheel with eight spokes is a symbol of the Noble Eightfold Path. The eightfold path includes teachings about Right Views, Right Aspirations, Right Speech, Right Behavior, Right Mode of Livelihood, Right Efforts, Right Thoughts, and Right Contemplation. Like the Ten Commandments, the Noble Eightfold Path forbids murder, unchastity, theft, falsehood, and, especially, covetous desire.

According to Buddhist teachings, all human suffering is caused by the desire to obtain things which do not satisfy the spirit. But those who follow the Noble Eightfold Path will be freed from every ignoble desire, and hence from all suffering. Eventually, they will reach a state called *Nirvana* in which all covetous desire is extinguished. *Nirvana* (from *nir* meaning "out," and *vana* meaning "to blow") refers to blowing out the flame of covetous desire and receiving in its place the Kingdom of Heaven—joy, peace, insight, and compassion for all living beings. This state, which is the supreme goal of the Noble Eightfold Path, might be called "Nirvana on earth."

The Open Word (New Church)

The symbol of the Open Word represents the perpetual presence of God with all people through the Sacred Scriptures. While the New Church focuses on the Old and New Testaments—and the Divine Humanity of Jesus Christ—it acknowledges that God comes to us, and speaks to us through the Sacred Scriptures of all the great religions.

In a thirty-volume revelation, written between 1749 and 1772, Emanuel Swedenborg describes the New Church as a new dispensation of God's Love and Wisdom, "coming in the clouds of heaven"—the opening of the internal meaning of the Word. Gifted with the ability to interpret sacred symbolism, and guided by the Lord alone, Swedenborg was allowed to open the book that had been "sealed with seven seals" (Revelation 5:5) and invite all people to "enter with understanding into the mysteries of faith" (*True Christian Religion* 508).

Selected Bibliography

Primary Sources:

The Bhagavad Gita for Daily Living. Translated by Eknath Easwaran. Petaluma, CA: Nilgiri Press, 1975.

The Book. Wheaton, Illinois: Tyndale House Publishers, 1986.

Enlightenment from the Aramaic: Selected Passages from the Khabouris Manuscript, An Ancient Text of the Syriac New Testament. Atlanta: The Yonan Codex Foundation, 1970.

The Hidden Words of Baha'u'llah. Translated by Shoghi Effendi. Wilmette, Illinois: Baha'i Publishing Trust, 1969.

The Holy Qur'ān: Text, Translation, and Commentary. Maryland: Amana Corporation, 1989.

The Holy Bible: Containing the Old and New Testaments. Nashville: Thomas Nelson. 1982.

The Interlinear Hebrew Greek English Bible. Lafayette, Indiana: Associated Publishers and Authors, 1981.

The Jewish Encyclopedia. New York: Funk and Wagnalls, 1910.

Oneness: Great Principles Shared by All Religions. Arranged by Jeffrey Moses. Introductory comments by Mother Theresa and the Dalai Lama. New York: Fawcett Columbine, 1989.

The Religion of Islam: A Comprehensive Discussion of the Sources, Principles and Practices of Islam. U.S.A.: The Ahmadiyya Anjuman Isha'at Islam, 1990.

Swedenborg, Emanuel. *Angelic Wisdom about Divine Providence.* Originally published in Latin. Amsterdam, 1764. Translated by W. Wunsch. New York: Swedenborg Foundation, 1963.

_____. *Angelic Wisdom concerning the Divine Love and Wisdom.* Originally published in Latin.

Amsterdam, 1763. Translated by C. Harley and D. Harley. London: Swedenborg Society, 1990.

_____. *Apocalypse Explained*. Volumes 1-6. Originally written in Latin. Stockholm, 1759. Published posthumously. Translated by J. Whitehead. New York: Swedenborg Foundation, 1976.

_____. *Arcana Coelestia*. Volumes 1-12. Originally published in Latin. London, 1749-1756. Translated by J.F. Potts. New York: Swedenborg Foundation, 1969.

_____. *The Delights of Wisdom concerning Conjugial Love after which follow the Pleasures of Insanity pertaining to Scortatory Love*. Originally published in Latin. Amsterdam, 1768. Translated by Samuel Warren. Revised by Louis Tafel. New York: Swedenborg Foundation, 1971.

_____. *The Doctrine of Life for the New Jerusalem from the Ten Commandments*. Originally published in Latin. Amsterdam, 1763. Translated by J.F. Potts. London: Swedenborg Society, 1990.

_____. *Heaven and Its Wonders and Hell: From Things Heard and Seen*. Originally published in Latin. London, 1758. Translated by J. Ager. New York: Swedenborg Foundation, 1978.

_____. *The Spiritual Diary: Records and Notes made by Emanuel Swedenborg between 1746 and 1765 from his Experiences in the Spiritual World*. Translated from the Swedish by A.W. Acton. London: Swedenborg Society, 1977.

_____. *True Christian Religion containing the Universal Theology of the New Church*. Originally published in Latin. Amsterdam, 1771. Translated by Wm. C. Dick. London: Swedenborg Society, 1950.

A Sourcebook in Indian Philosophy. Edited by Sarvepalli Radhakishnan and Charles A. Moore. Princeton: Princeton University Press, 1957.

Worldwide Laws of Life: 200 Eternal Spiritual Principles. Arranged by John Marks Templeton. Philadelphia: Templeton Foundation, 1997.

World Scriptures: A Comparative Anthology of Sacred Texts. Edited by Andrew Wilson. St. Paul, Minnesota: Paragon House, 1995.

243

Secondary Sources:

Alcott, Louisa May. *Little Women*. New York: Grosset and Dunlap, 1915.

Alcoholics Anonymous. New York: Alcoholics Anonymous World Services, 1987.

Beck, Aaron T. *Love is Never Enough*. New York: Harper Perennial, 1989.

Burnham, Sophy. *A Book of Angels: Reflections on Angels Past and Present and True Stories of How They Touch Our Lives*. New York: Ballantine Books, 1990.

Burns, David D. *Feeling Good: The New Mood Therapy*. New York: Avon Books, 1980.

Castiglione, Baldesar. *The Book of the Courtier*. Translated from the Italian by Charles S. Singleton. New York: Doubleday & Company, 1959.

Davis, John D. *Dictionary of the Bible*. Grand Rapids, Michigan: Baker Book House, 1980.

Dostoevsky, Fyodor. *Crime and Punishment*. New York: Barnes and Noble, 1994.

Easwaran, Eknath. *Meditation: A Simple Eight-Point Program for Translating Spiritual Ideals into Daily Life*. Petaluma, California: Nilgiri Press, 1991.

Fraser, James. *The Golden Bough: A Study in Comparative Religion*. New York: Macmillan, 1935.

Gibran, Kahlil. *Tears and Laughter*. New York: Philosophical Library, 1949.

Gorski, Terence T. and Merlene Miller. *Staying Sober: A Guide for Relapse Prevention*. Independence, Missouri: Herald House / Independence Press, 1986.

Huxley, Aldous. *The Perennial Philosophy*. New York: Harper and Row, 1945.

Junge´, Kent. *Living Commandments*. Unpublished Manuscript, 1985.

Keller, Helen. *Light in My Darkness*. Revised and edited by Ray Silverman. West Chester, PA: Chrysalis Books, 2000.

Kingslake, Brian. *Angel Stories*. Evesham, England: Arthur James Limited, 1982.

Kirven, Robert H. *Angels in Action: What Swedenborg Saw and Heard*. West Chester, PA: Chrysalis Books, 1994.

Konieczka, Richard Lee. *A Survival Manual for the Romantic Lover*. University of Michigan Doctoral Dissertation, Department of English Language and Literature, Ann Arbor, Michigan, 1980.

Mother Teresa. *A Simple Path*. New York: Ballantine Books, 1996.

O'Neil, Nena and George O'Neil. *Open Marriage: A New Life Style for Couples*. New York: M. Evans, 1972.

Peck, Scott. *The Road Less Traveled*. New York: Simon and Schuster, 1998.

Sex and Love Addicts Anonymous. Boston: The Augustine Fellowship, 1986.

Shakespeare, William. *The Tragedy of Hamlet, Prince of Denmark*. In *Shakespeare: The Complete Works*. Edited by G.B. Harrison. New York: Harcourt, Brace, and World, 1952.

_____. *The Tragedy of Julius Caesar*. In *Shakespeare: The Complete Works*. Edited by G.B. Harrison. New York: Harcourt, Brace, and World, 1952.

_____. *The Tragedy of Macbeth*. In *Shakespeare: The Complete Works*. Edited by G.B. Harrison. New York: Harcourt, Brace, and World, 1952.

Van Dusen, Wilson. *Returning to the Source*. Moab, Utah: Real People Press, 1996.

Index

ᴰ

K

N

O

P

❧❧❧

❧ *T* ❧

Notes

Notes

Notes

Notes

Notes

Notes

Notes

Notes

Notes

Notes

Notes

Notes

Notes

Even as a deep lake is clear and calm,

so also wise men become tranquil

after they have listened to the laws.

—WORDS OF THE BUDDHA
THE DHAMMAPADA 6:7